HERTFORDSHIRE GARDEN HISTORY

Volume II

Gardens pleasant, groves delicious

HERTFORDSHIRE GARDEN HISTORY

Volume II

Gardens pleasant, groves delicious

Edited by Deborah Spring

HERTFORDSHIRE PUBLICATIONS
an imprint of the
University of Hertfordshire Press

First published in Great Britain in 2012 by
University of Hertfordshire Press
College Lane
Hatfield
Hertfordshire
AL10 9AB

British Library Cataloguing in Publication Data
A catalogue record for this book is available from the British Library

ISBN 978-1-907396-81-6

Design by Arthouse Publishing Solutions Ltd
Printed in Great Britain by Hobbs the Printers Ltd

*In memory of Esther Gatland and her valued contribution
to the work of the Hertfordshire Gardens Trust*

Contents

	List of figures	ix
	List of plates	xiii
	Notes on contributors	xv
1	The London connection: Gardens of the sixteenth and seventeenth centuries *Deborah Spring*	1
2	Hertfordshire's lost water gardens 1500–1750 *Anne Rowe*	31
3	Hadham Hall and the Capel Family *Jenny Milledge*	60
4	Mr Lancelot Brown and his Hertfordshire clients *Helen Leiper*	92
5	Gardens and industry: The landscape of the Gade Valley in the nineteenth century *Tom Williamson*	121
6	Some Arts and Crafts gardens in Hertfordshire *Kate Harwood*	148
7	Planting the gardens: The nursery trade in Hertfordshire *Elizabeth Waugh*	177
8	Salads and ornamentals: A short history of the Lea Valley nursery industry *Kate Banister*	202
	Index	231

Figures

1.1   Hertfordshire gardens of the sixteenth and seventeenth centuries.

1.2   Detail of John Norden's map of Hertfordshire, 1598. 942.58/NOR. Reproduced by kind permission of Hertfordshire Archives and Local Studies (HALS).

1.3   The remains of Sir Nicholas Bacon's house at Gorhambury. Photograph by Deborah Spring.

1.4a and b Sir Nicholas Bacon, sixteenth century, British School, and Sir Francis Bacon. Reproduced by kind permission of the Masters of the Bench of the Honourable Society of Gray's Inn.

1.5   Site of the Oak Wood at Gorhambury. Photograph by Deborah Spring.

1.6   The Pondyards: detail of Gorhambury estate map of 1634. D/EV P1. Reproduced by kind permission of HALS.

1.7   Detail of John Norden's map of London, 1593. Reproduced by kind permission of HALS.

1.8   Estate map of Benington Park in 1628. Private collection.

1.9   Drapentier's engraving of Aspenden Hall, c.1700. Reproduced by kind permission of HALS.

2.1   Map showing the locations of important water gardens in the county.

2.2   Detail of the First Edition OS map sheets XLIII (1868–83) and XLIV (1877), 6 inches to the mile, showing the household moat of The More. Reproduced by kind permission of HALS.

2.3   Reconstructed ground plan of The More, c.1529, by Simon Thurley. Reproduced by kind permission of Simon Thurley.

2.4   Plan of The More, c.1547, by Simon Thurley. Reproduced by kind permission of Simon Thurley.

2.5   Detail of First Edition OS map sheet XLI (1882), showing the site of the former 'Royal Palace' and the eighteenth-century mansion called 'Theobalds Park'. Reproduced by kind permission of HALS.

2.6   Aerial photograph from 1946 showing the surviving fragments of the sixteenth- and seventeenth-century designed landscape. Off Acc 300, 4049

CPE/UK/1779. Reproduced by kind permission of HALS.

2.7   View of Bushey Hall from the west by J. Drapentier. Reproduced by kind permission of HALS.

2.8a and b   Details of Drapentier's illustrations of Bushey Hall from the south and from the north. Reproduced by kind permission of HALS.

2.9   Detail of Paul Sandby's illustration of Brocket Hall showing the Chinese boat built for Sir Benjamin Truman. DE/X55/Z2/12. Reproduced by kind permission of HALS.

2.10   Detail of OS map sheet XXXV (1883), 6 inches to the mile, showing the wood called Popes Pondholes. Reproduced by kind permission of HALS.

3.1   Hadham Hall. Plan of the old buildings by W. Minet. DE/X10/Z1. Reproduced by kind permission of HALS.

3.2   The gatehouse or 'Entry'. Photograph taken by W. Minet, c.1902. CV. Had. Lt. 21. Reproduced by kind permission of HALS.

3.3   Engraving of Hadham Hall from 'Views of Hertfordshire' – a collection of drawings by J.C. Buckler (1793–1894). DE/Bg. Reproduced by kind permission of HALS.

3.4   Hadham Hall, south front. Photograph taken W. Minet, 1900. 70899. Reproduced by kind permission of HALS.

3.5   Hadham Hall, the seat of Arthur Baron Capel, c.1648. 64322A. Reproduced by kind permission of HALS.

3.6   The Holbein Porch, Wilton. Photograph by Jenny Milledge.

3.7   Memorial to Charles Morrison and his wife, by Nicholas Stone, St Mary's Church, Watford. Photograph reproduced by kind permission of A. Skelton.

3.8   Detail of Dury and Andrews' county map, 1766, showing Hadham Hall. Reproduced by kind permission of HALS.

3.9   Detail of OS Drawing 1800, sheet number 141. Reproduced by kind permission of British Library Board.

3.10   Engraving of Hadham Hall, c.1880. 70899. Reproduced by kind permission of HALS.

3.11   Hadham Hall, east front. Photograph taken by W. Minet, 1900. 70899. Reproduced by kind permission of HALS.

4.1   'The Hoo' by J. Drapentier. Reproduced by kind permission of HALS.

4.2   Watercolour painting of 'The Hoo' by an unknown artist, n.d. KIM/9. Reproduced by kind permission of HALS.

4.3   Map of Hertfordshire, showing the twelve Hertfordshire parks where Brown is thought to have been consulted.

4.4   Portrait of William, second Earl Cowper, attributed to Bartholomew Dandridge. Private Collection. Supplied by the Courtauld Institute of Art. (Every effort has been made to trace the copyright holder and to obtain their permission for the use of this material. The publisher apologises for any errors or omissions and would be grateful if notified of any corrections that should be incorporated in future reprints or editions of this book.)

4.5   Detail of Dury and Andrews' map, 1766, showing the landscape features at

Cole Green Park. Reproduced by kind permission of HALS.

4.6   View of Cole Green, by John Charnock. Reproduced by kind permission of the National Maritime Museum.

4.7   View of Colegreen House and park by an unknown artist. CV HERTING/39. Reproduced by kind permission of HALS.

4.8   Plan of Youngsbury with proposals for improvements. HALS DE/A 2845. Reproduced by kind permission of the Hon. C.A. Savile.

4.9   Portrait of David Barclay. Reproduced by kind permission of Barclays Group Archives.

5.1   Parks and industry in the valley of the Gade in the second half of the nineteenth century.

5.2   Cassiobury, The Grove and Russells Farm, as depicted on the First Edition OS map, 6 inches to the mile, 1877.

5.3   Apsley Mills, with decorative planting of Lombardy poplar and conifers. Undated sketch, early nineteenth century, by Harriet Dickinson. Reproduced by kind permission of Apsley Paper Trail.

5.4   The ornamental bridge carrying the main drive to The Grove across the Grand Union Canal.

5.5   Abbots Hill, as shown on the Abbots Langley Tithe Award map of 1839. Reproduced by kind permission of HALS.

5.6   Shendish and Abbots Hill, as shown on the First Edition OS map, 6 inches to the mile, 1877.

5.7   Design by Edward Kemp for the grounds at Shendish, 1866. Reproduced by kind permission of Apsley Paper Trail.

6.1   New Place, Welwyn. Photograph by Kate Harwood.

6.2   Diamond Court, Temple Dinsley. Photograph by Kate Harwood.

6.3   Hertfordshire Gardens Trust plan of the Rose Garden restoration at Putteridge Bury.

6.4   Rothamsted garden. Photograph by Kate Harwood.

6.5   Sparrows Herne Hall. Reproduced by kind permission of HALS.

6.6   Letchworth Garden City. Photograph by Kate Harwood.

7.1   John Tradescant depicted on a carved newel post at Hatfield House. Reproduced by kind permission of Heritage House Groups and the Marquess of Salisbury/Hatfield House.

7.2   *Tradescantia virginiana* (Virginia spiderwort).

7.3   Diagrams for planting in Moses Cook, *The Manner of Raising, Ordering and Improving Forest Trees* (2nd edn, 1679).

7.4   Engraving of Cassiobury by J. Kip and L. Knyff, 1707. WATF/58. Reproduced by kind permission of HALS.

7.5   Brocket Hall account book 1772–3. Reproduced by kind permission of HALS.

7.6   Frontispiece to William Malcolm's *Catalogue of Hot-House and Green-House Plants, Fruit and Forest Trees, Perenniel and Annual Flower Seeds, Garden Mats and Tools* (London, 1771). Reproduced by kind permission of RHS Lindley

Library.

7.7   Bill from Thomas Rivers Nursery, to Mrs Delme Radcliffe, Hitchin Priory,
         20 May 1842. Reproduced by kind permission of HALS.

7.8   Welwyn Garden City, an aerial view down Parkway, c.1950. Reproduced by
         kind permission of HALS.

8.1   Map of Lee Valley. Based on map of Lee Valley Park Authority
         <http://www.visitleevalley.org.uk>. Reproduced with permission.

8.2   Light in market hall at Covent Garden, late nineteenth century. Pen and ink
         drawing by Diana Jones, 2012.

8.3   Advertisement for Tuck's flower pots, 1954. Reproduced by kind permission
         of Epping Forest District Museum.

8.4.   Advertisement for South's calendar for 1960. Reproduced by kind
         permission of Epping Forest District Museum.

8.5   William Paul, 1822–1905.

8.6   Advertisement from gardening journal, 1887.

8.7   Royal Nurseries, Waltham Cross, 1899. *Country Life*, 30 September 1899,
         p. 406. Reproduced with permission.

8.8   Waltham House, Waltham Cross, 1901. *Country Life*, 2 February 1901, p. 137.
         Reproduced with permission.

8.9   George Paul, 1841–1921. *Gardeners' Chronicle*, 1921. Reproduced by kind
         permission of Haymarket Publishing.

8.10   *Rosa*, Goldfinch, bred in 1907 by George Paul. Photograph reproduced by
         kind permission of Peter Beales Roses.

8.11   View in Messrs Paul's Garden in Broxbourne, 1880s. Wood engraving from
         photograph © St Albans Museums.

8.12   Turnford Hall, c.1953. Photograph reproduced by kind permission of
         Lowewood Museum.

8.13   Picking melons at Mr E. Rochford's nursery, 1913. Photograph reproduced
         by kind permission of Lowewood Museum.

8.14   Workforce at Rochford's nursery, c.1895. Photograph reproduced by kind
         permission of Lowewood Museum.

8.15   Palm House at Rochford's nursery. Photograph reproduced by kind
         permission of Lowewood Museum.

8.16   Storm damage at Nazeing, 6 January 1976. Photograph reproduced by kind
         permission of the *Evening Standard*.

8.17   Women workers picking cucumbers, 1916. Photograph reproduced by kind
         permission of Lowewood Museum.

Plates

1.1   Detail of Gorhambury estate map of 1634. D/EV P1. Reproduced by kind permission of HALS.

1.2   Lord Burghley on his mule in the gardens at Theobalds. Late eighteenth- or early nineteenth-century copy of a sixteenth-century original. Reproduced by kind permission of the Masters of the Bench of the Honourable Society of Gray's Inn.

2.1   Detail of a map of *c*.1575 showing fields belonging to the manors of Theobalds and Cullings. MS Gough Drawings a.3. Fol. 27. Reproduced by kind permission of The Bodleian Library, University of Oxford.

2.2   Digitised tracing of part of the plan of Theobalds by J. Thorpe held in the British Library. Cotton MS Aug.I.i.75.

2.3   Detail of a plan of the Bushey Hall estate, 1685. DE/Hx/P2. Reproduced by kind permission of HALS.

2.4a and b   A comparison of the water features depicted on the 1685 plan and the view of Bushey Hall from the west by J. Drapentier, 1700. DE/Hx/P2. Reproduced by kind permission of HALS.

2.5   Detail of a 'Plan of the manor of Holbatches alias Popes … belonging to Mrs Rebecca Asheton surveyed by Taylor and Chilcott in the year 1785'. CPM Supp 69. Reproduced by kind permission of the Marquess of Salisbury © The Marquess of Salisbury.

2.6   Portrait of Sir Benjamin Truman by T. Gainsborough, *c*.1770–4. Reproduced by kind permission of the Tate Gallery.

3.1   Detail of Little Hadham Tithe Map, 1844. Tracing on Linen by W. Minet. DE/X10/P1. Reproduced by kind permission of HALS.

3.2   Painting of Hadham Hall, East Wing, *c*.1640, artist unknown. Reproduced by kind permission of Hertford Museum.

3.3   Portrait of the Capel Family by C. Johnson, *c*.1641. Reproduced by kind permission of the National Portrait Gallery.

4.1   Portrait of Lancelot Brown by Sir N. Dance, R.A., *c*.1769. Reproduced by kind permission of The Burghley House Collection.

4.2   'View of Moor Park', west front, by R. Wilson, *c*.1765. Photographed
        by Jerry Hardman-Jones. Reproduced by kind permission of the Zetland
        Collection.

4.3   Detail of a survey map showing William Cowper's estate, drawn by J.
        Halsey, 1703/4. D/EP/P 4. Reproduced by kind permission of HALS.

5.1   GIS-generated viewshed showing areas visible from Shendish house.

5.2   GIS-generated viewshed showing areas visible from Abbots Hill house.

6.1   Fanhams Hall Japanese gardens. Photograph by Kate Harwood.

7.1   Rivers Early Prolific Plum painted by May Rivers, daughter of the
        nursery director, *c*.1890. Reproduced by kind permission of the
        Rivers Archive.

8.1   Lithograph of *Rosa centifolia Perpetuelle* Mauget by James Andrews.

Notes on contributors

Kate Banister

After gaining a Classics degree from Oxford in 1961 Kate spent twenty years teaching, mostly in Hertfordshire and Bedfordshire. Following retirement in 2000 she completed a four-year Garden History course at Capel Manor, Enfield, and joined the Hertfordshire Garden Trust as an active member. It was while living in Waltham Cross that Kate developed an interest in the historic gardens and nurseries of the area.

Kate Harwood

Kate Harwood is a lecturer and writer on garden history, and holds an MA in Garden History from Birkbeck College. She contributed a chapter to the previous Hertfordshire Gardens Trust book, *Hertfordshire Garden History: A Miscellany*, and is currently working on Arts and Crafts gardens in Hertfordshire.

Helen Leiper

Helen Leiper is a graduate of Leeds University and taught modern languages. She has been a member of the Hertfordshire Gardens Trust since 2000, writing reports for the research group and conservation team and is currently the honorary librarian. She has an MA in Garden History from Birkbeck College. Research for her dissertation into the eighteenth-century gardens at Cole Green House led to an interest in the work of Lancelot Brown in Hertfordshire. She contributed to *Marshalswick: The Story of a House and its Estate* (2008).

Jenny Milledge
Jenny Milledge has lived in Hertfordshire for much of her life. After a Garden History diploma, which combined her long-standing interest in all things related to gardening with her interest in social history, Jenny gained a Masters degree at Birkbeck College in 2007 and has since given occasional lectures. She is an active member of the Hertfordshire Gardens Trust research team, and has a particular interest in the seventeenth and early eighteenth centuries, having studied the work of Charles Bridgeman at Sacombe Park near Ware for her dissertation, later published in the *Journal of Garden History*, 2009.

Anne Rowe
Anne Rowe is a freelance landscape historian and author who lectures on various aspects of landscape and garden history. She has co-ordinated the Research Group of the Hertfordshire Gardens Trust since 1998 and edited *Hertfordshire Garden History: A Miscellany* (2007). Her recent publications include *Medieval Parks of Hertfordshire* (2009) and several chapters in *An Historical Atlas of Hertfordshire* (2011). She is currently collaborating with Tom Williamson on a new book about the landscape history of the county.

Deborah Spring
Following a degree in Archaeology and Anthropology, Deborah Spring became an academic publisher. An interest in gardening led her to horticulture courses at Capel Manor college, where she discovered garden history. She completed an MA in Garden History at Birkbeck, University of London in 2007, and joined the Hertfordshire Gardens Trust as a member of the research group. She is interested in the historical context of garden-making, and has written on the development of the gardens of the Inns of Court in the sixteenth and seventeenth centuries.

Elizabeth Waugh
Although she gained degrees in English Language and Literature from American universities (BA Bryn Mawr, MA University of Richmond), Elizabeth Waugh has lived and worked in the UK since 1972. She has taught in colleges from Paris, to Harlow, to Harvard. A natural progression from acting as archivist for the Rivers Nursery and Orchard Site Group was preparing a history of the company, published

as: *Rivers Nursery of Sawbridgeworth, The Art of Practical Pomology* in 2009. An interest in gardening and in spending long hours chasing historical information led her to join the Hertfordshire Garden Trust research group.

Tom Williamson

Tom Williamson was born in Bushey and is Professor of Landscape History at the University of East Anglia. He has written widely on landscape archaeology, agrarian history, and the history of designed landscapes. His books include *Polite Landscapes: Gardens and Society in Eighteenth-century England* (1995); *The Archaeology of the Landscape Park* (1998); *Suffolk's Gardens and Parks* (2000); *Chatsworth: A Landscape History* (2005); and *The Origins of Hertfordshire* (2000; revised edition 2010). He is currently working with Anne Rowe on a book called 'Hertfordshire: a landscape history'.

CHAPTER ONE

The London connection: Gardens of the sixteenth and seventeenth centuries

Deborah Spring

Earth now is greene, and heaven is blew,
Lively Spring which makes all new,
Iolly Spring, doth enter;
Sweete yong sun-beames doe subdue
Angry, agèd Winter.

Blasts are milde, and seas are calme,
Every meadow flowes with balme,
The Earth weares all her riches;
Harmonious birdes sing such a psalme,
As eare and heart bewitches.

Reserve (sweet Spring) this Nymph of ours,
Eternall garlands of thy flowers,
Greene garlands never wasting;
In her shall last our *State*'s faire Spring,
Now and for ever flourishing,
As long as Heaven is lasting.

John Davies, *Hymnes of Astraea*, 1599[1]

The reign of Elizabeth I was often symbolised as springtime, when winter was defeated and nature could flourish, as this acrostic verse in her praise illustrates. The time from her accession in the mid-sixteenth century into the first decades of the seventeenth century and James I's reign was one of relative stability and prosperity in England, when some of the greatest gardens of the English Renaissance were created.[2] There was a sense of bringing order from confusion, commonly expressed in the imagery of the time by reference to the taming and ordering of nature.[3] This period saw an evolution of ideas about the natural world, from the allegorical focus of the Renaissance, when a garden was viewed as a series of emblematic representations, to the beginnings of scientific thought and experiment, as gardens became the setting for the cultivation and study of botanical specimens. The first gardening manuals were published in the mid-sixteenth century, bringing expert advice on practical horticulture and husbandry.[4] With the introduction from Europe of humanist thought, drawing on classical sources, came a revival of the ideal of rural villa life and philosophical thinking about nature and cultivation, which influenced the design of gardens. The return of Inigo Jones from travels in Italy in 1615 coincided with the adoption in England of the concept of symmetry in the garden and in its relationship to the house.[5] The garden became a classically influenced, structured retreat from the active world, the setting for reflection and

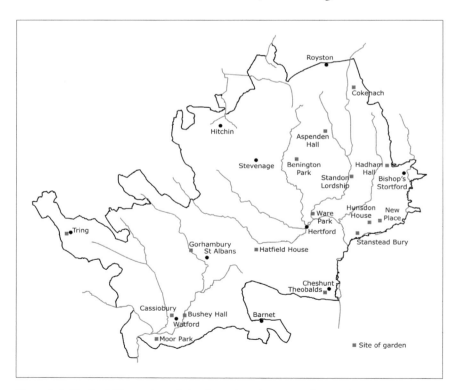

Figure 1.1 Hertfordshire gardens of the sixteenth and seventeenth centuries.

rational discussion, masques, sports and entertainments. Gardens were designed with more direct reference to the Italian Renaissance, using symbolic designs and complex water effects.

The London connection

By the mid-seventeenth century, Hertfordshire had many of the finest gardens in England. While those shown in Figure 1.1 have long disappeared, with only the revival of part of the gardens at Hatfield reminding us of their past scale and structure, enough evidence remains for the study of some of their individual histories, the context in which they were made, and the motives of those who committed substantial resources to developing them. This chapter explores how the great early modern gardens of Hertfordshire were to a degree distinctive from those in other rural settings in England, because of the different context in which they were created. Long favoured as a convenient location for royal hunting parks and residences, Hertfordshire was now also settled by newly rich lawyers, officials and City merchants. Easily accessible, Hertfordshire was an attractive place to live, away from the crowds and disease of the city. In his 1598 survey of the county, John Norden described it as 'much repleat with parkes, woodes and rivers', where 'the ayre for the most part is very salutary, and in regards thereof, many sweete and pleasant dwellings, healthful by nature and profitable by arte and industrie are planted there'.[6]

Norden added that Hertfordshire 'is much benefited by thorow-fares to and from London Northwards', and the inns are good: 'no one Shire in England for the quantitie commes neere it for thorow-fare places of competent receipt'. His map of Hertfordshire (Figure 1.2) shows settlements, rivers and – unusually for maps of the time – roads, in the late sixteenth century. Direct communications between London and Hertfordshire were crucial to the county's increasing prosperity. Four major roads linking London to the Midlands and the North crossed Hertfordshire and can be seen on the map: Watling Street (now the A5183); Akeman Street (now the A41); the Great North Road (so called by 1663, now the A1) from Islington through Barnet and Hatfield; and the Old North Road, formerly Ermine Street, the Roman military road north (now the A10), which left London at Bishopsgate and went due north via Cheshunt, crossing the Lea west of Ware and continuing north via Stamford. During Elizabeth's reign Watling Street and Ermine Street became post roads, providing the means to exchange post within a day with the city.[7] By 1637 regular coach services as well as carrier routes were in place between London and Hertfordshire destinations.[8]

People of wealth and influence who wanted to live outside the city, but have regular and easy access to it, took advantage of the opportunities afforded by Hertfordshire's road system. Proximity to London and major roads north drew in individuals whose resources depended on lucrative office in the capital, rather than on rents and revenues from great landholdings. Successful mid-sixteenth-century incomers, whose Hertfordshire houses and gardens are recorded, include William Cecil (Lord Burghley) (1521–98), principal adviser to

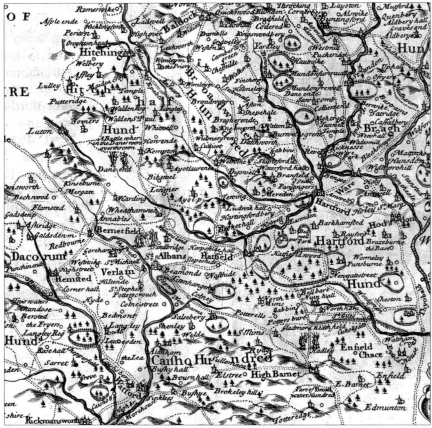

Figure 1.2 Detail of John Norden's map of Hertfordshire, 1598. From *Speculum Britanniae, an Historical and Chorographical Description of Middlesex and Hartfordshire* (1723 edn). 942.58/NOR. REPRODUCED BY KIND PERMISSION OF HERTFORDSHIRE ARCHIVES AND LOCAL STUDIES (HALS).

Elizabeth I, at Theobalds, and his brother-in-law Sir Nicholas Bacon, Lord Keeper of the Privy Seal, at Gorhambury. A senior treasury official, the Queen's Remembrancer Thomas Fanshawe (*c*.1533–1601), acquired and developed an estate at Ware Park. Sir Julius Caesar (1558–1636), an upwardly mobile lawyer who became both Master of the Rolls and Chancellor of the Exchequer, acquired land in Hertfordshire for his sons, including an estate at Benington Park. The substantial earthworks at this site have recently been identified by Hertfordshire Gardens Trust as important remains of a garden of this period.[9] The Freman brothers, successful City merchants who bought an estate at Aspenden, similarly established their family as landowners with both local and national status.

These were socially mobile individuals, whose estates with their new houses and gardens were often further developed by their equally successful sons, among them Francis Bacon at Gorhambury, Robert Cecil at both Theobalds and Hatfield, and Henry Fanshawe at Ware Park, consolidating the status and wealth of their families in Hertfordshire in the next generation. This chapter will look at some gardens which no longer survive but for which evidence is available. As Hatfield is well documented and can still be visited, it is not addressed in detail here.[10] Some houses and gardens for which evidence is very limited were once places of importance. The royal residence Hunsdon House was given by Elizabeth I to her cousin Henry Carey – a soldier and statesman who worked closely with Lord Burghley – on her accession, and traces remain of the gardens of other great Elizabethan houses and gardens at Stanstead Bury and Standon Lordship. The noted gardens at Moor Park may have been made by Lucy Harrington, Countess of Bedford. The gardens at Hadham Hall, where the house was rebuilt in the 1570s by Henry Capel, another new member of the gentry, are discussed elsewhere in this volume (see Chapter 3), as is the important forest garden made by his descendant the Earl of Essex, at Cassiobury (see Chapters 5 and 7), while Chapter 2 explores Robert Cecil's development of water gardens in Theobalds park.

The great rebuilding

The sixteenth century was a period of population rise and price inflation. In Hertfordshire, the population increased in parallel with that of London and became concentrated in the south of the county, which became the focus of stylistic innovation: the most important houses were in a band across the south-east falling within a twenty-mile radius of London (see Figure 1.1).[11] The landscape and its management changed following the dissolution of the monasteries, when most monastic houses in Hertfordshire were converted to domestic use. Sixteen parks changed from monastic to private owners, and more than a quarter of the county's land overall changed hands.[12] By 1550 foundations for thirty large houses had been laid, many within old parks.[13] New purchasers were building more frequently than established gentry. The influx of rising gentry and new money from London into Hertfordshire continued for centuries to come, and was central to the development of garden style in Hertfordshire.[14] The London focus remained significant, to the extent that no large urban centre developed in Hertfordshire because of the dominance of London.[15]

At this period in Hertfordshire, estates were smaller and changed hands more frequently than in other counties. There were large numbers of comparative newcomers, and the social elite was unusually unstable: at the outbreak of the Civil War in 1641 only 10 per cent of the gentry summoned to take sides had families that were established before 1485, and 42.5 per cent had arrived since 1603.[16] The 'great rebuilding' that took place in England during the sixteenth and early seventeenth centuries started earlier in Hertfordshire than elsewhere, beginning in the 1530s, and was heavily dependent on the dispersal of land that had belonged to the Church or Crown: a third of the country houses built by 1640 were on ex-monastic land.

Success and display

For many Hertfordshire incomers, continuing success required their frequent presence in London. They were part of the metropolitan elite of their day, with substantial financial resources and the desire to create settings for themselves that signalled their status, wealth, education and culture. A wider pool of families sought higher education in the universities and the Inns of Court.[17] This became a pathway to social mobility, achievement, wealth, and the Italian Renaissance ideal of the cultivated man, for ambitious members of the yeoman, mercantile and professional classes:

> I know many yeomen in divers provinces in England which are able to spend betwixt £300 and £500 yearly by their lands and leases, and some twice and

some thrice as much; but my young masters, the sons of such, not contented with the states of their fathers ... but must skip into his velvet breeches and silken doublet and, getting to be admitted to some Inn of Court or Chancery, must ever after think it scorn to be called any other than gentleman.[18]

In order to become fully established, and even more to establish one's family and become part of a local elite, an essential first step, bringing recognition and prestige, was acquiring a country seat.[19]

There was great social pressure on those with wealth to build grand houses and provide lavish hospitality. Personal identity was marked by possessions, display and the cultivation of important networks of kin and patronage. Country houses became centres of power as well as display.[20] At these houses conspicuous entertaining took place and the house might be kept fully open at all times so that neighbours and passing visitors could be entertained in style whether the owner was at home or not. At Theobalds, in the summer of 1584, the Earl of Leicester and friends arrived without warning at three o'clock in the afternoon, to look at the new garden walks and buildings. Although Lord Burghley was away, they were invited to hunt in the park and eat dinner. Leicester was impressed by the generous hospitality offered in his host's absence – he wrote that they found 'both meat and good drink of all sorts there, too much for such sudden guests', and had killed a young hind.[21] The garden was an aspect of country life that could be used to great effect to display wealth, fashion and taste, and to impress visitors. Gardens were part of the way in which owners advertised their culture as well as their understanding of the values of a well-ordered society.[22] Their new country settings helped to define owners' local and/or national image, and it was important both that they got the visual signals right, and that observers recognised them.[23]

Gorhambury

Nicholas Bacon was a successful lawyer who rose through education, hard work and post-Reformation land transactions to become a powerful and influential adviser to Elizabeth I. He made his fortune, attained high office and consolidated his position with property. He systematically bought land to pass to his five sons, with the intention of building estates that would establish a Bacon dynasty. His interests ranged from education, the classics and oratorical style to poetry and architecture. These interests, held in common with a small number of his contemporaries, were central to the English Renaissance.[24] Through the study of classical sources, including Pliny, Columella and Virgil, educated landowners like Bacon developed a new awareness of the horticultural aspects of gardening, and the virtue of self-sufficiency. Yet the revival of classical learning also supported the idea of an almost moral obligation to create a display. Aristotle wrote that display is a virtue, and even a public duty, for a man of wealth, standing and nobility of mind – in contrast to a mere show of opulence by the vulgarian.[25] This view is echoed in the sixteenth-century manual for courtiers, Castiglione's *The Book of the Courtier* (*Il Cortegiano*), which directed the courtier to 'erect great buildings both to win honour in his lifetime and to give a monument of himself to posterity'.[26]

Nicholas Bacon followed the precepts of Seneca and Cicero for a balanced life. The stoic philosopher Seneca was the source of ideas that

Figure 1.3 The remains of Sir Nicholas Bacon's house at Gorhambury: porch with classical details. PHOTOGRAPH BY DEBORAH SPRING.

justified the garden as reconciling, on the one hand, wealth and comfort, and, on the other, the belief that virtue could be achieved by living according to nature. Bacon decorated his gallery, garden and garden buildings at Gorhambury with scholarly quotations. While one of these read, 'One needs many things to live, few to live happily', his house was nevertheless large and comfortable, and to receive the queen he built on a gallery and loggia, including a large statue of Henry VIII.

Nicholas Bacon bought Gorhambury in 1561, the year of his youngest son Francis's birth. He had already built a house in Suffolk, but needed to be nearer London because of pressing duties at Court: he was by now Lord Chancellor. His second marriage made him brother-in-law to William Cecil. He pulled down the old medieval hall house and began building in 1563, spending just over £3,000 on the project by 1568.

The resulting house was one of the first in England to show classical features, plastered and painted white, with portraits in relief, and fine marble work on the porch (Figure 1.3). Although Nicholas Bacon and William Cecil were developing their Hertfordshire houses and gardens in parallel over the same period – indeed Bacon had begun building three years before Cecil – and Elizabeth did visit again, in 1577, Bacon never expressly set up his house to receive the queen and her court as Cecil did at Theobalds. He designed his gardens as a retreat, for the enjoyment of solitude and private discussion, and as the expression of his moral and philosophical attitudes.

The estate map of 1634 (Plate 1.1) shows the main Gorhambury garden to have been one of the most extensive of its time, and, given Nicholas Bacon's classical scholarship, it may represent the revival of ideas about gardens and their settings derived from Italian villa gardening and the study of the classical sources that inspired them. It has been suggested that his son Francis Bacon's famous essay, 'Of Gardens' (1625), which provides one of the most detailed contemporary descriptions of a great garden, is an idealised version of the garden that Nicholas Bacon (Figure 1.4a) made at Gorhambury.[27] This would go some way to explaining the enigma that the princely garden described in the essay appears to look back to earlier Tudor gardens, and is very unlike the fashionable water garden Francis Bacon (Figure 1.4b) was making for himself at the time it was published.[28]

The map of Gorhambury (Plate 1.1) shows a garden with three enclosed areas, extending to approximately twenty-eight acres. There is

Figures 1.4a and b Sir Nicholas Bacon, sixteenth century, British School, and Sir Francis Bacon. REPRODUCED BY KIND PERMISSION OF THE MASTERS OF THE BENCH OF THE HONOURABLE SOCIETY OF GRAY'S INN.

a rectangular court of some three acres to the south front of the house, edged on three sides with a herber or trees. It is coloured to indicate turf, with two ornamental gates in its north wall giving access to the house and to the loggia below the gallery. Francis Bacon's essay proposes 'a green in the entrance … I like well, that four acres of ground be assigned to the green'. In his parallel essay, 'Of Building' (1625), he is more specific: 'Let the court not be paved, for that striketh up a great heat in summer, and much cold in winter. But only some side Alleys with a cross, and quarters to graze, being kept shorn, but not too near shorn … Let there be an inward court of the same square and height, which is to be envirened with the Garden on all sides … And let there be a fountain or some fair work of statues in the middle of the court, and to be paved…'[29]

Beyond the entrance court can be seen the main garden, consisting of further courts to the west, north and south of the house with an irregular outline bordering the Oak Wood. To the east side are outbuildings, and trees that may have been an orchard.

The 'heath or desert' specified by Francis Bacon in 'Of Gardens' was an actual, striking feature of Gorhambury. It was walled, with summer houses or belvederes at each corner; it parallels the description of the heath in the essay, 'framed, as much as may be, to a natural wildness', planted with thickets of shrubs underplanted with flowers, together with 'little heaps, in the nature of mole-hills' topped with herbs and bushes, and surrounded by alleys of shrubs and fruit trees, with at each corner, 'a mount of some pretty height, leaving the wall of the enclosure breast high, to look abroad into the fields'. It has been suggested that the 'desert' was a clever device to integrate gardens with parkland, sited within the landscape so that it created an area of transition between the geometrical garden layout and the local terrain.[30]

The Oak Wood (Figure 1.5) lay beyond the boundary of the formal garden. Old oaks still grow in the parkland that was once the Oak Wood.

Francis Bacon inherited the house at Gorhambury from his older brother Anthony in 1601, but did not live there until after his mother's death in 1610, although he began to make notes about creating a water garden there.[31] Once installed at Gorhambury, Francis Bacon 'trimmed and dressed' the house and garden built by his father. Towards the end of his life, when his income finally matched his expectations, he spent lavishly on his house and entertainments.

Figure 1.5 Site of the Oak Wood at Gorhambury.
PHOTOGRAPH BY DEBORAH SPRING.

In his life, Francis Bacon modelled himself on the authors who had shaped his early outlook: Cicero, Demosthenes and Seneca. He drew on the writings of Anaxagoras, a natural philosopher praised by Socrates as a scholar of nature and the cosmos. For Bacon, the purpose of understanding nature, through both experiment and philosophy, was to control it: 'nature is only truly understood when we operate upon the world and learn to produce a variety of effects at will rather than rely on the accidental arrangement of qualities existing in unaltered nature'.[32]

Bacon adapted and improved gardens wherever he lived.[33] He created a new scientific understanding of nature, based on observation and experiment, wrote extensively on aspects of natural history, and was knowledgeable about plants and gardening. Bacon recorded detailed practical experiments, many relevant to gardening, such as careful trials of the different rates of germination in different conditions. He challenged unscientific ideas such as the sympathy and antipathy of plants, 'idle and ignorant conceits'; and set out a series of experiments that could be used to test the transmutation of plants, an idea that one plant could change into another, or into an animal. Other experiments covered grafting;

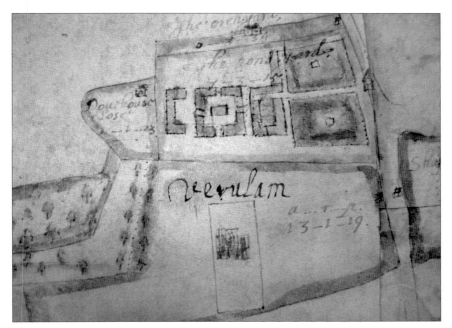

Figure 1.6 The Pondyards: detail from Gorhambury estate map of 1634. D/EV P1.
REPRODUCED BY KIND PERMISSION OF HALS.

improving fruits and plants; the possibility of hybridisation; the principal differences between plants; the properties of medicinal plants; compost-making; artificial training and dwarfing. The descriptions, observations, ideas for experiments, and conclusions where they appear, are based on close first-hand knowledge of plants, including their structure, and a careful accumulation of facts.[34]

The stained-glass panels that survive at Gorhambury from Francis Bacon's time illustrate his interest in all aspects of the natural world. They include examples of plants and creatures discovered in exploration of the New World.[35]

Another detail from the 1634 map (Figure 1.6) shows what Francis Bacon added to his father's estate. He built a long-planned summer house of his own design, overlooking new water gardens at the Pondyards a mile from the main house, next to the river Ver. The avenue connecting Verulam House and the Pondyards with the main house at Gorhambury was a sequence of eight species planted in a repeating pattern. The avenue was distinctive for its dramatic scale and for the effect of the planting of different species in sequence, 'severall stately trees of the like groweth and heighth, viz. elme, chestnut, beach, hornebeame, Spanish ash, cervice-tree'. It was seventy feet wide with side walks extending to a further thirty feet; the middle section was wide enough for three coaches abreast. The avenue afforded 'a most pleasant variegated verdure' viewed from the roof of Verulam House, according to notes made by John Aubrey in 1656.[36] Trees used in decorative sequence were a feature of gardens created by Bacon. A 1609 plan of the garden at Twickenham House, which he occupied before inheriting Gorhambury, shows limes and birches planted in concentric rings.[37] The plan for the water garden at Gorhambury includes boundaries similarly planted with rows of birch and lime. The Walks laid out by Bacon at Gray's Inn from 1598 prefigured the Gorhambury triple avenue on a smaller scale, with lower and upper walks planted with beech, elm and sycamore.[38]

Verulam House was an unusual and innovative building, and comparison with classically influenced Italian country villas of the mid-sixteenth century shows what might have informed the design.[39] But by 1665 this building, on which Francis Bacon had spent extravagantly (up to £10,000), was sold off and demolished for the value of its materials.

Bacon created four acres of water gardens, using the existing pondyards, the site of which still exists as earthworks.[40] These were highly fashionable gardens. His cousin Robert Cecil had already created water gardens at Hatfield, and Bacon's planning note includes his intention to consult Cecil about Gorhambury. Aubrey in 1656 saw a pond paved with coloured pebbles, and a Roman banqueting house paved in black and white marble. Bacon's notes show his intention was to have a series of islands, each with its own building or statue, and a boundary of trees.[41]

Francis Bacon brought both horticultural expertise and a sense of theatre to his gardens. Once he finally had money, late in life, he spent it extravagantly. Yet he still kept the classical concept of the garden as a place of scholarly retreat and meditation: Aubrey writes that Bacon's assistant Thomas Hobbes 'walked with him in his delicate groves where he did meditate', and had the task of writing down Bacon's ideas there in the garden.

Theobalds

The great house of Theobalds, at Cheshunt, of which only fragments of the building and a garden wall now remain, was built by William Cecil from about 1567. A survey of 1611 shows the house, its green entrance courts and 'great garden' to the side divided into compartments, with ponds and park beyond, but there is little detail in the representation of the house and gardens.[42] Situated on the Old North Road, Theobalds had direct access both south into London, and north to Cecil's family home at Burghley, near Stamford.

At Theobalds, it has been said, William Cecil tried to create in England for the first time the splendour of Italian villa life, transforming the natural world into a perfected cosmos. He was a 'new man' of Elizabethan England, for whom culture principally meant the cultivation or fabrication of an identity; for such a man, 'to build greatly is first of all to construct one's own magnificence'.[43] In the case of Theobalds, the private life and existence of the house was eclipsed by royal obligations and the house metamorphosed into a palace. The turning point was Elizabeth's visit in 1571, shortly after Cecil had been created baron. For fifteen years after this, the house was transformed into a royal palace in all but name. Elizabeth and her retinue visited it frequently during her annual summer 'progresses' around the country, for extended stays of up to six weeks. Both house and garden were continually added to and changed to suit the Queen, and Theobalds eventually did become a palace when James I took it over from Robert Cecil.

The gardens were subject to constant alteration, and both William and Robert Cecil were actively involved. There was a great garden with a fountain, and a canal so that visitors could pass through the garden by boat. In a summer house were statues of twelve Roman emperors, imported from Venice in 1561, and an ornamental pool.[44] The gardens at Theobalds were described by Burghley's biographer as 'perfected most costly, bewtifully and pleasantly' and by a visitor after Burghley's death as 'an extremely rich garden'. Like his brother-in-law Nicholas Bacon, but more visibly worldly in his creation of a personal palace on an enormous scale, Burghley took a close interest in the planning and development of his new house and garden. He created a setting that, like Gorhambury, was laden with symbol and allegory. Nature came into the house: the Green Gallery was decorated with realistic trees on which were displayed the arms of the noble families of England, 'all England represented by 52 trees, each tree representing one county', and in the great chamber was an indoor grotto with life-size figures.[45] Cecil and Bacon were among the first to use the classical loggia, a feature which became popular in houses of the period, to connect house and garden. Francis Bacon's description of the ideal princely palace, which may have been based on Theobalds, includes an open loggia: 'Upon the ground story, a fair gallery, open, upon pillars; and upon the third story likewise, an open gallery upon pillars, to take the prospect and freshness of the garden'.[46] Cecil added five loggias to the house at Theobalds.[47] Despite its size and reputation, there are few contemporary descriptions of the garden. Foreign visitors occasionally include a glimpse of its splendours in their correspondence. They describe entering the garden 'of immense extent', on which no expense had been spared, through a loggia, and the long gravel walks, where 'one might walk two Myles'; the waterway surrounding it, 'large enough for one to have the pleasure of going in a boat, and rowing between the shrubs', a great variety of trees and plants, labyrinths, wooden columns and pyramids.[48] Water spouted from a marble fountain to surprise passers-by, there was an alabaster sundial, and a further fountain in the shape of a ship, 'complete with cannon, flags and sails'.[49]

Burghley, his wife and daughter were on the move almost every day. Cecil House on the Strand, fourteen miles away from Theobalds by road, was his London base. Cecil House was conveniently placed for the road to Hertfordshire.[50] Burghley tried to be at Theobalds as often as he could and would often return there to dine in the evening, even in bad weather. The London house had a substantial garden with views north that can be seen in Norden's map (Figure 1.7). The garden included formal compartments, a mount, a banqueting house and an orchard, and guests could be further entertained in the bowling alley and tennis court. John Gerard, the herbalist and plant collector, author of *The Herball* (1597), and Thomas Hill, who wrote one of the earliest practical gardening books, *The Gardener's Labyrinth* (1577), both dedicated their books to Burghley, reflecting his knowledge and involvement in planning his gardens at the Strand and Theobalds. Burghley employed Gerard, who lived in Holborn, as the superintendent of his gardens.

As he got older, Burghley repeatedly stressed his wish to withdraw from active life to Theobalds, although he was never free from the pressures of work and continued in office until his death. Theobalds was always a workplace as well as a retreat (Plate 1.2). His anonymous biographer wrote: 'if he might ride privately in his garden upon his little mule or lie a day or two at his little lodge at Theobalds retired from business or too

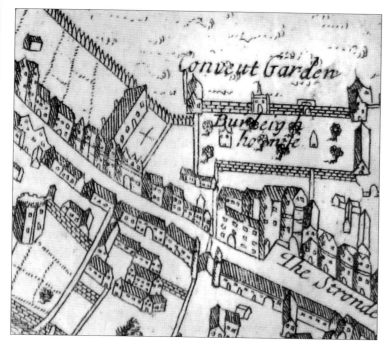

Figure 1.7 Detail of John Norden's map of London, 1593. From *Speculum Britanniae*. REPRODUCED BY KIND PERMISSION OF HALS.

much company, he thought it his greatest and only happiness'. The 'little lodge' would have been away from the main house in the park (a lodge is shown in the map of Theobalds park, see Chapter 2, p. 39).

After Burghley's death, his son Robert Cecil (1563–1612) inherited Theobalds. Like his father, he held political power as senior minister, first to the queen, then to James I, and was dedicated to the service of the Crown. On his progress from Scotland to London for his accession in 1603, the new king stayed for four nights at Theobalds before entering the city. He continued to visit it frequently to hunt, and in 1607 Cecil handed over the house and estate in exchange for the old palace of Hatfield. There, Cecil built a new house using the most expensive materials.[51] Following his father's example, he surrounded it with spectacular gardens that included terraces, waterworks and fountains by Salomon de Caus, fruit trees given by the Queen of France, a vineyard stocked with 20,000 vines supplied by the French ambassador's wife, and rare plants acquired by his gardener John Tradescant (see Chapter 7, pp. 180–2).[52]

Ware Park

Thomas Fanshawe was a close adviser to William Cecil, and held the powerful and lucrative post of Queen's Remembrancer. He was able to raise his family to a position of considerable wealth and influence. In 1575 he purchased Ware Park near Hertford, which remained the family home for over a century. In 1601 his son Henry Fanshawe inherited both his father's position, with the large house in Warwick Lane, London, which served as the Remembrancer's office, and Ware Park. This was convenient professionally, because during times of plague in London the exchequer moved to Hertford. It was also useful to be within reach of the Cecils at Theobalds and Hatfield House.[53]

The gardens at Ware Park, which included a fountain, stream and simple flower garden, were praised by Sir Henry Wotton for their fruits, flowers and herbs – being described as 'a delicate and diligent curiosity, surely without parallel among foreign nations' – and for the care taken by Sir Henry in planning the planting:

> he did so precisely examine the tinctures and seasons of his flowers, that in their settings, the inwardest of which that were to come up at the same time, should be always a little darker than the outmost, and so serve them for a kind of gentle shadow, like a piece, not of Nature, but of Art.[54]

John Chamberlain, a friend of Henry Fanshawe's, wrote letters that give a vivid contemporary account of the garden's development:

> And such a coil about gardening that a man cannot be idle though he do but look on ... here have been every day since my coming above forty men at work, for the garden is wholly translated, new levelled, and in a manner transplanted, because most of the first trees were dead with being set too deep. And in the midst of it, instead of a knot, he is making a fort in perfect proportion, with his ramparts, bulwarks, counterscarps, and all other appurtenances, so that when it was finished it is like to prove an invincible piece of work.[55]

A huge labour force was used in 1606 to make the garden fort. Not only did Fanshawe spend money twice over on trees, after the first ones that were planted died, but, if Chamberlain's report from another visit in 1609 is to be believed, the general outlay to acquire plants for the garden display could be astonishingly high: 'I never knew this place sweeter, though much fairer and richer in show; and yet we have now four or five flowers from Sir Ralph Winwood's, that cost £12.'[56]

In 1613 Chamberlain, who was a frequent visitor, recorded more expensive upheavals in the garden at Ware Park, as the fort was demolished and fashionable water gardens were installed. Fanshawe was no doubt influenced by the garden canal winding through shrubs, and the fountains and ornamental ponds of nearby Theobalds, and the new gardens at Hatfield:

> we are busied about new works and bringing of waters into the gardens, which have succeeded so well that we have a fine fountain with a pond in the lower garden where the fort was ... and a running stream from the river in the upper garden between the knots and ranks of trees in the broad walk or alley, wherein we hope to have plenty of trouts fed by hand. These works with industry and cost are brought almost to perfection...[57]

In 1614 Chamberlain wrote to friends in Venice thanking them for vine plants, seeds and plumstones, and he describes other sources and exchanges that helped stock his friends' gardens:

> Lady Winwood ... takes great delight in flowers and plants, and is as busy herself in setting and tending of melons as any gardener of them all ... We have had some plants of muscadine grapes from her that were sent out of the Low Countries for excellent good, and we truck and live much by exchange that way, for we furnished her with melon seed in the spring and sent her some grown plants from Ware Park before Whitsuntide.[58]

Fanshawe's income was said to be £4,000 per annum. Although he had a large retinue, and outlay on large projects such as the changes to the gardens must have been heavy, he left no debts and was able to provide £1,500 apiece for his five surviving daughters.

Benington Park

In September 1612 Sir Julius Caesar, Chancellor of the Exchequer, arrived to stay with the Fanshawes at Ware Park.[59] The son of Caesar Adelmare, an Italian physician at Queen Elizabeth's court, he created an eye-catching name by adopting 'Caesar' rather than 'Adelmare' as his surname. Caesar qualified as a lawyer in the 1580s and used a network of

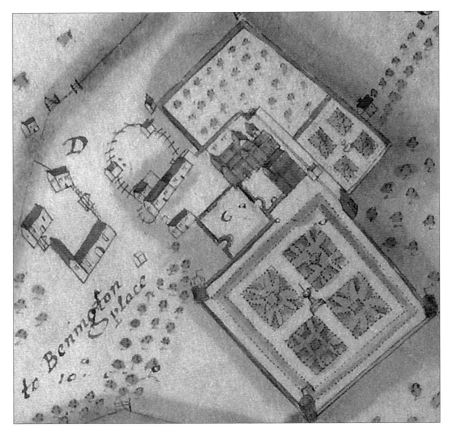

Figure 1.8 Estate map of Benington Park in 1628. PRIVATE COLLECTION.

influential patrons – including Lord Burghley and Francis Walsingham – and advantageous marriages, the third of which was to Francis Bacon's niece, to attain high office and to acquire property in Hertfordshire, Lincolnshire, Norfolk, Essex and Kent.[60] Caesar was visiting his treasury colleague Fanshawe on his way home to Kent, after staying at a house he had recently bought in the Hertfordshire parish of Sandon for his son John.[61] In 1613 he bought the estate of Benington Park and it was conveyed in 1614 to his older son Charles (1590–1642),[62] who was knighted at Theobalds and married that year.

A series of massive terraces formed by cutting into the side of a valley and including a raised walkway, which are still visible at Benington Park, may date from this period. This important site has been recently surveyed and analysed.[63] While it has so far proved difficult to reach any firm conclusion about the date and layout of the early gardens, there is nevertheless evidence from an estate map of 1628 of a garden divided into compartments, walled, with parterres and a fountain and a separate wooded area (Figure 1.8). Questions remain as to when the terraces were excavated, and why the garden shown in 1628 appears old-fashioned. This site illustrates the difficulty of dating historic gardens of this period and interpreting the available evidence. Could it have been planned by Sir Julius, to a design he was familiar with from earlier gardens, rather than by his son? He bought Benington to establish Charles, who had just married, in a house suitable as a seat for a landed family. It has been suggested that details of the 1628 plan indicate it may have been Sir Julius who made the decisions about extending and updating the house – a formerly dilapidated medieval manor house – and laying out the garden, because some features are more typical of a garden of the late sixteenth century than the first decades of the seventeenth century: the enclosed garden, only partly visible from the house, with domed corner pavilions or summer houses, would initially appear to date from the 1590s. Yet the plan also shows parterres and fountains, more appropriate for a later garden.

It could be that further updating was undertaken, or planned, following Charles Caesar's second marriage in 1625. The 1628 plan of Benington Park, which he commissioned, is the earliest known plan of the buildings and gardens. We cannot be sure it is accurate: sometimes plans were made to illustrate proposals that were not carried out, or only partly implemented, or changed. Such plans were often made to mark a major change such as inheritance or marriage – as may be the case here. The Benington plan includes the whole estate, and appears to be accurate when compared to park boundaries, fields, roads, tracks and buildings that still exist. The garden boundaries also seem to be correct. Yet the large-scale terraced garden is not shown – it first appears in a much later map of 1743. This is a puzzle, since the terraces are made in a natural valley, and it is unlikely that the earlier garden was made before they were cut into the hillside. The researchers conclude that the garden on the 1628 plan never could have existed exactly as it is shown, but no interpretation of the evidence available so far can provide a certain answer about the dating of the terraces.

ASPEDEN HALL

Figure 1.9 Drapentier's engraving of Aspenden Hall, c.1700. From H. Chauncy, *Historical Antiquities of Hertfordshire*. REPRODUCED BY KIND PERMISSION OF HALS.

Aspenden Hall

Many of the features that characterised high-status gardens by the end of the period can be seen at Aspenden Hall (Figure 1.9). Drapentier's engraving shows how it looked by the late seventeenth century.

The owners of Aspenden Hall had long been closely associated with the London elite. It has been noted that because of the social mobility and changing fortunes of their owners, many Hertfordshire estates stayed in the same hands for only one or two generations. The history of Aspenden Hall is an example of the way property went through multiple ownership in Hertfordshire, its owners' London connections over several generations, and the way it changed as a setting for their aspirations and achievements. Its mid-fifteenth century owner was Ralph Jocelin, a Lord Mayor of London. In Henry VIII's reign the manor passed to the Crown, and it changed hands a further five times before being sold to two brothers, William and Ralph Freman, clothiers of London, who acquired Aspenden in 1607 and settled there together. They extended the small manor house into a larger house with courtyards. Ralph, the younger brother, became another Lord Mayor. He significantly raised the profile and status of the family by putting on a spectacular New Year procession and masque in the City in 1633, in the presence of the king and queen. The historian Henry Chauncy devotes five pages of description to the glories of the parade and the lavish entertainments that followed it, but while it brought much honour to Sir Ralph, he died shortly afterwards. His nephew, another Ralph, inherited Aspenden, and settled down as a person of established wealth and status in the county. He had twelve children, and lived quietly during the dangerous years of the Civil War. Chauncy records that at this time, 'he did quit all public Imployments, affected a retired life, and pleased himself with the Conversation of his Children … He made his house neat, his gardens pleasant, his Groves delicious … He had a general insight in Architecture and Husbandry.' He was succeeded by his son, a third Ralph, who resumed the upward family trajectory, moving from local to national prominence as an MP. He carried on the improvements to the garden: 'He has cased and adorned this Manor House with brick, beautified the Gardens with delicious Greens, the Grove with pleasant Walks, and made all things neat and curious to the Spectator.'[64] His daughter Mary married another Charles Caesar, the great-great-grandson of Sir Julius, and went to live at Benington Park where she carried on the family interest in garden-making.

The engraving shows how the buildings and gardens had been updated, with irregular early Tudor buildings still visible behind the new façade. They were altered to conform to new ideas about the closer relationship between building and garden design, and the ways in which gardens were laid out and used.

The first half of the sixteenth century saw service buildings moved away from central public spaces to be replaced by lodgings or open courts. Gardens became more regular in shape and more directly related to buildings, although they remained essentially an enclosure divided into a privy garden and wider grounds for public display. At Aspenden we see how these essential features have been put in place, as house and garden were improved to reflect the success and status of the owners. The busy farmyard is hidden from the main approach to the house, which is uncluttered, formal and symmetrical. A decorative dovecote signifies status. There is a private garden near the house, the elegant 'Grove with pleasant Walks' can be seen at the top of the picture, as well as a wide walk or bowling green edged with the 'delicious Greens' (i.e. evergreens) of the description, where games are being played, and there is a fountain. Well-dressed, leisured people stroll along neat walks which are kept in order by the gardener, while others are equipped for hunting in the well-stocked deer park – an important indicator of the owner's wealth and status – visible beyond the garden.

One of the key symbols of the elite and therefore an immediate signifier of status was the replacement of old-style gatehouses and lodges by gate piers – Hunneyball notes they were the one consistent feature of most gardens, regardless of which other elements were present.[65] Creating an immediate impression on the visitor at the entrance to a property, gate piers signalled the owner's awareness of fashionable garden style and could be adapted to suit resources, from simple and plain to elaborate. They clearly feature in the entrance to Aspenden, where the piers are surmounted by heraldic emblems.

As we have seen, open loggias, lodges and banqueting houses connected outside and inside in new ways from the mid-sixteenth century, and the garden's setting within the landscape became more important. Views over the garden and beyond were highly valued. 'He that builds a fair house upon an ill seat,' wrote Francis Bacon, 'committeth himself to prison.'[66] At Aspenden, a loggia was added to the older building, lending classical symmetry to the garden side of the house, with a terrace on top from which the gardens could be viewed, while other garden buildings provided locations for entertaining, private conversation and admiring the views from the garden boundary. Even though the depiction by Drapentier is later, it can be seen that many of the features of the earlier but clearly influential gardens such as Theobalds, Hatfield and Gorhambury were still being emulated at the end of the seventeenth century by the upwardly mobile Freman family.

New-feathered gentlemen

From the second half of the sixteenth century, the numbers classed among the gentry or aristocracy in Hertfordshire significantly expanded, and they worked hard to become accepted into the local elite. William Cecil still counted himself a 'new-feathered gentleman' of Hertfordshire in 1586, when he was long established at Theobalds.[67] This chapter has reviewed how some of these individuals came to achieve success and settle in Hertfordshire, and the factors that influenced the development of their gardens. With only limited evidence available, our knowledge of the gardens is variable. What we can establish is that Hertfordshire's location near London was important in determining who settled in the county during this period, and the approach the incomers took to developing their houses and gardens. They were socially mobile and innovative, without the debts and obligations of the traditional landed class. For these families, country life was centred on leisure, not economic need. It reflected the Renaissance revival of the classical concept of *villeggiatura,* or villa life, and the ancient Roman ideal of *otium* (learned leisure or restorative withdrawal) as an antidote to urban *negotium* (business).

The more prominent incomers were educated thinkers, whose lives were focused on the city. By creating houses and gardens larger and more elaborate than the medieval manors and monastic buildings they replaced, families enhanced their status, signalled their awareness of the newest ideas, and displayed their knowledge and culture.

Notes

1. J. Davies, *Hymnes of Astraea in acrosticke verse* (London, 1599).
2. R. Strong, *The Renaissance Garden in England* (London, 1979), pp. 7–10.
3. For a full discussion of this concept, see J. Francis, 'Order and Disorder in the Early Modern Garden, 1558–*c*.1630', *Garden History*, 36/1 (2008), pp. 22–35.
4. They included T. Hill, *The Gardener's Labyrinth* (London, 1577), J. Gerard, *The Herball* (London, 1597), William Lawson, *A New Orchard and Garden* (London, 1617) and J. Parkinson, *Paradisi in Sole, Paradisus Terrestis* (London, 1629).
5. Strong, *Renaissance Garden*, p. 10.
6. J. Norden, *Speculum Britanniae, An Historical and Chorographical Description of Middlesex and Hartfordshire* (London, 1723), 'Hartfordshire', p. 2.
7. P. Plumb, 'Coaching Routes, Post Roads and Inns', in D. Short (ed.), *An Historical Atlas of Hertfordshire* (Hatfield, 2011), p. 42.
8. P.M. Hunneyball, *Architecture and Image-Building in Seventeenth Century Hertfordshire* (Oxford, 2004), p. 12.
9. A. Rowe, C. Taylor and T. Williamson, 'The History of the Gardens at Benington Park', report for the Hertfordshire Gardens Trust (2008). HALS 712.6.
10. See, for example, Strong, *Renaissance Garden*, pp. 103–10; discussion of aspects of the garden's history in P. Henderson, *The Tudor House and Garden* (New Haven, CT and London, 2005); and S. Snell, *The Gardens at Hatfield* (London, 2005).
11. Hunneyball, *Architecture and Image-Building*, p. 67.
12. H. Prince, *Parks in Hertfordshire since 1500* (Hatfield, 2008), p. 17.
13. *Ibid.*, pp. 18–19.
14. Tom Williamson discusses the influence on style of the proximity of London in these and later centuries in 'The Character of Hertfordshire's Parks and Gardens', A. Rowe (ed.), *Hertfordshire Garden History: A Miscellany* (Hatfield, 2007), pp. 11–23.
15. N. Goose, 'Urban growth and economic development in early modern Hertfordshire', in T. Slater and N. Green (eds), *A County of Small Towns: The Development of Hertfordshire's Urban Landscape to 1800* (Hatfield, 2008), p. 119.
16. Hunneyball, *Architecture and Image-Building*, p. 13.
17. The Inns of Court were known as England's 'third university' and often used as a London base by wealthy young men.
18. T. Wilson, 'England in 1600', quoted in L. Stone (ed.) *The Crisis of the Aristocracy 1558–1641* (Oxford, 1965), p. 115.
19. L. Stone and J. Stone, *An Open Elite? England 1540–1880* (Oxford, 1984), p. 295.
20. *Ibid.*, p. 299.
21. S. Alford, *Burghley: William Cecil at the Court of Elizabeth I* (New Haven, CT and London, 2011), p. 253.
22. N. Cooper, *Houses of the Gentry 1480–1680* (New Haven, CT and London, 1999), p. 11.
23. Hunneyball, *Architecture and Image-Building*, p. 185.
24. R. Tittler, *Nicholas Bacon: The Making of a Tudor Statesman* (London, 1976), p. 67.
25. N. Cooper, *Houses of the Gentry*, p. 185.
26. B. Castiglione, *The Book of the Courtier, done into English by Sir Thomas Hoby, anno 1561* (London, 1900).
27. F. Bacon, 'Of Gardens', *Essays or Counsels, Civil and Moral* (London, 1625; Folio Society edn, London, 2002).
28. For an examination of the contradictions, see H. Smith, 'The Gardens of Sir Nicholas and Sir Francis Bacon: An Enigma Resolved and a Mind Explored', in A. Fletcher and P. Roberts (eds), *Religion, Culture and Society in Early Modern Britain* (Cambridge, 1994), pp. 125–60. For more on the contemporary context of Bacon's essay, see P. Henderson, 'Sir Francis Bacon's essay "Of Gardens" in context', *Garden History*, 36/1 (2008), pp. 59–84.
29. F. Bacon, 'Of Building', *Essays or Counsels, Civil and Moral* (London, 1996 edn), pp. 160–1.
30. Smith, in Fletcher and Roberts (eds), *Religion, Culture and Society*, p. 149.

31. J. Spedding, *The Letters and Life of Francis Bacon*, vol. iv (London, 1857–9), pp. 76–7.
32. J.R. Solomon and C.G. Martin, *Francis Bacon and the Refiguring of Early Modern Thought* (Farnham, 2005), pp. 183–4.
33. Henderson, 'Sir Francis Bacon's Essay', p. 69.
34. F. Bacon, *Sylva Sylvarum: Or a natural history in ten centuries* (1627, Kessinger Publishing edn, n.p., n.d.), p. 3.
35. M. Archer, 'Beest, Bird or Flower: Stained Glass at Gorhambury House', *Country Life*, 3 June 1976, p. 451.
36. J. Aubrey, 'Francis Bacon', in *Brief Lives* (1680, Folio Society edn, London, 1975), p. 42.
37. R. Smythson, 'Lord Bedford's House at Twickenham, Middlesex'. Illustrated in M. Girouard, *Robert Smythson and the Elizabethan Country House* (New Haven, CT and London, 1983), p. 169.
38. The role of Francis Bacon in developing the Gray's Inn Walks is discussed in D. Jacques, '"The Chief Ornament" of Gray's Inn: The Walks from Bacon to Brown', *Graya*, 110 (1999), pp. 54–75; and D. Spring, 'James Dalton and Francis Bacon: Two Garden-makers of the Inns of Court', *The London Gardener*, 14 (2008–9), pp. 11–20.
39. Compare, for example, Palladio's Villa Rotunda of 1567, and the Villa Emo Capodilista near Padua, both of which still exist. They have much in common with the structure shown in John Aubrey's sketch of Verulam House. See <http://www.villevenetecastelli.com/it/provincia-di-padova/45-la-montecchia/66-la-montecchia.html>, accessed 7 February 2012.
40. See P. Henderson, 'Sir Francis Bacon's Water Gardens at Gorhambury', *Garden History*, 20 (1992), pp. 116–31.
41. Spedding, *Letters and Life*.
42. J. Thorpe, 'Survey of Cheshunt Park in 1611', British Library, Cotton MS Aug.I.i.75.
43. T. Comito, 'Renaissance Gardens and the Discovery of Paradise', *Journal of the History of Ideas*, 32/4 (1971), p.497–8.
44. Henderson, *Tudor House and Garden*, p. 196.
45. Description of Theobalds in 1602, quoted in M. Girouard, *Elizabethan Architecture* (New Haven, CT and London, 2009), p. 229.
46. F. Bacon, 'Of Buildings', p. 162.
47. M. Airs, 'Pomp or Glory: The Influence of Theobalds', in P. Croft (ed.), *Patronage, Culture and Power: The Early Cecils* (New Haven, CT and London, 2002), p. 4.
48. The Duke of Wurtemberg's visit in 1592, recorded by Rathgeb, and Hentzer's visit of 1598. See Henderson, *Tudor House and Garden*, pp. 84–5.
49. Baron Waldstein, visiting in 1600; Henderson, *Tudor House and Garden*, pp. 84–5.
50. Theobalds Road in Holborn is still the start of the route north.
51. N. Cooper, *The Jacobean Country House* (London, 2006), pp. 44–50.
52. Strong, *Renaissance Garden*, pp. 105–7.
53. S.M. Jack, 'Fanshawe, Thomas (*c.*1533–1601)', *Oxford Dictionary of National Biography (ODNB)*, (Oxford, 2004), online edn, January 2008, <http://www.oxforddnb.com.ezproxy.londonlibrary.co.uk/view/article/9150>, accessed 7 February 2012.
54. H. Wotton, 'Architecture', in *Reliquiae Wottonianae* (London, 1672), pp. 64–5, <http://books.google.co.uk/books?id=3iZEAAAAcAAJ&pg=PA64&lpg=PA64&dq=wotton+a+delicate+curiosity&source>, accessed 7 February 2012.
55. Thomson (ed.), *The Chamberlain Letters* (London, 1966), p. 61.
56. T. Birch, *The Court and Times of James the First*, vol. i (London, 2005 edn), p. 94. An outlay of £12 in 1609 is the equivalent of over £1,000 today.
57. Thomson (ed.), *The Chamberlain Letters*, p. 99.
58. *Ibid.*, p. 157.
59. *Ibid.*, p. 93.
60. Alain Wijffels, 'Caesar, Sir Julius (*bap.* 1558, *d.* 1636)', *ODNB*, (Oxford, 2004), online edn, January 2008, <http://www.oxforddnb.com.ezproxy.londonlibrary.co.uk/view/article/4328>, accessed 7 February 2012.

Bibliography

Primary sources
Calendar of State Papers, Domestic, Elizabeth I/12/193/28 (1586).

British Library:
Cotton MS Aug.I.i.75, Thorpe, J. 'Survey of Cheshunt Park in 1611'.

Hertfordshire Archives and Local Studies (HALS):
Chauncy, H., *The Historical Antiquities of Hertfordshire*.
D/EV P1, Map of the manor of Gorhambury 1634, by Benjamin Hare.
712.6, Rowe, A.,Taylor, C. and Williamson, T., 'The History of the Gardens at Benington Park', report for the Hertfordshire Gardens Trust (2008).
942.58/NOR, Norden, J., *Speculum Britanniae, an Historical and Chorographical Description of Middlesex and Hartfordshire* (London, 1723).

Secondary sources
Alford, S., *Burghley: William Cecil at the Court of Elizabeth I* (New Haven, CT and London, 2011).
Aubrey, J., *Brief Lives* (1680; Folio Society edn London, 1975).
Bacon, F., *Essays or Counsels, Civil and Moral* (1625; Folio Society edn, London, 2002).
Bacon, F., *Sylva Sylvarum: Or a natural history in ten centuries* (1627; Kessinger Publishing edn n.p., n.d.).
Birch, T., *The Court and Times of James the First*, vol i (London, 2005).
Castiglione, B., *The Book of the Courtier, done into English by Sir Thomas Hoby, anno 1561* (London, 1900).
Chauncy, H., *The Historical Antiquities of Hertfordshire* (London, 1700; 2nd edn 1826).
Cooper, N., *Houses of the Gentry 1480–1680* (New Haven, CT and London, 1999).
Cooper, N., *The Jacobean Country House* (London, 2006).
Croft, P. (ed.), *Patronage, Culture and Power: The Early Cecils* (New Haven, CT and London, 2002).
Davies, J., *Hymnes of Astraea in acrosticke verse* (London, 1599).
Fletcher, A. and Roberts, P. (eds), *Religion, Culture and Society in Early Modern Britain* (Cambridge, 1994).
Gerard, J., *The Herball or generall historie of plantes* (London, 1597).
Girouard, M., *Robert Smythson and the Elizabethan Country House* (New Haven, CT and London, 1983).
Girouard, M., *Elizabethan Architecture* (New Haven, CT and London, 2009).
Henderson, P., *The Tudor House and Garden* (New Haven, CT and London, 2005).
Hill, T., *The Gardener's Labyrinth* (London, 1577).
Hunneyball, P.M., *Architecture and Image-Building in Seventeenth Century Hertfordshire* (Oxford, 2004).
Lawson, W., *A New Orchard and Garden* (London, 1617).
Page, W. (ed.), *VCH Hertfordshire*, vol. iii (London, 1912).
Parkinson, J., *Paradisi in Sole, Paradisus Terrestis* (London, 1629).
Prince, H., *Parks in Hertfordshire since 1500* (Hatfield, 2008).
Rowe, A. (ed.), *Hertfordshire Garden History: A Miscellany* (Hatfield, 2007).
Short, D. (ed.), *An Historical Atlas of Hertfordshire* (Hatfield, 2011).
Slater, T. and Goose, N. (eds), *A County of Small Towns: The Development of Hertfordshire's Urban Landscape to 1800* (Hatfield, 2008).
Snell, S., *The Gardens at Hatfield* (London, 2005).
Solomon, J. R. and Martin, C.G., *Francis Bacon and the Refiguring of Early Modern Thought* (Farnham, 2005).
Spedding, J., *The Letters and Life of Francis Bacon*, vol. iv (London, 1857–9).

Stone, L. (ed.), *The Crisis of the Aristocracy 1558–1641* (Oxford, 1965).
Stone, L. and Stone, J., *An Open Elite? England 1540–1880* (Oxford, 1984).
Strong, R., *The Renaissance Garden in England* (London, 1979).
Thomson, E. (ed.), *The Chamberlain Letters* (London, 1966).
Tittler, R., *Nicholas Bacon: The Making of a Tudor Statesman* (London, 1976).

Journals

Archer, M., 'Beest, Bird or Flower: Stained Glass at Gorhambury House', *Country Life*, 3 June (1976), p. 451.
Comito, T., 'Renaissance Gardens and the Discovery of Paradise', *Journal of the History of Ideas*, 32/4 (1971), pp. 497–8.
Francis, J. 'Order and Disorder in the Early Modern Garden, 1558–*c*.1630', *Garden History*, 36/1 (2008), pp. 22–35.
Henderson, P. 'Sir Francis Bacon's Water Gardens at Gorhambury', *Garden History*, 20 (1992), pp. 116–31.
Henderson, P., 'Sir Francis Bacon's Essay "Of Gardens" in Context', *Garden History*, 36/1 (2008), pp. 59–84.
Jacques, D., '"The Chief Ornament" of Gray's Inn: The Walks from Bacon to Brown', *Graya*, 110 (1999), pp. 54–75.
Jones, A.,'Turnpiking the Old North Road', *Hertfordshire's Past*, 31 (1991).
Rowe, A., Taylor, C. and Williamson, T., 'The Earthworks at Benington Park, Hertfordshire: An Exercise in Dating an Archaeological Garden', *Landscape History*, 32/2 (2011), pp. 37–55.
Spring, D., 'James Dalton and Francis Bacon: Two Garden-makers of the Inns of Court', *The London Gardener*, 14 (2008–9), pp. 11–20.

Web sources

Davies, J., 'Hymnes of Astraea in ackrosticke verse' (London, 1599). *The Works in Verse and Prose (including hitherto unpublished Mss.) of Sir John Davies: for the first time collected and edited: With memorial-introductions and notes: By the Rev. Alexander B. Grosart* (Blackburn, 1869), p. 239. Online edition (Cambridge, 1992), <http://gateway.proquest.com/openurl/openurl?ctx_ver=Z39.88-2003&xri:pqil:res_ver=0.2&res_id=xri:ilcs&rft_id=xri:ilcs:ft:e_poetry:Z300335271:3>, accessed 7 February 2012.
Jack, S.M, 'Fanshawe, Thomas (*c*.1533–1601)', *Oxford Dictionary of National Biography* (Oxford, 2004), online edn, January 2008, <http://www.oxforddnb.com.ezproxy.londonlibrary.co.uk/view/article/9150>, accessed 7 February 2012.
Jack, S.M. 'Fanshawe, Sir Henry (1569–1616)', *Oxford Dictionary of National Biography* (Oxford, 2004), online edn, January 2008, <http://www.oxforddnb.com.ezproxy.londonlibrary.co.uk/view/article/9148>, accessed 7 February 2012.
Villa Emo, <http://www.villevenetecastelli.com/it/provincia-di-padova/45-la-montecchia/66-la-montecchia.html>, accessed 7 February 2012.
Wijffels, A., 'Caesar, Sir Julius (*bap.* 1558, *d.* 1636)', *Oxford Dictionary of National Biography* (Oxford, 2004), online edn, January 2008, <http://www.oxforddnb.com.ezproxy.londonlibrary.co.uk/view/article/4328>, accessed 7 February 2012.
Wotton, H. 'Architecture', in *Reliquiae Wottonianae* (London, 1672), pp. 64–5, <http://books.google.co.uk/books?id=3iZEAAAAcAAJ&pg=PA64&lpg=PA64&dq=wotton+a+delicate+curiosity&source>, accessed 7 February 2012.

CHAPTER TWO

Hertfordshire's lost water gardens 1500–1750

Anne Rowe

Introduction

Hertfordshire has provided the setting for some iconic water gardens.[1] The most famous of these are perhaps those created at Theobalds near Waltham Cross in the late sixteenth century by Lord Burghley, and those created a generation later by his son, Sir Robert Cecil, Lord Salisbury, at Hatfield House, and by Cecil's cousin, Sir Francis Bacon, at Gorhambury near St Albans. While none of these survive as water gardens today, as we saw in Chapter 1 each has been the subject of much research by eminent garden historians who have drawn together a variety of evidence to build up a picture of what the gardens looked like 400 years ago.

There have been many other water gardens in Hertfordshire besides these three and this chapter will consider the evidence for four which are less well known, but are nevertheless important: The More near Rickmansworth, Theobalds park near Waltham Cross, Bushey Hall near Bushey and Popes near Hatfield. Each was created in a different period of history – the first nearly 500 years ago in the early sixteenth century during the reign of Henry VIII, the second at the end of the reign of his daughter Elizabeth I, the third during the reigns of James II and William and Mary in the late seventeenth century, and the last in the Georgian era of the mid-eighteenth century.

As can be seen in Figure 2.1, all these water gardens, together with the three famous ones, were located in the south of the county, suggesting that access to the capital was important for their owners. Indeed, most were created by important statesmen who spent much of their time at the royal court. From the evidence of this small sample, it appears that it was only in the later seventeenth century that men slightly lower down the social scale started to create water gardens. A source of water was, of course, a prerequisite for any water garden and most were established on the flood plain of one of the county's rivers or utilised the water of a tributary. However, as we shall see, where no natural watercourse was available, it was not beyond the wit or wealth of at least one landowner to create an artificial river in his park.

The water gardens at The More, Theobalds park and Bushey Hall all incorporated a pre-existing moat, presumably dug around the site of a house in the medieval period. The original purpose of these household moats has long been the subject of debate. Although no doubt a deterrent to intruders, few moats could have provided much resistance to a determined attack and most historians now believe that the primary motivation for digging a moat had more to do with fashion than defence. A moat may also have improved the drainage of the house site and many were stocked with fish destined for the table. Ornamental ponds in water

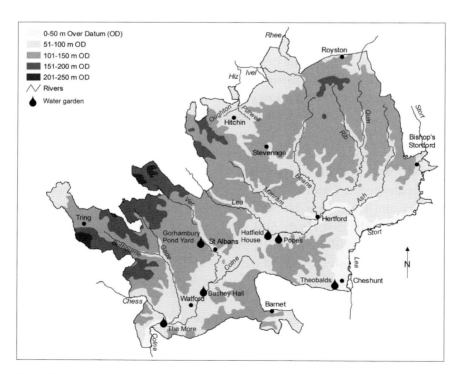

Figure 2.1 Map showing the locations of important water gardens in the county. The gardens at Theobalds and in Theobalds park are represented by a single symbol.

gardens were also dual-purpose and functioned as valuable fish stores into the eighteenth century.

The More, Rickmansworth

The earliest water garden in Hertfordshire for which evidence has been found was at the manor of The More near Rickmansworth. It has to be admitted that the evidence is only circumstantial but it nevertheless seems very likely that Cardinal Thomas Wolsey, Chief Minister to Henry VIII, had an impressive water garden around his house here in the early sixteenth century. Wolsey acquired The More when he became the titular abbot of St Albans in 1521. A high-status manor house had been built at The More in the mid-fifteenth century within a moat just to the south of the river Colne (Figure 2.2).[2] The house was built of brick and crenellated and further enhanced by the creation of an extensive deer park on the rising ground to the south-east, incorporating perhaps 600 acres of woodland and heath in the parishes of Rickmansworth and Watford.[3]

The manor of The More was held by some prestigious men in the late fifteenth century, including Archbishop George Neville and King Edward IV, and we know that there were significant gardens before Wolsey's time because in 1484 Richard III granted custody of his manor 'of Le More with all its gardens' to Edward Gower, one of the ushers of the King's chamber.[4] No record of the form of these gardens has been found.

Cardinal Wolsey is perhaps best known for the building work he undertook at Hampton Court beside the Thames in Surrey, a property he held from 1514. But he was one of the most active builders of his day, with major works at another seven sites including York Place, his London residence beside the Thames at Westminster, Esher Place in Surrey and another Hertfordshire house belonging to the abbey of St Albans at Tyttenhanger, about twelve miles upstream from The More.[5] The house Wolsey created at The More was comparable in size and splendour with Hampton Court; one contemporary report even describes The More as more magnificent than Hampton Court.[6] Wolsey spent much of each summer at one or other of these two houses, using them both for entertaining visiting ambassadors and royalty.[7] Work began to improve The More in 1522 and, as at Hampton Court, Wolsey's development of the house seems to have been influenced by his enthusiasm for gardens.[8]

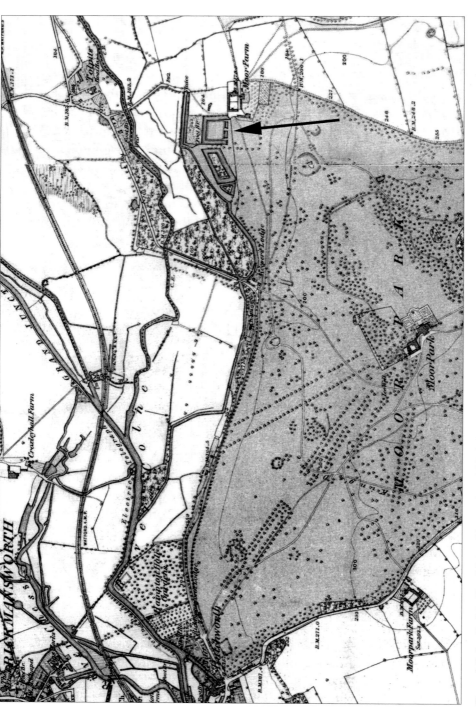

Figure 2.2 Detail of the First Edition OS map sheets XLIII (1868–83) and XLIV (1877), 6 inches to the mile, showing the household moat of The More (arrowed) at the north-east corner of Moor Park. (Not reproduced at the original scale.) REPRODUCED BY KIND PERMISSION OF HALS.

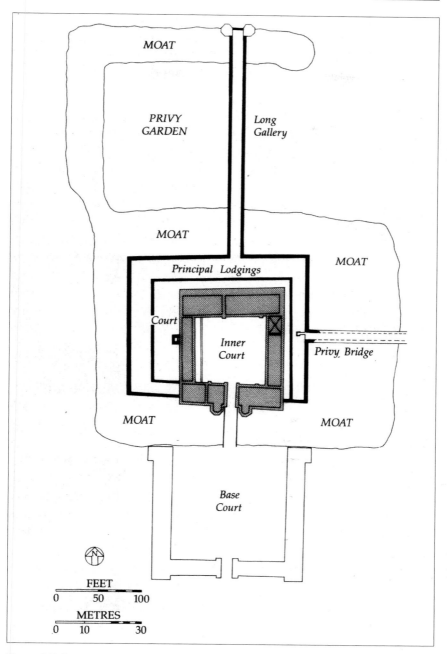

Figure 2.3 Reconstructed ground plan of The More, c.1529, by Simon Thurley. The shaded areas represent the pre-existing house. Taken from 'The Domestic Building Works of Cardinal Wolsey', in S.J. Gunn and P.G. Lindley (eds), *Cardinal Wolsey: Church, State and Art* (Cambridge, 1991), p. 92. REPRODUCED BY KIND PERMISSION OF SIMON THURLEY.

He enclosed the original courtyard house within a larger courtyard house, leaving narrow courts between the two and taking up all the ground within the moat (Figure 2.3). The new buildings incorporated accommodation for Henry VIII and Queen Katherine and a new base court south of the moat was built to accommodate the royal household. These facilities were well used: the king made at least eight visits to The More between 1515 and 1528, staying for twenty-one days in total.[9] From the east range of his enlarged house, Wolsey constructed a bridge which gave access to an orchard. From the north range, he built a long gallery which extended for 253 feet across the moat, through the privy garden and across an extension to the moat, ending with two towers. The privy garden, surrounded by water on three sides, was presumably accessed from the long gallery.

Research by Simon Thurley and others has revealed that a distinctive feature of Wolsey's buildings was the innovative form of his long galleries. Unlike other early sixteenth-century galleries which were incorporated within the house, Wolsey's were free-standing, extending from the house out into the gardens. Of the six for which evidence survives, we know that:

- All were about 250 feet long. They were glazed on both sides and were dead ends – that is, you walked along the gallery not to get to somewhere else, but simply for the exercise and the pleasure of looking out of the windows.
- Like the gallery at The More, those at Hampton Court and Esher Place also ended in two small towers.
- At York Place, Esher Place and The More, water was a major feature of the view – either running alongside, or running beneath, the gallery. At Hampton Court, too, the view from one side of the gallery was probably over water – into the garden which became known as The Pond Gardens.[10]

Mario Savorgnano, a visitor from Venice, described Wolsey's galleries as 'long porticoes or halls, without chambers, with windows on each side, looking on gardens or rivers'.[11] Taken together, the evidence (both documentary and archaeological[12]) for the gallery and the extended moat, and for Wolsey's use of The More for entertaining prestigious guests, as well as his known predilection for gardens and water, all

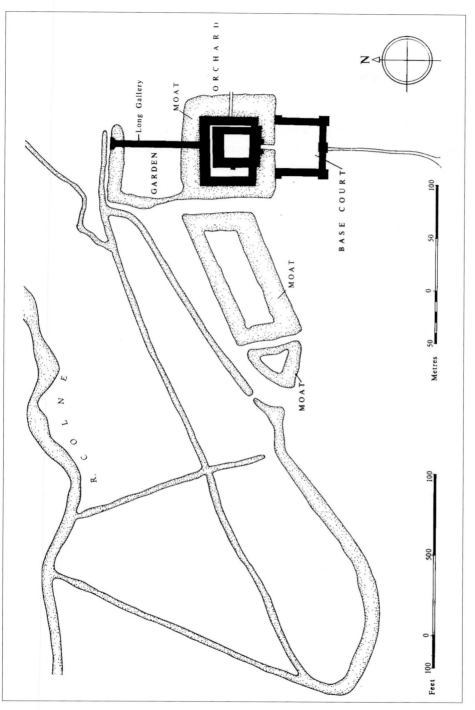

Figure 2.4 Plan of The More, c.1547, by Simon Thurley, showing the layout of manor and gardens. Taken from *The Royal Palaces of Tudor England* (Newhaven, CT and London, 1993), Plan 9. REPRODUCED BY KIND PERMISSION OF SIMON THURLEY.

supports the theory that there were beautiful water gardens around The More in the 1520s. There are, unfortunately, no surviving descriptions or illustrations of the gardens but the fact that Wolsey is reported to have spent between £40 and £50 a year on their maintenance hints at a high level of sophistication.[13]

In 1529, following Cardinal Wolsey's fall from power, The More became one of the King's houses. He paid 6d a day for a man to care for the garden, ponds, orchard and 'les sluces' in the 1530s and a special boat was purchased to help keep the ponds and moat clear of grass and weeds to allow 'the kings grace to fysche'.[14] These fishponds were probably the water features that lay to the west of the house within the deer park which Wolsey had extended northwards to surround his sumptuous residence (Figure 2.4).[15] Whether the ponds date from Wolsey's time or an earlier period is not known. All we do know is that, in 1539, 'a branch of the moat was filled … to make a clear way for the coursing'[16] – so the water features shown in Figure 2.4 are not entirely the remains of what existed in Wolsey's time.

The More seems to have been used less frequently from the middle of the sixteenth century, and the house was in need of costly repairs by 1568, so it seems unlikely that the gardens would have been maintained.[17] There is conflicting evidence for the subsequent fate of The More: it may have been demolished by the end of the sixteenth century but a reference in 1642 to the 'ould Mansion house' along with the 'ground called the Pondyardes, together with the ponds and fishinges thereof' suggests that it continued in use, albeit at a much reduced status, well into the next century.[18] By 1627 the first of a series of grand houses – and equally grand gardens – had been constructed on a new site located on higher ground within the deer park.[19]

The moat of the Tudor house was partially filled with clay from road widening before 1939, and then entirely filled in 1957, but not before archaeological investigations were undertaken in 1952–5.[20] The site now lies beneath the playing fields of a school.

Theobalds park, Waltham Cross
The park at Theobalds was created by William Cecil, Lord Burghley, to provide an appropriate setting for the magnificent house he built from 1563 and the famous gardens he laid out around it (see Chapter 1). An excellent map of his estate, drawn *c*.1575, shows the landscape to

the south and west of his new house and gardens before the park was created.[21] His lands were bounded to the south by the county boundary (the 'shyre dyche'), to the north by 'wood grene layne' (now called Theobalds Lane), to the west by 'Bulcroslaine', and to the east by fields on the west side of the Old North Road. The estate incorporated the manors of Theobalds and Cullings and perhaps a third manor to the west, unnamed on the map.[22]

Lord Burghley's plans for his new park are indicated by a double row of dots leading southwards in a straight line from the south wall of his garden at Theobalds, and across the 'Conygarth' and three fields to the hedged walk or lane surrounding two fields belonging to the manor of Cullings. Later maps show that this became a tree-lined walk linking the gardens of Theobalds to the hedged walk and then leading west and south towards a moat. This moat is labelled 'The manoer place in Coelyns Wodde' on the c.1575 map and probably originated as the homestead moat of the manor of Cullings. By the time this map was drawn, however, it already had the appearance of a garden, the central island divided by paths into four square plats (Plate 2.1). This moated garden was to become an important feature in the designed landscape of Theobalds park created by Lord Burghley and his son, Sir Robert Cecil, at the turn of the sixteenth and seventeenth centuries.

The extent of Lord Burghley's park is not known but an early seventeenth-century petition by the inhabitants of Cheshunt records that 'Lord Burghley, late Lord Treasurer of England, took 16 acres in Cullers [the manor of Cullings] into Theobalds park'.[23] The earliest known map to show the park is the county map by Norden, published in 1598, the year Lord Burghley died.[24]

Sir Robert Cecil made major improvements to Theobalds park in the years following the death of his father. A survey made by Israel Amyce recorded that Cecil had enlarged the park in 1600 and again the following year. As a result of these enlargements the park contained 313 acres.[25] One of the features shown on a map drawn by Amyce in 1602 was The Lodge, a substantial three-storey building which overlooked an open area of parkland labelled 'The Cowrse'.[26] This lodge is likely to have been the retreat favoured by Lord Burghley when he wished to escape from the pressures of court and government.[27]

In 1602 Cecil embarked on a major project to create a 'new river' through the park. The work was undertaken by Adrian Gilbert, the younger brother of the famous Sir Humphrey Gilbert, seaman and explorer, and the older half brother of the even more famous Sir Walter Ralegh. During the 1590s Adrian Gilbert was closely involved with Ralegh's affairs, living at his estate at Sherborne Castle, Dorset, and undertaking much of the responsibility for the building of Ralegh's new house 'Sherborne Lodge' and the construction of its gardens.[28] Intriguingly, this work included 'drawing the River through rocks into his garden'. Gilbert appears to have taken a keen interest in gardening, and research by John Roberts suggests that he may have been connected with the creation of several important gardens, some of which, like Sherborne, included water works.[29]

This previous experience of manipulating water may explain why Adrian Gilbert was employed by Sir Robert Cecil to create the artificial river in Theobalds park. The river formed part of a suite of water features depicted on a plan of Theobalds park by John Thorpe in 1611 (see Plate 2.2 for a digitised tracing of part of this plan).[30] The plan shows the garden in the Cullings moat as well as a number of other ponds, some or all of which may have been initiated by Lord Burghley before 1598 to embellish his new park. Alternatively, the ponds may have been created for Sir Robert Cecil between 1598 and 1607.

There is no doubt, however, that the artificial river was constructed for Cecil because letters written to him by Adrian Gilbert as the work was proceeding survive in the Hatfield House Archives. In the first of these, written at the end of June 1602, Gilbert set out his proposals for obtaining water to supply the 'new river'. A spring had been brought 'through the wood' to supply the lodge and the surplus was then to be directed 'to the great pond by your Honour's house', which would be the source of water for the 'new river'.[31] On 11 July Gilbert wrote that he wanted Cecil to see the newly-dug channel 'before the end of the next week, before they bring in water', in case Cecil would have it broader or deeper.[32] A month later he states he 'has made Cecil a river in his park better than if it were natural, and has less impediments, more pleasure, more profit and [is] more beautiful'. He had 'made four or five fords for the deer to go through, and be fit places for the herons to feed on the shoals, which they cannot do on the high banks'. Whatever fish were put in 'none can go away, if it be less than a minnow or an eel, or as big as a goose quill'. Gilbert also mentioned a 'fair square pond' and considered that his work was 'worth half Cecil's house and park'.[33] He recommended that the banks of the channel should be left to stabilise during the coming winter before being planted up with 'sagge' [?sedge], rushes and bushes the following spring.[34] Subsequent letters written during August and September suggest that there were problems obtaining sufficient water to fill 'the wounded ground where my river is cut' and Cecil was given estimates for the cost of bringing water from a spring at Wood Green using lead pipes (over £300) or brick (about £200).[35]

As well as the artificial river, Thorpe's plan also shows several clearly man-made ponds which appear to be ornamental and were probably also fishponds. These include two ponds – perhaps deliberately aligned with the lodge – and a pair of small rectangular ponds lying side by side on the east bank of the artificial river. The 'fair square pond' mentioned by Gilbert may perhaps be identified as the square pond containing the green blobs depicted by Thorpe (Plate 2.2). Just what these green blobs represent is problematic: the shade of green paint used by Thorpe on his plan is the same as that used for trees in the park, but it seems unlikely that trees could grow successfully in fairly deep water. The blobs appear to have had elliptical shading applied to them, suggesting that they might be islands, but there is no supporting evidence for this theory surviving on the ground today. One possible explanation is that Thorpe thought that the pond would be improved with the addition of some islands so used artistic licence to embellish his plan.

An alternative location for the 'fair square pond' is the former household moat of the manor of Cullings. By 1611 this moated garden was connected to the palace gardens by formal tree-lined paths and Thorpe depicted additional, apparently ornamental, details over the moat; it is not really clear what they were but perhaps pavilions at the corners of the moat and a bridge. It is possible that the elaboration of this moated garden was the work of neither Lord Burghley nor Sir Robert Cecil, but may instead have been undertaken for King James after he became the owner of Theobalds in 1607. No expenditure relating to these gardens appears in the *History of the King's Works*, however, until the year of the king's death, 1625/6, so the features shown on Thorpe's plan are most likely to have been the work of Cecil or his father.

Sir Robert Cecil's artificial river was to last just a decade before it became incorporated into a much larger artificial river – the New River – which was opened in 1613. This innovative scheme to carry fresh water to London from the river Lea at Ware was enthusiastically backed by King James, who happily allowed the New River to pass through his park and make use of part of the channel dug earlier by Adrian Gilbert.

At least some of the ponds shown on Thorpe's plan remained ornamental features in Theobalds park during King James's lifetime. A 'great pond' recorded in 1625/6 contained 'an island, planted with cherry, plum and other fruit trees, while strawberries, primroses and violets were set "round about the border of the Pallisadoe"'.[36] Theobalds was perhaps King James's favourite palace and works completed shortly before he died there in 1625 included the 'making of twoe new pondes and frameing of a mount, and a new stand about a tree at the head of the lower pond'. 'The "old crooked brooke" was 'levelled up answerable to the side of the pondes', equipped with 'gates and sluces with the piramids and arches belonging to them', and with 'diverse bridges'. 'The earth round one or both ponds was reinforced with timber and laid with green turfs.' A survey of 1650 recorded 'the Kings Pond' with a 'decayed Barge and Barge house' and 'an arbour in the midst of the Pond', together with stairs, rails, water gates and grates.[37]

Charles I spent much less time at Theobalds and after the Civil War and the king's execution, the magnificent palace, its gardens and the park were all dismantled by Parliament. A number of houses were constructed on the site of the former palace in the eighteenth century but they were subsequently demolished and fragments of the former palace, a garden wall and the large Elizabethan 'great pond' can still be found in Cedars Park today (Figure 2.5). The land which had formed Theobalds park was divided up and reverted to agricultural use. A new mansion was built in the later eighteenth century on a new site lying to the west of the New River. Parkland was re-established to the east of the mansion, incorporating the New River which was appropriated and modified to form a lake-like feature to ornament the park in the way that was fashionable at the time.

By the middle of the twentieth century a new by-pass for Cheshunt and Waltham Cross (the A10) had been constructed, severing the site of the old palace from its former parkland, and much of the pasture had been converted to arable. Nevertheless, an aerial photograph taken by the RAF in 1946 reveals several traces of the early seventeenth-century landscape (Figure 2.6).[38] In addition to the New River, which was still supplying water to London, the adjacent pair of rectangular ponds can

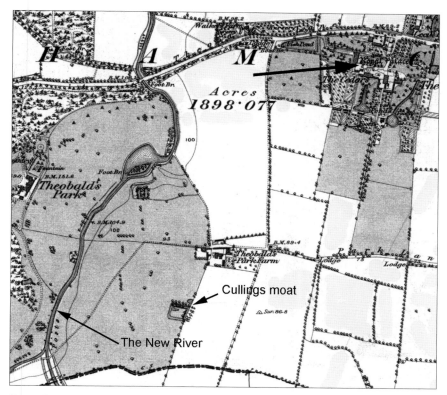

Cullings moat

The New River

Figure 2.5 Detail of First Edition OS map sheet XLI (1882), showing the site of the former 'Royal Palace' (arrowed) and the eighteenth-century mansion called 'Theobalds Park'. The New River and the Cullings moat are also annotated. REPRODUCED BY KIND PERMISSION OF HALS.

still be seen. Nearby, the earthwork banks of the large square pond and the site of the moated garden can be identified within an area of unploughed pasture. The moated garden was partially in-filled in the late twentieth century but the site was excavated by the Enfield Archaeological Society in 2009. They discovered that the ground enclosed within the moat was partly terraced: the northern two-thirds was lower than the southern third. Paths dividing the garden into quadrants were recorded, resulting in a site plan that is noticeably similar to the sixteenth-century map shown in Plate 2.1. In addition, a leat was found to have supplied water to the south-west corner of the moat. Most of the pottery recovered during the dig dated from the seventeenth to the nineteenth centuries.[39]

The land around the former square pond and the moated garden was ploughed up during the later twentieth century. The part of the square pond lying north-west of the public footpath which crosses the site was

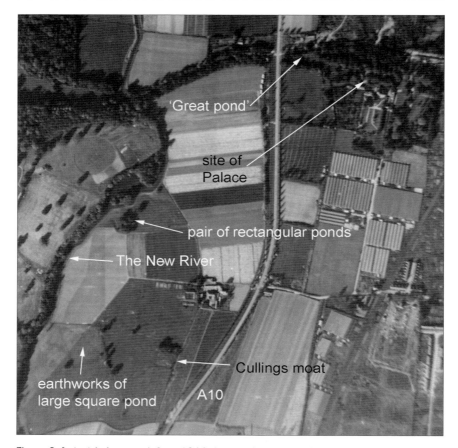

Figure 2.6 Aerial photograph from 1946 showing the surviving fragments of the sixteenth-
and seventeenth-century designed landscape. Off Acc 300, 4049 CPE/UK/1779. REPRODUCED
BY KIND PERMISSION OF HALS.

also ploughed up and the earthwork banks around this part of the pond
were largely destroyed, but it remains a distinctly damp area of the field
and the darker colouration of the soil can be seen on aerial photographs.
The remaining two-thirds of the former pond, lying south-east of the
footpath, remained unploughed until 2010, protected by the massive
banks and a line of trees and shrubs growing on the bank along the
north-eastern side.

     This pond was about 100 metres square and even today the north-
eastern bank is about 12 metres wide and rises about 1.5 metres above
the base of the pond. English Heritage was alerted to the discovery of
this important and very rare piece of archaeology surviving from the early

seventeenth century in June 2011. The artificial river and the associated ponds in Theobalds park represent an important and very unusual water garden, not only because of the high profile of the Cecil family in British history, but because they are precursors to what Sir Robert Cecil went on to create at the much more famous gardens around Hatfield House.

Bushey Hall, Bushey

The creation of the water garden at Bushey Hall can be closely dated to between 1685 and 1700 when the house and its gardens were beautifully illustrated, with no fewer than three different views, in the county history by Sir Henry Chauncy.[40] According to Chauncy, Sir George Walker had 'erected a fair House upon the River Colne' and he was created first Baronet Walker of Bushey Hall in 1679.[41] Walker's new house succeeded another grand house built in the fifteenth century by the Earl of Salisbury.[42] It is not known whether the fifteenth-century house stood within the household moat which lay a short distance from Baronet Walker's house, or whether the latter house incorporated the site, and perhaps some of the structure, of the previous building. The new house was depicted on a plan of the estate surveyed in 1685 (Plate 2.3).[43]

It seems likely that Sir George Walker was responsible for initiating the formal designed landscape around his new house, which can be seen on the plan in Plate 2.3. This included a courtyard garden on the south side of the house with corner pavilions, a circular bowling green encircled by trees on the north front and avenues approaching the house from the north and south. This plan was not, however, drawn for Sir George, but for the next owner of Bushey Hall, Sir Robert Marsham, who was in possession of the estate by May 1685. Sir Robert was from Kent and he was one of the Six Clerks in Chancery, a position he had inherited from his father. He had been knighted in 1681 and his father, Sir John Marsham, died at Bushey Hall in 1685.[44] The 1685 plan does not show any water gardens. To the west of the house lay a rectangular pond and, beyond that, a moat overlooked by a dovecote. North of the moat was the mill and its associated land bordered the river Colne. Neither the pond nor the moat was depicted as an ornamental garden feature. So in the last fifteen years of the seventeenth century Sir Robert Marsham must have created the water gardens between the house and the river, as depicted on a view of Bushey Hall prepared by J. Drapentier for Sir Henry Chauncy's county history of 1700 (Figure 2.7).

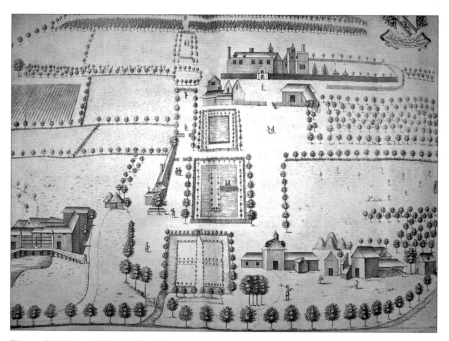

Figure 2.7 View of Bushey Hall from the west drawn by J. Drapentier. The mill is shown bottom left. REPRODUCED BY KIND PERMISSION OF HALS.

Turning the drawing to match the orientation of the plan allows us to examine how Marsham created his water gardens, which take the form of a series of rectangular ponds or moats heading west from the house towards the river Colne (Plates 2.4a and b). The probable former homestead moat (closest to the river) was joined to the river by a channel, and a small rectangular pond along its west side appears the same in 1685 and 1700. By 1700 a causeway had been built at the western end of this moat to match the one at its east end and a border of trees had been planted along its north, south and west sides. On the east side was an arched entrance and the trees were significantly smaller – perhaps fruit bushes rather than trees – to allow a view into the garden from the house. The island within the moat was divided into quadrants by paths and each quadrant was bordered by small bushes. The outer border of the moat was edged with a short fence on the north, south and east sides. On the south side of the moat was a collection of farm buildings, including the square dovecote indicated on the 1685 plan.

The middle pond had been created by extending the previous pond northwards but leaving a rectangular island in an off-centre position.

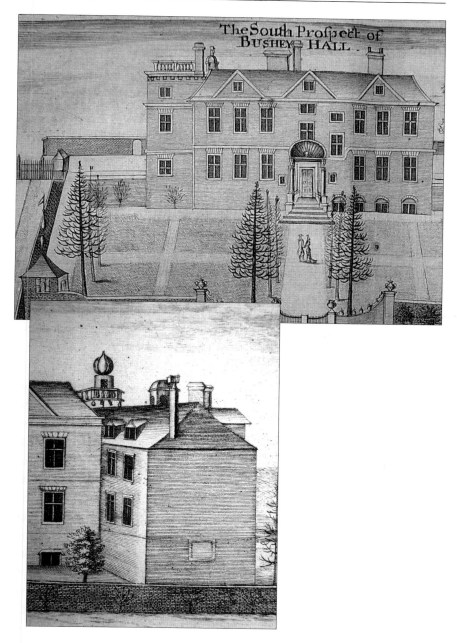

Figures 2.8a and b Details of two of Drapentier's illustrations of Bushey Hall. The view from the south shows the balustraded terrace on the roof giving elevated views of the water gardens laid out to the west. The view from the north (inset) suggests the terrace incorporated an ornately roofed stairwell or perhaps an observatory. Taken from H. Chauncy, *The Historical Antiquities of Hertfordshire* (1700), pp. 540–3. Reproduced by kind permission of HALS.

This island was accessed across the broadest stretch of water via an ornate bridge with a central support. The island and the margins of the pond or moat were planted with rows of small trees or bushes, enclosed within a wooden fence with rows of trees along the north and south sides. An additional rectangular pond had been created between the middle pond and a group of outbuildings close to the house. This pond was edged with a low fence and then bordered with an arrangement of trees and another fence which was similar to that depicted around the middle pond but constructed differently.

The water gardens were approached from the house through a grand archway in the courtyard wall but they were also meant to be enjoyed from a viewing platform located high up on the roof on the west side of the house (Figures 2.8a and b). This appears to have been constructed on an extension to the west end of the house built by Sir Robert Marsham and was perhaps deliberately planned to complement his new water gardens. A similar roof-top viewing platform was a feature of the house built by Sir Francis Bacon alongside the much more famous water gardens created in the early seventeenth century in the Pond Yard at Gorhambury (see Chapter 1).[45]

Sir Robert became the fourth Baronet Marsham on the death of his nephew in 1696.[46] He moved back to the family estate in Kent and sold Bushey Hall in 1701.[47] His water gardens did not survive for long after his departure and nor indeed did the house. The last known reference to Bushey Hall dates from 1732[48] and neither house nor garden was depicted on the county map by Dury and Andrews published in 1766.[49] The property seems to have continued as a farm and the site of Bushey Hall has now been lost under residential development. The household moat was still visible in the early twentieth century and was designated a Scheduled Ancient Monument in 1956. By 1975 only the north-west and south-west arms of the moat survived, both heavily silted and with a maximum depth of 1.8 metres, and the site has now been largely lost in the suburban expansion of Bushey.[50]

Popes, Hatfield

The extraordinary water garden that existed in the park at Popes in the eighteenth century is revealed on a beautiful estate map in the Hatfield House Archives dated 1785 (Plate 2.5).[51] Running across the park from west to east in the valley of a tributary of the river Lea was a string of ponds. These ponds were broadly formal in design but irregular in their layout. The sequence begins with a rectangular pool which feeds eastwards into a square pool and then an octagonal basin, outlined by trees planted for ornamental effect. A series of oddly shaped canals follows and these flow towards the largest body of water, which is roughly funnel-shaped, broadening eastwards to terminate abruptly at a straight dam across the valley. The dam is breached by a cascade which falls into a final pool at the eastern side of the park, a large rectangular sheet of water with a small round island in the middle and bordered by rows of trees along its north and south sides. The straight eastern side of the pool is another dam carrying a carriage drive to the house.

Other features depicted on this map show that a high degree of planning had gone into the design of the park and gardens. They include an avenue of trees which crossed the south side of the park aligned with a walk which formed the north side of a 'wilderness' garden lying south of the house. A Temple lay south of the avenue and opposite a path leading to the centre of the western wilderness garden. To the south of the Temple was a Mount, which was approached by a tree-lined walk aligned with a walk along the south side of the wilderness garden. The wilderness was divided into two distinct halves by a north–south path, the south end of which ended in an alcove, and the axis was continued south of the garden by another avenue of trees. The wilderness to the west of the path was laid out with a series of straight paths radiating from a central point. The eastern wilderness was embellished with a symmetrical arrangement of serpentine paths which crossed at the centre of the garden. To the north of the house was the walled kitchen garden, enclosed on its south side by an ornamental canal.

The formal character of these features in the park and gardens, and the plan of the water gardens, suggests that the whole design dates from the first half of the eighteenth century and the string of ponds, canal and avenue were certainly all in place before 1766 when they were depicted on the county map by Dury and Andrews.[52] The occupier of Popes at this time was the immensely wealthy London brewer, Sir Benjamin Truman, knighted in 1760 on the accession of George III, 'in recognition of his standing in the London business community and for large loans to the crown'.[53] In the same year he also served as sheriff of Hertfordshire.[54]

Truman took up residence at Popes in 1757 but was recorded living at Popes Farm in 1754, from where he perhaps oversaw the rebuilding of the mansion which had been destroyed by fire in 1746.[55] In about 1770–4 Truman commissioned Thomas Gainsborough to paint his portrait, and also those of two granddaughters and two great-grandsons. His portrait hung at Popes until it was removed to his London house at the brewery after his death, in accordance with the instructions left in his will. The portrait is described as 'one of the largest and most powerful canvases Thomas Gainsborough ever painted'[56] and portrays Truman standing beside a stream which is tumbling over a cascade in a pastoral scene, with a house in the background (Plate 2.6). The painting conveys no hint of a formal design but another portrait, painted by George Romney in the 1770s, depicts him sitting beside the columns of a classical building – perhaps the Temple – with a country house in the background and water to the left.[57] Both of these portraits *could* (allowing for a little artistic licence) portray scenes in the park at Popes in the mid-eighteenth century.

Confirmation of a possible fondness for water suggested by the Gainsborough portrait is provided by a record that Sir Benjamin Truman spent £300 on the construction of a Chinese boat. This boat was depicted floating on the Broadwater in nearby Brocket Park, Hatfield, in an illustration by Paul Sandby published in 1787, seven years after Truman died (Figure 2.9).[58] It seems likely that the Chinese boat was initially built to embellish the water gardens at Popes. Careful examination of the 1785 map shows a building on the north bank of

Figure 2.9 Detail of Paul Sandby's illustration of Brocket Hall showing the Chinese boat built for Sir Benjamin Truman. DE/X55/Z2/12. REPRODUCED BY KIND PERMISSION OF HALS.

the largest pool, straddling a narrow channel which extends northwards from the pool (Plate 2.5). This building must have been a boathouse and the scale of the earthwork channel which survives at this location today suggests that it would have been large enough to accommodate the Chinese boat depicted in Sandby's illustration.

The evidence suggesting that Sir Benjamin Truman enjoyed the water gardens at Popes does not necessarily mean, however, that he was responsible for creating them; he was, after all, a tenant and not the owner of the estate. Until 1744 Popes was owned and apparently occupied by David Mitchell (*né* Cooke) and it is possible that he was responsible for the formal design of the park, including the water gardens.[59] An estate map dating from 1722, when he inherited Popes from his uncle, Admiral Sir David Mitchell, pre-dates the avenues, Temple and formal gardens and shows a much simpler arrangement of ponds.[60] These comprised two large rectangles lying end to end along the valley at the east side of the park. The easternmost pond had a small building at its centre; the western one, somewhat improbably, had a tree at its centre.

The small amount of evidence that has been found concerning David Mitchell suggests that he lived the life of a country gentleman and, through his wife's family, he appears to have had connections with the social circle that included the poet Alexander Pope and the royal gardener Charles Bridgeman.[61] Mitchell had certainly enlarged the park by twenty acres by 1730, which could be construed as evidence of him 'improving' the landscape and would be entirely compatible with him establishing a fashionably formal design within it.[62]

In 1744 David Mitchell sold Popes to William Hulls, Esq., citizen and pewterer of London, and he must have been Sir Benjamin Truman's landlord in the 1750s.[63] Given that the house burnt down less than two years after Hulls bought it, and that he also owned an estate in Kent, it seems unlikely that Hulls was responsible for creating the water gardens at Popes.[64] In his will of 1760 Hulls left the Popes estate in trust for his daughter Rebecca Assheton and others.[65] Mrs Assheton was recorded as the owner of the estate in 1785 on the map by Taylor and Chilcott (Plate 2.5).

One other piece of evidence concerning who might have created the water gardens was discovered by Sarah Spooner. Her research has shown that the ornamental landscape of Popes extended beyond the

Figure 2.10 Detail of OS map sheet XXXV (1883), 6 inches to the mile, showing the wood called Popes Pondholes (not reproduced at the original scale). The shape of the wood should be compared with the water features shown on Plate 2.5. REPRODUCED BY KIND PERMISSION OF HALS.

estate boundary: the vista along the avenue heading west across the park continued through a grove to another temple on land belonging to John Church of Woodside Place, Hatfield. A field book belonging to Church and dating from the mid-1770s records an annual payment of £1 from Sir Benjamin Truman 'for leave to erect a temple in Pickbones Field – this is a view cut thro' Quails Wood from Popes Walk & like to be a standing Rent so long as any Gentleman lives there'.[66] This record suggests that it was Benjamin Truman who laid out the avenue – Popes Walk – and perhaps, therefore, the other landscape features as well. This temple and the vista cut through the wood were already present by 1766 when they were shown on Dury and Andrews' county map.

Whichever of the two men – Mitchell or Truman – created the string of ponds, it was not destined to survive far into the nineteenth century. After Truman's death in 1780, Popes continued to be let to tenants before being purchased by the Marquess of Salisbury in 1817 and absorbed into the huge Hatfield House estate.[67] By the time that A. Bryant carried out the survey for his county map, published in 1822, the mansion and park had gone and the remaining buildings were simply labelled 'Popes Farm'. Fragments of the former gardens and park landscape can be detected as lines of trees on the first edition OS map of 1883; High Wood had been felled and the string of ponds – labelled 'Popes Pondholes' – was enveloped in woodland (Figure 2.10). No ponds were shown, however, and it seems likely that the dams which had held the water back were deliberately broken to allow the land to drain. The beds of the former ponds were subsequently planted up with trees and managed for forestry.

The wood called Popes Pondholes has remained unchanged to the present day and under the protective canopy of the trees can be found the remarkable earthwork remains of the eighteenth-century water gardens.[68] Only by visiting the site can one appreciate the impressive scale of these former water features.[69] Some of the earthwork dams constructed to retain the water are massive structures which must have involved a huge amount of earth-moving and cost a great deal of money. The largest of these, between the two easternmost ponds, is still about five metres high and three metres broad across the top. The earthworks, surveyed and recorded with the kind permission of Lord Salisbury in 2012, constitute one of the most remarkable archaeological gardens in Hertfordshire.

Conclusion

The examples described in this chapter give an indication of the variety of water gardens that were established in the county between the early sixteenth century and the middle of the eighteenth century. The earliest water gardens were created on estates within easy reach of London by leading figures in the royal court, such as Cardinal Wolsey in the early sixteenth century and Sir Robert Cecil nearly a century later. Later examples were the work of less prominent individuals, such as Sir Robert Marsham at Bushey Hall. By the late seventeenth century wealthy tradesmen were beginning to make their mark on the county, buying their way into landed society and spending their money on creating fashionable landscapes, as perhaps Sir Benjamin Truman did at Popes.

Most water gardens were relatively short-lived, perhaps because they required a high level of maintenance to keep them looking good; owners needed both wealth and commitment. Their ephemeral nature may have been exacerbated by the regularity with which many Hertfordshire estates changed hands: wealthy London-based statesmen, politicians, lawyers, businessmen and merchants sought country estates within easy reach of the capital. New owners were often not only affluent but also fashion-conscious and, therefore, keen to remodel their houses, gardens and parks in the latest style. Proximity to London also meant that Hertfordshire's designed landscapes – and especially those in the south of the county – were particularly prone to redevelopment.

So the 'London factor' that led to the creation of some of the most prestigious water gardens in the country was also what ultimately led to their destruction. Changing fashions in garden design, together with a pressing need for land to grow food for the capital or trees for the timber trade, and spreading urbanisation, have all combined to erase most traces of these special places from today's landscape. Those traces which *have* survived need to be recorded, celebrated and cherished as an important aspect of Hertfordshire's landscape history.

Notes

1. A water garden is defined as 'an area within a garden in which water provides the main interest, with rocks, pools, cascades and a display of moisture-loving plants, or a large garden where water is the dominant feature, such as Studley Royal, North Yorkshire, with its river and Moon Ponds', M. Symes, *A Glossary of Garden History* (Princes Risborough, 1993), p. 131.
2. H. Falvey, 'The More Revisited', *The Ricardian*, 18 (2008), pp. 93–4.
3. A. Rowe, *Medieval Parks of Hertfordshire* (Hatfield, 2009), p. 180.
4. *Calendar of Patent Rolls 1476–1485*, p. 381.
5. Wolsey's building projects have been researched by several historians and their work has been summarised by Simon Thurley in 'The Domestic Building Works of Cardinal Wolsey', in S.J. Gunn and P.G. Lindley (eds), *Cardinal Wolsey: Church, State and Art* (Cambridge, 1991), pp. 76–102.
6. S. Thurley 'Building Works', p. 91, citing A.F. Pollard, *Wolsey* (London, 1929), p. 325; H.M. Colvin (ed.), *The History of the King's Works*, 4, 1485–1600 (Part II) (London, 1982), pp. 164–7.
7. Thurley, 'Building Works', p. 87.
8. T. Longstaffe-Gowan, *The Gardens and Parks at Hampton Court Palace* (London, 2005), p. 8.
9. He made sixteen visits to Hampton Court during the same period, staying eighty-seven days (Thurley, 'Building Works', pp. 84–5).
10. The Pond Gardens at Hampton Court are usually attributed to Henry VIII, who certainly embellished them, but they were possibly started by Wolsey as there is a record of fishponds being dug/repaired in 1518 (Longstaffe-Gowan, *Hampton Court Palace*, p. 56).
11. Thurley, 'Building Works', p. 98, citing *Calendar of State Papers, Venetian (UK)*, IV, 682.
12. M. Biddle, L. Barfield and A. Millard, 'The Excavation of the Manor of the More, Rickmansworth Hertfordshire', *Archaeological Journal*, 116 (1959), pp. 156–8.
13. H. Falvey, 'The More: Rickmansworth's Lost Palace', *Hertfordshire's Past*, 34 (1993), citing Letters and Papers, Henry VIII, vol. 5, entry 375.
14. TNA: PRO SC6/HENVIII/6012 and 1016 ministers' and receivers' accounts, 1536/7 and 1539/41; S. Thurley, *The Royal Palaces of Tudor England* (New Haven, CT and London, 1993), p. 193.
15. Wolsey enlarged the 600-acre park by nearly 200 acres by enclosing land belonging to a tenant called Tolpott. The road to Watford was diverted to accommodate the enlarged park, presumably to the north and west of the house.
16. Thurley, *Royal Palaces*, p. 192. Watching deer being chased along a course by dogs was a popular pastime in Tudor England.
17. Falvey, 'The More Revisited', p. 97.
18. For a detailed examination of the evidence regarding the demise of this important house, see H. Falvey, 'The More Revisited', pp. 92–9; HALS 45062 Agreement regarding Moor park, 1642.
19. HALS DE/GH/415 Bargain and Sale of Moor Park, 1631.
20. Biddle, Barfield and Millard, 'The Excavation of the Manor of the More', pp. 136–99.
21. Bodleian Library, MS Gough Drawings a.3. Fol. 27 Map of three manors in the south part of Cheshunt.
22. Lord Burghley acquired the manor of Cullings in 1573.
23. TNA: PRO E178/3900 petition re lands taken into Theobalds park 1608–26.
24. J. Norden, *Hartford Shire* (London, 1598).
25. Hatfield House Archives (HHA), CP349 survey of the Hertfordshire estates of Robert Cecil, 1600–01, by Israel Amyce.
26. HHA, CPM Supp 25 map of Theobalds park by Israel Amyce, 1602.
27. P. Henderson, 'A Shared Passion: The Cecils and their Gardens', in P. Croft (ed.), *Patronage, Culture and Power: The Early Cecils* (New Haven, CT, 2002), p. 99.

28. M. Nicholls and P. Williams, 'Ralegh, Sir Walter (1554–1618)', *Oxford Dictionary of National Biography (ODNB)*, (Oxford, 2004), online edn, January 2008, <http://www.oxforddnb.com/view/article/23039>, accessed 31 October 2010.

29. J.C. de V. Roberts, *Devon's Falstaff... the life and times of Adrian Gilbert* <http://jrmundialist.wordpress.com/devon-history/devons-falstaff/> chapters 12 and 14, accessed 9 August 2011. Although clear evidence is lacking, it is possible that Adrian Gilbert played a part in the creation of the water features in the gardens at Wilton where he lived at the end of his life.

30. British Library, Cotton MS Aug.I.i.75. The catalogue describes this as a map of Cheshunt Park but it is Theobalds park (in the parish of Cheshunt). Traced by kind permission of the British Library staff and subsequently digitised and coloured by the author.

31. Royal Commission on Historical Manuscripts, *Calendar of the manuscripts of the Most Honourable the Marquis of Salisbury, preserved at Hatfield House, Hertfordshire, Part XII (1602–3)* (Hereford, 1910), p. 206.

32. *Ibid.*, p. 221.

33. *Ibid.*, p. 292.

34. *Ibid.*, p. 317.

35. *Ibid.*, p. 318, letter dated 24 August 1602 from Roger Houghton to Sir Robert Cecil; p. 380, letter dated 18 September 1602 from Adrian Gilbert to Sir Robert Cecil.

36. Colvin, *The History of the King's Works*, 4, 1485–1660 (Part II), p. 277.

37. *Ibid;* TNA: PRO E317/Herts 27 Parliamentary survey of Theobalds Park, 1650.

38. HALS Off Acc 300, 4049 CPE/UK/1779 aerial photograph taken by the RAF, 10 October 1946.

39. M.J. Dearne and N. Pinchbeck, 'Fieldwalking and Excavation on the Site of Cullings "manor", Cheshunt, Herts', unpublished report of the Enfield Archaeological Society, 2009.

40. H. Chauncy, *The Historical Antiquities of Hertfordshire* (London, 1700), pp. 540–3.

41. Chauncy, *Hertfordshire*, p. 541. George Walker inherited the property in 1674 from his father, Sir Walter Walker, advocate to Catherine of Braganza. He was knighted in 1676 and married in 1677.

42. W. Page (ed.), *VCH Hertfordshire*, vol. ii (1908), Bushey parish, pp. 179–86, <http://www.british-history.ac.uk/report.aspx?compid=43267&strquery=bushey>, accessed 11 August 2010.

43. HALS DE/Hx/P2 Manuscript map of the Bushey Hall Estate, 1685.

44. E. Hasted (ed.), *VCH Kent*, vol. iii (1797), Cookstone parish, pp. 389–403, <http://www.british-history.ac.uk/report.aspx?compid=62869&strquery=Marsham>, accessed 11 August 2010.

45. Bodleian Library, MS Aubr. 6, fol. 72 Sketch by John Aubrey of Verulam House, 1656. Published in P. Henderson, 'Sir Francis Bacon's Water Gardens at Gorhambury', *Garden History*, 20/2 (1992), p. 125.

46. Hasted, *VCH Kent*, vol. iii (1797), Cookstone parish, pp. 389–403, <http://www.british-history.ac.uk/report.aspx?compid=62869&strquery=Marsham>, accessed 11 August 2010.

47. Page, *VCH Hertfordshire*, vol. ii (1908), Bushey parish, pp. 179–86, <http://www.british-history.ac.uk/report.aspx?compid=43267&strquery=bushey>, accessed 11 August 2010.

48. London Metropolitan Archives, ACC/0351/752–756b Lease, Release, Bargain and Sale, Assignments and note of a fine, 1732. A John Nicholl of Bushey Hall, Herts., gent., was party to this transaction.

49. A. Dury and J. Andrews, *A Topographical Map of Hartford-Shire, from an Actual Survey,* 1 mile: 1.95 inches (1766; repr. Hertford, 2004).

50. Hertfordshire Historic Environment Record Number 2579. The 'Moated site at Bushey Hall Farm' is Scheduled Ancient Monument 72:20727/16445 and an Area of Archaeological Significance.

51. HHA, CPM Supp 69 'Plan of the manor of Holbatches alias Popes … belonging to Mrs Rebecca Asheton surveyed by Taylor and Chilcott in the year 1785'.
52. Dury and Andrews, *Hartfordshire*.
53. P. Mathias, 'Truman, Sir Benjamin (1699/1700–1780)', *ODNB* (Oxford, 2004), online edn, <http://www.oxforddnb.com/view/article/50468>, accessed 29 October 2010.
54. TNA C 202/147/2/ Return of Writs: Herts. Oath of Benjamin Trueman, sheriff. 1759/60.
55. H.C.N. Daniell, 'Popes Manor, Essendon', *Transactions of the East Herts Archaeological Society*, 7/2 (1924), p. 155.
56. Mathias, 'Truman, Sir Benjamin (1699/1700–1780)', *ODNB* (Oxford, 2004), online edn, <http://www.oxforddnb.com/view/article/50468>, accessed 29 October 2010.
57. S. Spooner, 'The Diversity of Designed Landscapes: A Regional Approach *c*.1660–1830', PhD thesis, University of East Anglia, 2010, p. 113 (portrait in private collection).
58. W. Angus, *Seats of the Nobility* (1787); HALS DE/X55/Z2/12 illustration of Brocket Hall by Paul Sandby, 1787.
59. R. Eaton *et al.*, 'Pope's Manor, Hatfield: Its History and Excavation', *Hertfordshire's Past*, 7 (1979), p. 15, states that 'it was at this time that the landscaping of the gardens was undertaken' but no source is provided.
60. HHA, CPM Supp 67 A survey of the manor or lordship of Holbatches alias Popes belonging to David Mitchell Esq lying in the parishes of Hatfield and Essendon by John Senex and Richard Cushee, 1722.
61. Richard West, a minor poet and nephew of Mitchell's wife, died at Popes in 1742. His close friends included Horace Walpole, Thomas Ashton and Thomas Gray (see entry in *ODNB*).
62. Daniell, 'Popes Manor, Essendon', p. 155, citing the *Daily Post*, 11 March 1730, which contained an advertisement that Popes was available to let, including a park of 130 acres.
63. In 1744 David Mitchell made a conveyance to 'Wm Hulls and another of the manor of Holbeach alias Popes, manor house, capital messuage, site, gardens etc ground and park and deer therein adjoining the manor house 130ac and various lands', HHA Hatfield Manor Papers, Summaries 2 Sub-manors etc; see also HALS 75169A Deeds of the manor of Popes, 1744. Daniell, 'Popes Manor, Essendon', p. 155, states that this was the son of David Mitchell né Cooke, also called David.
64. J. Bernard Burke, *Genealogical and Heraldic Dictionary of the Landed Gentry* (Dublin, 1879), <http://www.archive.org/stream/genealogicalhera01byuburk/ genealogicalhera01byuburk_djvu.txt> searching for 'Assheton', accessed 7 August 2011.
65. HALS DE/H/790 Copy will of William Hulls, 1760. Rebecca had married Ralph Assheton, of Downham and Cuerdale, Lancashire.
66. Spooner, 'The Diversity of Designed Landscapes', p. 110, citing HALS D/EX55/E1.
67. Page, *VCH Hertfordshire*, vol. iii (1912), Hatfield parish, pp. 91–111, <http://www. british-history.ac.uk/report.aspx?compid=43587&strquery=Hatfield>, accessed 10 August 2011.
68. The remains of the ponds are not the only earthworks to survive from the eighteenth century: The Mount also appears to survive close to the margin of an arable field and the main paths around the wilderness south of the former house were recorded as surviving ridges in 1969–72 (Eaton *et al.*, 'Pope's Manor').
69. The site is on private land and is not accessible to the public.

Bibliography

Primary sources
Manuscript
Bodleian Library, Oxford:
MS Gough Drawings a.3, fol. 27 Map of three manors in the south part of Cheshunt.
MS Aubr. 6, fol. 72 Sketch by John Aubrey of Verulam House, 1656.

British Library:
Cotton MS Aug.I.i.75, the catalogue describes this as a map of Cheshunt Park but it is
    Theobalds park (in Cheshunt).

Hatfield House Archives, Hatfield (HHA):
CP349, survey of the Hertfordshire estates of Robert Cecil, 1600–01, by Israel Amyce.
CPM Supp 25, map of Theobalds park by Israel Amyce, 1602.
CPM Supp 69, 'Plan of the manor of Holbatches alias Popes … belonging to Mrs Rebecca
    Asheton surveyed by Taylor and Chilcott in the year 1785'.
Hatfield Manor Papers, Summaries 2 Sub-manors etc – conveyance by David Mitchell, 1744.
CPM Supp 67, A survey of the manor or lordship of Holbatches alias Popes belonging to
    David Mitchell Esq lying in the parishes of Hatfield and Essendon by John Senex and
    Richard Cushee, 1722.

Hertfordshire Archives and Local Studies (HALS):
45062, Agreement regarding Moor park, 1642.
DE/GH/415, Bargain and Sale of Moor Park, 1631.
Off Acc 300, 4049 CPE/UK/1779, aerial photograph taken by RAF, 10 October, 1946.
DE/Hx/P2, Manuscript map of the Bushey Hall Estate, 1685.
DE/X55/Z2/12, illustration of Brocket Hall by Paul Sandby, 1787.
75169A, Deeds of Manor of Popes, Holbeach, twenty cottages, two dovehouses, twenty
    gardens, 800 acres of land and 300 acres of meadow, 1744.
DE/H/790, Copy will of William Hulls, 1760.
D/EX55/E1, Field book of Woodside House and lands: two particulars of the house and
    Estate, 1772–9.
First Edition OS map sheets XLIII (1868–83) and XLIV (1877), 6 inches to the mile.
First Edition OS map sheets XXXV (1883), 6 inches to the mile.
First Edition OS map sheets XLI (1882), 6 inches to the mile.

Hertfordshire Historic Environment Record Number 2579 Moated Site, Bushey Hall Farm,
    Bushey.

London Metropolitan Archives:
ACC/0351/752-756b, Lease, Release, Bargain and Sale, Assignments and note of a
    fine, 1732.

The National Archives, Kew (TNA: PRO):
SC6/HENVIII/6012 and 1016 ministers' and receivers' accounts, 1536/7 and 1539/41.
E178/3900, petition re lands taken into Theobalds Park 1608–26.
E317/Herts 27 survey of Theobalds Park, 1650.
C 202/147/2/ Return of Writs: Herts. Oath of Benjamin Trueman, sheriff. 1759/60.

Printed
Dearne, M.J. and Pinchbeck, N., 'Fieldwalking and Excavation on the Site of Cullings
    "manor", Cheshunt, Herts', unpublished report of the Enfield Archaeological Society, 2009.

Secondary sources

Angus, W., *Seats of the Nobility* (Islington, 1787).

Calendar of Patent Rolls 1476–1485.

Chauncy, H., *The Historical Antiquities of Hertfordshire* (London, 1700).

Colvin, H.M., (ed.), *The History of the King's Works*, 4, 1485–1660 (Part II) (London, 1982).

Dury, A. and Andrews, J., *A Topographical Map of Hartfordshire* (London, 1766; reprinted by Hertfordshire Record Society, 2004).

Henderson, P., 'A Shared Passion: The Cecils and their Gardens', in P. Croft (ed.), *Patronage, Culture and Power. The Early Cecils* (New Haven, CT, 2002), pp. 99–120.

Longstaffe-Gowan, T., *The Gardens and Parks at Hampton Court Palace* (London, 2005).

Norden, J., *Hartford Shire* (London, 1598).

Pollard, A.F., *Wolsey* (London, 1929).

Rowe, A., *Medieval Parks of Hertfordshire* (Hatfield, 2009).

Royal Commission on Historical Manuscripts, *Calendar of the manuscripts of the Most Honourable the Marquis of Salisbury, preserved at Hatfield House, Hertfordshire, Part XII (1602–3)* (Hereford, 1910).

Spooner, S., 'The Diversity of Designed Landscapes: A Regional Approach *c.*1660–1830', PhD thesis (University of East Anglia, 2010).

Symes, M., *A Glossary of Garden History* (Princes Risborough, 1993).

Thurley, S., 'The Domestic Building Works of Cardinal Wolsey', in S.J. Gunn and P.G. Lindley (eds), *Cardinal Wolsey: Church, State and Art* (Cambridge, 1991), pp. 76–102.

Thurley, S., *The Royal Palaces of Tudor England* (New Haven, CT and London, 1993).

Journals

Biddle, M., Barfield, L. and Millard, A., 'The Excavation of the Manor of the More, Rickmansworth Hertfordshire', *Archaeological Journal*, 116 (1959), pp. 136–99.

Daniell, H.C.N., 'Popes Manor, Essendon', *Transactions of the East Herts Archaeological Society*, 7/2 (1924), pp. 148–60.

Eaton, R. *et al.*, 'Pope's Manor, Hatfield: Its History and Excavation', *Hertfordshire's Past*, 7 (1979), pp. 8–29.

Falvey, H., 'The More: Rickmansworth's Lost Palace', *Hertfordshire's Past*, 34 (1993), pp. 2–16.

Falvey, H., 'The More Revisited', *The Ricardian*, 18 (2008), pp. 93–4.

Henderson, P., 'Sir Francis Bacon's Water Gardens at Gorhambury', *Garden History*, 20/2 (1992), pp. 116–31.

Web sources

Burke, J.B., *Genealogical and Heraldic Dictionary of the Landed Gentry* (Dublin, 1879) seen at <http://www.archive.org/stream/genealogicalhera01byuburk/genealogicalhera01byuburk_djvu.txt>, by searching for 'Assheton', accessed 7 August 2011.

Hasted, E., *VCH Kent*, vol. iii (1797), Cookstone parish, pp. 389–403, <http://www.british-history.ac.uk/report.aspx?compid=62869&strquery=Marsham>, accessed 11 August 2010.

Mathias, P., 'Truman, Sir Benjamin (1699/1700–1780)', *Oxford Dictionary of National Biography* (Oxford, 2004), <http://www.oxforddnb.com/view/article/50468>, accessed 29 October 2010.

Nicholls, M., and Williams, P., 'Ralegh, Sir Walter (1554–1618)', *Oxford Dictionary of National Biography* (Oxford, 2004), online edn, January 2008, <http://www.oxforddnb.com/view/article/23039>, accessed 31 October 2010.

Page, W., *VCH Hertfordshire*, vol. ii (1908) Bushey parish, pp. 179–86, <http://www.british-history.ac.uk/report.aspx?compid=43267&strquery=bushey>, accessed 11 August 2010.

Page, W., *VCH Hertfordshire*, vol. iii (1912), Hatfield parish, pp. 91–111 <http://www.british-history.ac.uk/report.aspx?compid=43587&strquery=Hatfield>, accessed 10 August 2011.

Roberts, J.C. de V., *Devon's Falstaff... the life and times of Adrian Gilbert*, <http://jrmundialist.wordpress.com/devon-history/devons-falstaff/>, chapters 12 and 14.

Hadham Hall and
the Capel Family

Jenny Milledge

Introduction

Hadham Hall, an impressive Elizabethan mansion, stands proud above the Ash valley to the east of Little Hadham with commanding views across the fields which were formerly the Hall's park. Mentioned in Domesday, the manor was held by the Baud family for nearly four hundred years. When William Capel bought it in 1504, probably as an investment, there was already a brick manor house on the site. Three generations later, Henry Capel moved to Hadham and built a house which was sufficiently luxurious to attract Elizabeth I for a brief stay. However, the most important point in the history of the gardens of Hadham Hall occurred in the 1630s, just before the Civil War, when an Italianate garden with accompanying banqueting hall was built. This magnificent garden is featured in the background of the family portrait that Arthur Capel commissioned to celebrate his elevation to the peerage. This chapter will examine the history of Hadham Hall with particular attention to the house and garden as they were in the early seventeenth century. The manor remained in Capel ownership for nearly four hundred years but it was only occupied by the family between 1572 and 1668 – less than a century.

The history of Hadham Hall is well documented, largely due to the work of William Minet, fellow of the Society of Antiquaries. Minet was a descendant of French Hugenot, Isaac Minet, who escaped persecution in France and, in 1686, set up business with his brother, initially in Dover and later in London. Investments in land in Hayes (Middlesex) and Camberwell (now the borough of Lambeth) brought the family prosperity. In 1885 William Minet inherited these estates, which will have afforded him the necessary funds to purchase Hadham

Hall in 1901.[1] He also had the time, inclination and necessary resources to investigate its story, as well as build a new wing to his own design.[2] Research by Roy Strong, Paula Henderson and Dianne Duggan in early seventeenth-century garden design has been invaluable in evaluating the banqueting hall and Italianate garden at Hadham, affording the possibility of tentatively proposing those responsible for their design.

The early years
The village of Little Hadham, about three miles west of Bishop's Stortford in Hertfordshire, comprises several hamlets where the Roman road, Stane Street, intersects with the road that links the village to Albury and the Pelhams in the north and Much Hadham and Widford in the south. The Hadham Hall site has been occupied continuously from as early as 700 BC.[3] The manor of Little Hadham, or Hadham Parva, appears in Domesday. It was held by the Bishop of London, and the tenant in fee was 'William' (possibly) Baud. Certainly the property became known as Baud's Manor and was passed down through the Baud family, who are thought to have built at least two houses on the site. No visible trace remains of the first buildings, which were to the south-west of the existing house and which were all of timber construction, within a moat that enclosed about one acre. The earth dug for the moat was used to form the path leading down to the church and is known locally as 'Nut Walk' but described by Minet as the Church Causeway.[4] The site included house, barns and cattle sheds which might well have been built by a later William Baud, who was the first of the family to live at Hadham and had a park and free warren there in 1275.[5]

Six generations later, in 1440, Thomas Baud, no doubt to reflect his status as MP for the county, built a splendid brick house on a site east of the moat. The date of the house can be confirmed, as it was in that year (1440) that Thomas purchased Livery Wood in neighbouring Farnham to supply the necessary timber, and bricks were made from 'Brick Lea', a field south of the Hall.[6] Minet discovered the foundations for this house south-east of the present building and plotted its foundations on his plan dated 1903 (Figure 3.1).

Capel ownership
Knighted in 1494, Thomas Baud's grandson, also Thomas, incurred a liability for a substantial fine which forced him first to mortgage his

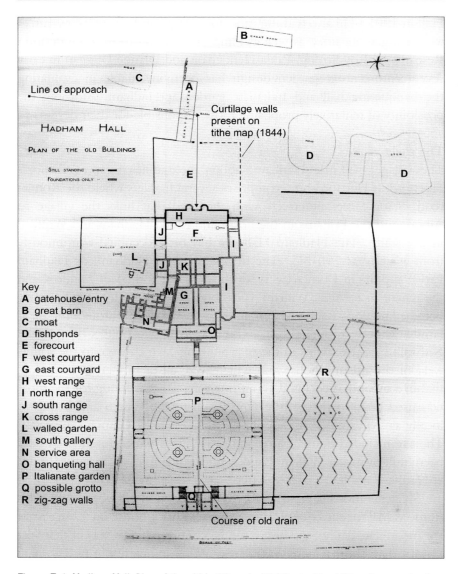

Key
A gatehouse/entry
B great barn
C moat
D fishponds
E forecourt
F west courtyard
G east courtyard
H west range
I north range
J south range
K cross range
L walled garden
M south gallery
N service area
O banqueting hall
P Italianate garden
Q possible grotto
R zig-zag walls

Figure 3.1 Hadham Hall. Plan of the old buildings by W. Minet with additional annotation by the author. DE/X10/Z1. REPRODUCED BY KIND PERMISSION OF HALS.

property in 1503, and then to sell Hadham in 1504 to Thomas Lord Darcy, who in the same year conveyed the property to Sir William Capell. William was the younger son of a squire, John Capell, of Stoke-by-Nayland in Suffolk.[7] He went to London to seek his fortune, becoming a member of the Worshipful Company of Drapers. William was twice

Lord Mayor, in 1503 and 1509, but the street name 'Capel Court' is the only surviving reference to his London mansion which once stood near the Bank of England.[8] William's principal country residence was further east along Stane Street, at Rayne Hall near Braintree. It would appear that William had a policy of investing in property, and Hadham, with good communications between London and Rayne and its sporting opportunities, would have been an attractive purchase: when William died he left his 'black colt in the park at Hadham' to his eldest son Gyles. Hadham appears to have served as the Dower House for Margaret, William's widow, who lived at Hadham after his death in 1515, and possibly before: she was already a life tenant of the estate when William died. On her death in 1522 Margaret made a bequest of 40 shillings to the church to pray for her soul, and another of £20 for the improvement of the road between Hadham and Bishop's Stortford.[9]

William's son Gyles succeeded him and he too lived at Rayne Hall. Gyles, a member of Henry VIII's court, was knighted in 1516, and distinguished himself in 1519 by accompanying Henry to the Field of the Cloth of Gold, where he was one of the Challengers.[10] When he died in 1556, his son Henry inherited the estate. Like his father, Gyles had kept a horse at Hadham and left his 'fine Bay' to John Howes in his will. Henry only survived his father by a year, and in 1557 his brother Edward inherited the estate.[11]

In 1578 Queen Elizabeth I visited Hadham while on progress, spending the night at the impressive new house 'where there was excellent good cheere and entertaynment'.[12] The bell ringers of St Michael's Church in Bishop's Stortford were paid when the queen travelled from 'Mr Capells throwe the towne'.[13] Her visit was just a year after Edward's son, Henry, had inherited, but to build a vast mansion in that time would have been impossible. This raises a question regarding who commissioned the new building. It would appear that Henry decided to build a new house at Hadham, after his first wife Katherine's death in 1572, as his elderly father Edward had chosen to live with his daughter and her family in Aspenden.[14]

As the queen approached the Hall from Stane Street along a straight drive, the scene would have been set by the large gatehouse with its impressive archway (Figure 3.2). Formerly a barn (during the Baud period), the gatehouse (known as the 'Entry' in the 1620s) was embellished on the south side with diaper work of vitrified brick

Figure 3.2 The gatehouse or 'Entry'. Photograph taken by W. Minet, *c.*1902. CV. Had.Lt. 21. REPRODUCED BY KIND PERMISSION OF HALS.

headers, and had been extended by Henry Capel to provide extra accommodation on the first floor. We know that some servants were fed here and it also had a garderobe.[15] The 'Entry' was an adornment that formalised the approach, but in addition its purpose was to provide security for the house.[16] Towards the end of the sixteenth century, gatehouses were less popular and often incorporated into the house.[17] It is interesting that Hadham retained its gatehouse as well as a turreted entrance to the main house.

As Elizabeth swept through the archway, the Great Barn to her left would have come into view and the fishponds would have mirrored the buildings.[18] The plan drafted by Minet (Figure 3.1) has been annotated by the author and shows the layout of the ancillary buildings (gatehouse and great barn: A and B), fragment of the moat (C), fishponds (D), and the hall and gardens (H–R).[19] To create a forecourt in front of the house (E), land south of the 'Entry' was enclosed by a curtilage wall, still present on the tithe map of 1844 (Plate 3.1). A sharp right-hand turn would have brought Elizabeth's cavalcade to the west front of the Hall where the many windows would have sparkled in the sunshine, the round-headed archway of the front door emphasised by a pair of semi-octagonal, embattled turrets in the centre of the symmetrical west range (H and Figure 3.3). Henry Capel's grandiose red-brick mansion, with attics and cellars, was arranged around two large courtyards – one closed (F) and one open (G) – and, as was the fashion of the period, reflected the influence of the Italian Renaissance: the archway had a classical entablature and stone frieze breaking forward over flanking pilasters (removed before 1832).[20] The windows were mullioned, the large ones transomed, and all had pediments.[21] The design is a statement of wealth and power.

The plan drafted by Minet shows the full extent of the building (Figure 3.1), and a painting of the East Wing, (*c.*1640) by an unknown artist, helps us to understand the appearance of the house (Plate 3.2). From the west range, two ranges projected east – a north (I) and a south range (J), connected at the centre by a cross range double the width of the others (K).[22]

A lantern rose above the roof and housed a bell (Plate 3.2). The south range (J) would have looked south over a court – now the walled garden (L) – where the bakehouse was located. The ground

Figure 3.3 Engraving of Hadham Hall from 'Views of Hertfordshire' – a collection of drawings by J.C. Buckler (1793–1894), vol ii, p. 59. DE/Bg. REPRODUCED BY KIND PERMISSION OF HALS.

floor had eight circular-headed windows and a central archway. It has been suggested by Smith that this was a colonnade, possibly glazed, underlying the gallery (J).[23] The cellars of this wing still exist and were lit by one west-facing and four south-facing windows. A south gallery (M) linked the mansion to the service buildings of the earlier Baud house of 1440, which Henry had retained (N).[24] These included a bakehouse, kitchen, pantry, dairy, bayley,[25] buttery and a brewery, which had a large, buttressed but simple chimney.[26] This older building is visible to the left of the banqueting hall in the *c.*1640 painting (Plate 3.2). The cross range separating the east and west courts would have accommodated the living apartments (K). The interior arrangement of rooms in the house changed considerably in the late seventeenth century.[27] With only the evidence of foundations, it is difficult to identify the purpose of individual rooms. However, the steward's account tells us that there was a Great Chamber, parlour, hall and nursery. All that remains of this house is the west range (originally the entrance area; Figure 3.3) and less than half of the south range (Figure 3.4). Although some minor details have been altered (a small door has

Figure 3.4 Hadham Hall, south front. Photograph taken by W. Minet, 1900. 70899.

been inserted to the south of the main entrance) this fraction of the original house has remained largely unchanged since it was built.[28]

The overall design of Hadham Hall in 1578 is very much in keeping with the fashion of the late sixteenth century. Classical principles were being adopted by the innovators of the time. Between 1547 and 1552, Edward Seymour, Duke of Somerset, commissioned Somerset House in the Strand. Its classical design, which includes engaged and super-imposed columns and aligned and pedimented windows, features also used at Hadham, is seen as a benchmark in sixteenth-century building.[29] Also in this period, service buildings were removed from the entrances to houses, and replaced by an open court.[30] At Hadham, the service buildings are located away from the entrance but they break the overall symmetry of the building. Similar irregularity can be found at Standon Lordship just four miles from Hadham, where Sir Ralph Sadleir built a new house from 1546. J.T. Smith has suggested that this inconsistency is in fact intentional and the irregularity of the service areas distinguishes them as inferior to the main formal rooms of the house.[31]

There is no evidence of the garden that must have complemented Henry's lavish mansion. However, in addition to the fishponds, which would have fulfilled an aesthetic as well as a practical purpose (discussed later), such gardens of this period often included a bowling green, knot gardens (visible from the principal rooms of the house), kitchen gardens, orchards and possibly a mount.

When Henry Capel died in 1588, his intention that Arthur, his son, should take up residence at Hadham is clear. His will instructed that the home at Hadham should be maintained until Christmas and that Arthur, who was then living at Rayne Hall, should leave bedding etc. for Henry's widow (Rayne therefore becoming the Dower House). Arthur married Margaret Grey, with whom he had nineteen children. He was Sheriff of Hertfordshire in 1592 and knighted in 1603.[32] Among his friends, Sir Arthur could number Robert Cecil, Earl of Salisbury, to whom he wrote letters 'from my poor house at Hadham'. He sent a fat buck and a pair of does from Hadham Park in recognition of Cecil's favours.[33] Perhaps the two men shared an interest in gardening, as Cecil, like his father, created gardens at Pymms and Theobalds – the latter so admired by James I that Cecil exchanged it for Hatfield House in 1607.[34]

Sir Arthur continued the family tradition of good hospitality, and the steward's accounts give us a picture of everyday life at Hadham during the late 1620s. It was a self-sufficient community where the food consumed was produced on the Capel estates; some rabbits were brought from Stebbing Park and deer from Walkerne Park.[35] The diversity and quantity of food enjoyed is an indication of the wealth and status of the family. In December 1628, the list included: beef, mutton, pork, venison, rabbits, pigeons, capon and woodcock. Different fish such as 'Storkefish', 'Haberdyne' and red herring as well as butter and eggs were consumed. Dinner was taken in the Great Chamber, the Parlour, the Hall, the Entry and also the Nursery. For three days over Christmas it appears that the whole village of Little Hadham was fed (about 340 meals each day) with more than 155 people served in the Hall on Christmas Day. The food is all meat-based except the reference to a 'tarte' and 'custard'. A good time was ensured with extra help in the kitchen, and with five musicians present there was ample singing and dancing.[36]

Arthur, Baron Capel, and his Italianate garden

When his eldest son, Henry, predeceased him in 1622 Sir Arthur took responsibility for the care of his grandson, Arthur. He rejected the suggestion that young Arthur should travel abroad to complete his education, arguing that the young man's calling was to be a country gentleman, 'wherein there is little or no use in foreign experience ... if God visit him with sickness he shall have no helpe abroad. His brother is so young and therefore if he dies it will be a greate hindrance unto the family'.[37] On the occasion of the grandson's marriage to Elizabeth in 1627, the manor was settled on him. Elizabeth was the only daughter and heiress of Sir Charles Morrison, of Cassiobury Park, Watford. Five years later Arthur inherited the Hadham estate and became one of the richest commoners in England. He held lands in ten counties with a reputed annual income of £7,000 (£624,000 in modern terms).[38] He carried on the life of a country gentleman as his grandfather had wanted, at first avoiding national affairs, probably because he was initially disaffected with the government of Charles I.[39] Between 1632 and 1640 Arthur invested in his estate at Hadham. He added 500 acres to the park (making a total of 740 acres). A survey in the early 1630s shows the 'Old Way', which was to be replaced by the 'New Way' thus enabling the road to Bishop's Stortford to be diverted around the enlarged park. Arthur extended the house and commissioned a new banqueting hall and Italianate garden in the latest fashion.[40] Sadly, no descriptions by contemporary visitors during this phase of development have been discovered. However, there is visual evidence: a portrait of the Capel Family by Cornelius Johnson *c*.1641 (Plate 3.3), the painting of the East Wing *c*.1640 (Plate 3.2), which looks back towards the banqueting hall from the park, and a nineteenth-century copy of a naive

Figure 3.5 Hadham Hall, the seat of Arthur Baron Capel, *c*.1648. Nineteenth-century copy of an original picture dated *c*.1648. 64322A. REPRODUCED BY KIND PERMISSION OF HALS.

three-dimensional depiction of the garden, which is perhaps a little later (Figure 3.5). These, together with the plan drawn by Minet after his archaeological excavations (Figure 3.1), contribute to our understanding of the banqueting hall and the classical garden which it overlooked.

The Johnson portrait (Plate 3.3) is thought to celebrate Arthur's new title when, in 1641, Charles I created him Lord Capel of Hadham Parva. It depicts Baron Capel as a devoted husband and father. This family scene closely emulates the portrait by Sir Anthony Van Dyck of Charles I with his wife Henrietta Maria and their two eldest children in an equally intimate family pose.[41] Arthur's wife, Elizabeth, is gazing lovingly at him while their five children are arranged in close contact. The Italianate garden in the background is depicted in great detail, with the park beyond stretching into the distance. Johnson's portrayal of Baron Capel with his wife and children is a method of not only displaying his wealth and success, but also of placing him firmly as a member of the court of Charles I. Notably, the garden has sufficient importance to cover about a quarter of the canvas.

The painting looks out to the garden through a window in the banqueting hall. From the balcony a central flight of steps leads down to a terrace running along the western side of a large square walled garden. The wall nearest to the banqueting hall screens the adjacent service area from view and is topped with an ornate fence, perhaps of wooden slats or wire, with posts at intervals supporting urns of flowers. Three sets of steps (one central and one at each end) lead from the terrace down to the garden, which is divided into quarters by wide walks. Paths form a simple geometric pattern in the closely cut grass or *parterre de gazon*. Fountains and statuary are the major form of decoration in this garden. Each quarter has a fountain with a lobed basin and water spurting from an urn-like centrepiece, closely resembling a design by Dutch architect Hans Vredeman de Vries,[42] while four life-size statues on pedestals, one in each quarter, emphasise the symmetry. The three-dimensional drawing shows a different layout of paths and six statues (Figure 3.5), but Minet's excavations, carried out in 1902 after a dry summer revealed parch-marks of the paths, confirm that there were indeed four bases for both statues and fountains (P – Figure 3.1). Only two are visible, and Strong suggests that one is Ceres holding a cornucopia, and the other holds an eagle, indicating Jupiter.[43] The opposite (east) wall of the garden has a balustraded terrace along its entire length which overlooks the park and the garden. Beneath the terrace, at its centre, is a building flanked by architectural stairs, each with a large half-landing leading to a grass terrace. These stairs closely resemble in design those at Bramante's Belvedere Court at the Vatican in Rome.[44] The terrace building is divided by a passage which leads to four rooms and through a door to the park beyond. The rooms have windows looking either inwards to the garden or out to the park. The intended purpose of this building is unclear but will be discussed later. At each end of the east terrace is a two-storey banqueting house or summer house with windows overlooking both the garden and the park. The central point of the north and south walls is marked by a classical garden gate after the style of Inigo Jones,[45] and espalier fruit trees decorate these walls.

At Hadham, Arthur created a sculpture garden, perhaps drawing inspiration from Thomas Howard's revolutionary garden beside the Thames at Arundel House in London. Following his tour of Italy with Inigo Jones from 1613 to 1614, Howard, aristocrat and collector of all things Italian, peopled his terraced garden with life-size statuary, depicted in the background of a portrait attributed to Daniel Mytens (*c.*1627).[46] Classical ornament demonstrated an awareness of continental art and architecture, and – even though Arthur had not been permitted to travel to the Continent – his garden is an indication of this awareness.[47]

Flowers are depicted only in the urns on the west terrace. These are tulips and carnations. The carnation was the symbol of love while the tulip was a high-status plant introduced into England at the end of the sixteenth century. Rare sports, which produced striped blooms, were highly prized and led to 'Tulipomania' in the Netherlands in the 1630s.[48] The axial line from the doors of the banqueting hall is continued not only into the garden, but also out into the park where a vista has been cut through the trees. This essay in perspective includes the park and woodland to complete the scene of Arthur Capel's estate.

The painting of the East Wing of Hadham Hall (Plate 3.2) depicts the nine-bay banqueting hall, which is of red-brick construction with white detailing and closes the east court of the 1570s house. Overlooking the garden, the long, rectangular windows of this large room on the first floor have single mullions and transoms, and a central glazed door opens onto a balustraded balcony running the full length of the hall. Above each window, separated by a moulded cornice, is a round niche containing a bust; but there is insufficient detail to identify it. The stables at Wilton House are of the same period. Designed by Isaac de Caus for Lord Pembroke, the building of red brick with white detailing has a similar frieze. Roundels depicting busts were a feature of the entrance porch at Francis Bacon's Elizabethan mansion at Gorhambury, Hertfordshire, and of the Holbein Porch at Wilton (Figure 3.6). Six columns, probably of the Ionic order, support the balcony, creating a wide five-bay arcade or loggia below. Such Italianate features became a fashionable addition to gardens of the period and provided a transitional space between house and garden. Robert Cecil rebuilt Hatfield House in 1612 and the south front features an arcaded loggia that can still be seen today. However, at Hadham, perhaps the English climate proved too chilly, as the three-dimensional drawing depicts a slightly different view and shows six arches which have been in-filled, forming rooms lit by six windows, alternately round-headed and Venetian (Figure 3.5). To complement the architecture of the banqueting hall, the north range appears to have been remodelled at this time (Plate 3.2). It is terminated by an east-facing canted bay window rising through the height of the whole range. On the roof above, a small belvedere topped with a cupola affords fine views of the gardens below and out across the park beyond. The parkland in the foreground has considerable detail: a man fishing in a stream, another walking with two dogs, and a third on horseback with a long gun. The herd of deer in the foreground seem remarkably relaxed, considering all the activity going on around them! This stylised painting depicts all the activities – hunting, shooting and fishing – that one could pursue in the wonderful park at Hadham Hall.

Was there a grotto?

The building at the centre of the east terrace is fifty-six feet deep by forty-six feet wide, divided into four rooms, each with a window looking either in to the garden or out to the park. One or more of these rooms might feasibly have housed a grotto (Q – Figure 3.1). The presence of a drain, discovered by Minet during his excavations, supports this suggestion. The drain runs from a point level with the two fountains nearest the banqueting hall, through the centre of the garden and ends in the centre of the room beneath the east terrace (marked with a broken line – Figure 3.1). Although the purpose of this drain is not confirmed, it might well have been part of a hydraulic system that fed the four fountains and then led to a grotto. The grotto, or *nymphaeum*, had become increasingly

Figure 3.6 The Holbein Porch, Wilton. PHOTOGRAPH BY JENNY MILLEDGE.

popular in the early seventeenth century and symbolised a link with classical gardens of antiquity, a 'perfectly contrived mixture of art and nature, also found in the great gardens of Italy and France'.[49] Grottoes featured mythological creatures, statues and naturalistic columns, often with fountains. The walls would be decorated with shells, mirrors and semi-precious stones, producing mosaics and three-dimensional friezes.

The best example of the appearance of such grottoes is at Woburn Abbey, where one created in the 1630s still exists. This, like the contemporary grotto at Wilton, was designed by Isaac de Caus and Nicholas Stone.[50]

Who designed the garden?

The architect of the lavish banqueting hall and gardens is another subject of conjecture. In *The Renaissance Garden in England,* Strong suggests that the gardens could well have been inspired by Inigo Jones. Certainly the garden closely resembles the garden scene of the court masque *The Shepherds' Paradise* (1633) designed by him. That scene depicts a garden with a parterre, central fountain, Italianate stairs and banqueting house. Jones, who had visited Italy on two occasions, had not only viewed the works of such architects as Palladio, Serlio and Bramante but had also seen masque designs for Medici spectacles by Parigi.[51] Jones became Surveyor of the King's Works in 1615 and one of his most important royal commissions was the Banqueting House, created at Whitehall Palace for James I in the early 1620s, which was used for court masques and public ceremonies and included a grotto.[52] Although Jones was the architect, he was assisted on the project by Nicholas Stone and Isaac de Caus. These three men were regularly involved in projects for members of the royal court and the most likely inference would be that they collaborated on such commissions.

Nicholas Stone, who is best known for his work as a sculptor – especially of funerary memorials – was appointed the King's Master Mason in 1632.[53] In his later book, *The Artist and the Garden,* Strong argues in favour of Stone as the architect at Hadham. This argument draws on the link between Arthur's wife, Elizabeth Capel (née Morrison), who commissioned Stone to design memorials to her father and mother (Figure 3.7). Stone's notebook confirms that he completed that work in 1630 for the sum of £400.[54] Architectural work attributed to Stone includes Balls Park, in Hertford, and the gardens and banqueting house at Oxnead Hall, Norfolk, designed for Sir William Paston in the 1630s.[55] Although now demolished, these gardens were drawn by John Adey Repton in 1809 and depict a banqueting hall with a 'Frisketting Room' (perhaps a grotto) beneath.[56] The hall overlooks a square walled enclosure divided into quarters and featuring statuary – Cupid, Jupiter, Venus and Flora – a central fountain, espaliered fruit trees, a summer house and a monumental garden gate.

Figure 3.7 Memorial to Charles Morrison and his wife, by Nicholas Stone, St Mary's Church, Watford. PHOTOGRAPH REPRODUCED BY KIND PERMISSION OF A. SKELTON.

However, recent research by Dianne Duggan has linked Stone's name with Isaac de Caus, hydraulic engineer and grotto and garden designer, whose first work in England was the grotto beneath the Whitehall Banqueting House. De Caus and Stone are thought to have worked together at Woburn Abbey, Wilton House and on the

Piazza at Covent Garden in the 1630s, the last of these being another development where Inigo Jones worked as architect.[57] The similarity of the architectural design of the Wilton Stables by Isaac de Caus, as well as his known abilities as a garden and grotto designer, strongly points to his involvement at Hadham. Without further evidence, the designer of the garden cannot be definitively identified, but the most likely answer seems to be a collaboration between Jones, Stone and de Caus.[58]

Other garden areas

The Italianate garden was the most lavish at Hadham, but evidence suggests that it was but one of a series. The Tithe map of 1844 (Plate 3.1) describes an area of just under twelve acres as 'Homestall',[59] and this includes the Italianate garden with two flanking enclosures, to the north and south, as well as the court to the west front of the house and the area where the barns and fishponds are located. Indeed, the symmetrical nature of the north and south enclosures is an indication that these were part of the gardens.

The enclosure to the north was found to have foundations for a series of zig-zag walls, twenty-seven feet apart (R – Figure 3.1). Although Minet considered these walls could have been used to protect grape vines (and therefore a vineyard), another purpose could have been a shelter for a range of fruit trees. In the Netherlands, zig-zag walls, known as *slingermuren*, were the precursor of crinkle-crankle walls, and were used to train tender fruits such as apricots, cherries, pears, plums, nectarines and peaches, as well as grape vines – all of which benefit from the warmth of a protective wall.[60] This is confirmed by the depiction of a zig-zag wall in the garden of plant collector Gaspar Fagel (1633–88), who created a garden at Leewenhorst, the Netherlands, from *c*.1680.[61] Dr L. Albers, landscape historian in the Netherlands, considers that the zig-zag arrangement was possibly experimental, as research has found that the temperature in the angles is hardly greater than on a straight wall.[62] Here, at Hadham, is a sophisticated version of an orchard, an important element of Stuart gardens. William Lawson in his treatise *A New Orchard and Garden* (1623) describes an orchard as a place where profit and pleasure are combined: 'the greater the Orchard is ... the better it is ... And it shall appear that no ground a man occupieth (no not the cornfield) yieldeth more gaine to the purse, and housekeeping, (not to speak of the unspeakable pleasure) quantitie for quantitie, than a good

Orchard.'[63] Orchards would also have included flowers, with borders planted with roses and berries, and the size of the enclosure at Hadham would have accommodated such borders.[64] We have no indication of the purpose of the south enclosure in the 'Homestall' but this is likely to have been a kitchen garden where fruit and vegetables, or indeed an orchard of standard fruit trees such as apples, might have been planted.[65]

Also within the 'Homestall' area is a series of fishponds to the north-west of the house as well as the remnants of the moat to the south-west, which pre-date the Capel house (Plate 3.1). Medieval *servatoria*, or holding ponds, were located near the house, where fish that had been bred in outlying and larger *vivaria*, or breeding ponds, would be transferred to provide an accessible supply. Until the early eighteenth century, freshwater fish were considered status symbols.[66] The ponds at Hadham would have been both ornamental and useful, as they are aligned on the 'Entry' archway which all visitors would have passed through.[67] It is possible that the ponds, being higher than the Italianate garden, might have been adapted to provide water for the fountains there.

Arthur Capel – royalist supporter

In 1640, Arthur Capel became more active in Parliament and delivered a petition from the freeholders of Hertfordshire complaining of 'ship money, projects, monopolies, Star Chamber' and other issues, the first of its kind to be presented to the House.[68] In 1641 he was appointed Baron Capel of Hadham Parva by Charles I in recognition of his support for the Crown. The Civil War must have had a dramatic effect on the house and park at Hadham. By 1642 the country was rapidly dividing into two factions. Although Arthur was 'more puritan, he became a constitutional royalist' and raised 800 horses and advanced Charles £12,000.[69] In August, while Arthur was away fighting, Parliamentarians raided Hadham Hall, seizing arms for 1,000 troops. In 1643 the house and park were charged with an annuity of £10,000 to the Earl of Essex, captain of the Parliamentary forces.[70] The Parliamentarians returned to Hadham in March 1644–5 and 44 horses as well as cattle and stores were taken, leaving the stables empty. With Arthur away pursuing the royalist cause, his mother, Theodosia, remained at Hadham. However, Elizabeth, his wife, took the children to her childhood home of Cassiobury Park, but eventually fled to Oxford in 1643. In an endeavour to protect the estate,

William Capel, Arthur's kinsman, negotiated with the local Sequestration Committee to become the main tenant at Hadham and the rent collector for the Capel estates.[71] In 1644 he paid a fine to prevent trees being cut down in the park, but, because William was away, the Committee ruled that '888 pollarde trees in Hadham Parke and 500 pollarde trees in Walkerne also owned by Arthur Capel should be rooted up' in order to raise money for two widows.[72] William felt the huge responsibility of looking after these estates, which is recorded in a letter he wrote to Arthur c.1646.[73] Arthur, who saw active service but was not a successful soldier, returned to Hadham in 1647, but was fighting again in 1648, until his capture under siege in Colchester. He was a prisoner, first at Windsor and then at the Tower of London, and even managed to escape by wading through the Tower's moat. However, he was arrested two days later in Lambeth. He was tried, appearing before the court five times, but was finally beheaded at Westminster in March 1649 because of his loyal support for the king.[74]

Perpetuating our memory

Arthur Capel was a man who took life seriously. Honest and loyal to Charles I, he had an unswerving Christian faith.[75] He was inclined towards Puritanism, and among his books were the works of Saint Augustine and Eusebius.[76] While imprisoned and awaiting execution, he wrote his 'Daily Observations or Meditations Divine, Morall. Written by a Person of Honour and Piety', in which he expresses his thoughts and feelings: 'Rarity deceives the judgement ... In many things this age examples this: for new and incommodious fashions of building, diet, cloaths, are more sought after then the despised, yet wise customs of our forefathers.'[77] It might therefore seem surprising that he indulged in creating such a lavish garden. However, man's relationship with the natural world became a metaphor for divine order.[78] The garden, a tangible form of paradise, also symbolised wild nature tamed.[79] Fountains were high-status features, and had symbolic meaning: life, knowledge, purification and deception. Perhaps this is the reason for four fountains at Hadham.[80] Strong observes that grottoes, a fundamental feature in Renaissance gardens, combined science and art, and demonstrated man's power to control the physical universe.[81] Arthur's motives for commissioning the banqueting hall and Italianate garden – which should be considered as a set piece – reflect not only his elevated social status but also his desire to achieve immortality. In one of 250 meditations in his 'Daily Observations', Arthur wrote: 'These four are the chief ways of perpetuating our memory: Books, which require a good Head; Valiant acts, which require a courageous Heart; Children, which require an ability of Body; and Building, which requires a replenished purse.'[82]

We must not forget the influence of Elizabeth, Arthur's wife, who might also have taken an interest in the development of the Hadham gardens. Her grandfather, Sir Baptist Hicks, Viscount Campden, laid out a notable garden at Chipping Campden in 1612–16 which featured a pair of banqueting houses, terraces and parterres.[83] Perhaps Elizabeth, like her grandfather, had an interest in garden-making? Theirs was not a marriage of convenience: Arthur's last letter to her expresses his unequivocal love,[84] and therefore he might have granted any wish of hers for a fashionable garden.

The Earl of Essex

When Hadham was recovered in 1651 by Arthur's son, Arthur, the manor must have been a shadow of its former glory. He was created Viscount Malden and Earl of Essex in 1661 by Charles II after his restoration.[85] Perhaps the Earl had become fond of Cassiobury Park, his mother's childhood home, during his stay there in the 1640s. In the light of his duties as a member of the House of Lords he will have appreciated its proximity to London. His decision to remove to Cassiobury must have been before 1670 when Hugh May was commissioned to remodel the old-fashioned house, and planting in the new gardens had begun under the supervision of the Earl's gardener, Moses Cook. Cassiobury was the only Hertfordshire seat to feature in *Britannia Illustrata*,[86] which no doubt contributed to the acclaim of the highly influential gardens. Cassiobury was one of the earliest pleasure grounds, with a forest garden which extended almost to the house. Under the Earl's patronage Cook wrote *The Manner of Raising, Ordering, and Improving Forrest Trees* in 1676.[87] The book has tantalising details of the preparations he carried out in cultivating plants at Hadham for the new garden at Cassiobury. He grew 296 lime trees for a double avenue which he raised from seeds and layers (cuttings) at Hadham, lifting the trees in November 1672. They were successfully established at Cassiobury, after having been transported over thirty miles.[88] Cook's description of an experiment tells us that in March 1666 he put a pot of earth and purslane (possibly seed or small plants) in a 'little room at Hadham Hall', which 'joined upon the bakehouse' and then put the pot out into the hot beds until May, when he set it under a south wall and 'at the latter end of August I took the pot of earth and set it in a south window of a Banquetting House' – no doubt one of the small pavilions at the corner of the Italianate garden.[89]

The Earl did not have long to enjoy Cassiobury. He was arrested under suspicion of plotting against the king in 1683 (in a conspiracy known as the Rye House Plot) and before he could be tried he was found dead in the Tower of London with his throat cut.[90]

Hadham after 1683

Initially the fabric of Hadham was left untouched after the family moved away, but by 1686 a large proportion of the house had been demolished and the remaining part was adapted into a farmhouse. The estate was divided into three farms – Hadham Hall, Wickham Hall and Hadham Old Park Lodge Farm – the two new farmhouses being built with materials from the old house. Minet discovered that the square walled garden adjoining the south range of the remodelled house comprised walls from three distinct periods (L – Figure 3.1). The lower part of

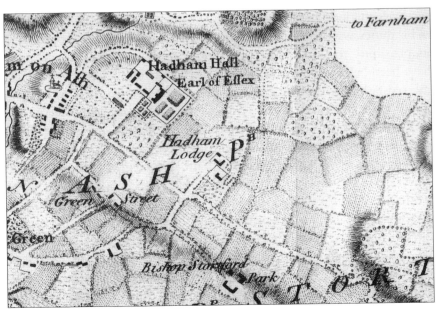

Figure 3.8 Detail of Dury and Andrews' county map, 1766, showing Hadham Hall.
REPRODUCED BY KIND PERMISSION OF HALS.

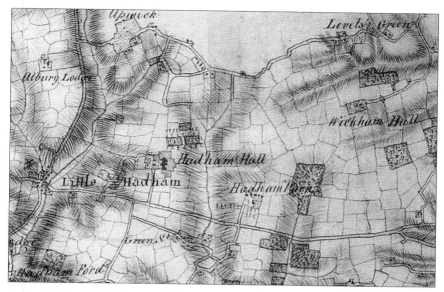

Figure 3.9 Detail of OS Drawing 1800, sheet number 141. REPRODUCED BY KIND PERMISSION OF BRITISH LIBRARY BOARD.

the east wall dates to 1440 and must be part of the Baud house. Most of the south wall, with evidence of an archway and possibly a porter's lodge, is from the 1570s period. The remaining west wall to complete the enclosure is built from reclaimed bricks from the old house, therefore built *c*.1680.[91]

It was at this time that the deer from the park were moved to Epping Forest and Bagshot.[92] Until at least 1702 Thomas Scott was paid £4 in the capacity of caretaker for 'looking to Hadham Hall' and the house contained an apartment suitable for entertaining. In 1698 Arthur's son Algernon entertained William III after a visit to Newmarket races.[93] From 1725 until its sale in 1901 Hadham Hall was leased. A local family, the Scotts, and their descendants by marriage were tenants until 1850 when it was let to John Betts from Kings Langley, not far from Cassiobury. His sons John and Samuel managed the farm. In 1855 Samuel married Elizabeth Scott (so bringing the Scotts to Hadham once more) but Samuel moved to Bury Green when Hadham Hall was sold in 1901 to William Minet.[94]

We rely on maps to provide evidence of the house and gardens while Hadham Hall was leased during the eighteenth and nineteenth centuries. The Dury and Andrews map (1766) depicts the much-reduced house

with two areas of enclosed gardens (Figure 3.8). One to the east of
the house is larger, and the second, smaller garden is to the south, but
no ponds are included. Three rectangular enclosures north-east of the
gardens are depicted on the Ordnance Survey Drawing of 1800 (Figure
3.9). A single row of trees is planted along the longest boundary of each
enclosure except the north side. A small fragment of the most northerly
enclosure called 'Newwood Spinney' is shown as woodland on the 1844
tithe map (Plate 3.1). The name has become 'Newwood Spring' on the
Ordnance Survey map of 1878.[95] Although there is also a field of just
over twenty-five acres named 'New Wood' on the tithe map (in the area
of the enclosures), by 1844 its purpose is arable. It seems likely that
the three enclosures are plantations which were part of Moses Cook's
nursery, where he propagated such trees as the limes for the double
avenue at Cassiobury. These nursery sites will have become redundant by
1681 when Cook's work at Cassiobury was finished.

While in the care of tenants, the pleasure grounds at Hadham had
been laid out in the High Victorian fashion. The sale particulars in 1900
reveal that the estate, of just under 400 acres, featured 'picturesque old
Pleasure grounds laid out in lawns, walks and flower beds, adorned with
shrubberies and well matured timber. Flower and kitchen gardens and
several enclosures of rich old pasture and arable land.'[96] These details are
augmented by an engraving (*c*.1880) of the west front which depicts a
croquet lawn with a rustic seat in front of a low wall (Figure 3.10). The

Figure 3.10 Engraving of Hadham Hall, *c*.1880. 70899. REPRODUCED BY KIND PERMISSION OF HALS.

Figure 3.11 Hadham Hall, east front. Photograph taken by W. Minet, 1900. 70899.
REPRODUCED BY KIND PERMISSION OF HALS.

lawn, scattered with deciduous and fir trees, is divided by a curving drive which sweeps up to the front door through gate piers topped with urns. Fastigiate yew trees and box balls flank the front door while another pair of urns emphasise the straight path leading from it. The house has creeper on the south walls and a trained shrub on part of the west front.[97] Photographs taken by Minet in 1900 complete the picture: in the walled garden (attached to the south front) beds of herbaceous flowers border the straight path (Figure 3.4). To the east, the house is again swathed in trained shrubs, and specimen conifers decorate the lawn. The area to the east of the first terrace has become a field – all evidence of the Italianate garden is lost (Figure 3.11).

Conclusion

Although Hadham Hall was in Capel ownership for nearly 400 years, only four generations of the family lived there and for less than a century in total. Henry Capel chose to build a new house at Hadham and moved there in time for Elizabeth I's visit in 1578. The mansion, built in the fashionable style of the day, reflected classical principles, which announced Henry's position of prosperity. He may have wanted to impress his peers, or even his second wife, but it was certainly a magnificent and appropriate residence in which to entertain a queen. Henry's great-grandson, Arthur, was prevented from foreign travel and the possibility of experiencing Renaissance art, architecture and gardens by the premature death of his father. However, his garden at Hadham was an essay in Renaissance principles and contained all the features that represented the 'Caroline Italian garden style' – the approach through the banqueting hall via a terrace, down steps into a symmetrical, walled garden in which fountains and statuary dominated. There are several inconsistencies between Figure 3.5 and the two paintings (Plates 3.2 and 3.3): the different number of statues, the pattern of paths and the details of the loggia below the banqueting hall. Minet's archaeological evidence suggests that the paintings are correct and, although the detail of the loggia is interesting, without supporting evidence the accuracy of this detail is subject to conjecture. The terrace directly opposite the house, with flights of stairs and possibly a grotto below, are all architectural features that were *de rigueur* in the fashionable gardens of the Stuart court. Although to our modern eyes, this extravagant garden might seem to conflict with Arthur's sober personality, he would have regarded the new banqueting hall and garden as an investment for future generations. As one of the wealthiest men in the country, he would have considered this an appropriate adjunct to his house. When he planned the project he would have had no concept of the impending Civil War and its disastrous consequences. It is not surprising that, after the Restoration, his son Arthur, Earl of Essex, decided to move to Cassiobury where the family could make a fresh start. When William Minet bought Hadham in 1901 its story captured his imagination, and his diligence in collating archival material has revealed much of the history of the house and garden. No doubt his choice of Hadham enabled him to advance his practical skills in archaeology and research. His work was meticulous, but we must remember that his conclusions are derived from his own work and opinions. Archaeological excavations were carried out by the Hertfordshire Archaeological Trust in 1992 and were interpreted using Minet's plan (Figure 3.1).[98] This work confirmed his findings in relation to the Baud and 1572 house, and the banqueting hall, but no trenches were dug in the area of the Italianate garden and further research and examination of the archaeology still remaining in this area would be worthwhile. We can also perhaps tentatively suggest that the design of the banqueting hall and Italianate garden was a collaboration between Inigo Jones, Isaac de Caus and Nicholas Stone. This possibility leads us to ask new questions and calls for further research. It would be interesting to find the statuary or fountains that are featured in the paintings and also to discover if there ever was a grotto beneath the east terrace. If Arthur had not chosen it as the backdrop for the family portrait, knowledge of his garden might have been lost forever.

Acknowledgements

I am indebted to Dr Sally Jeffery and Mr Andrew Skelton who have provided constructive comments on my work.

Notes

1. Myatt's Fields, Denmark Hill and Herne Hill: Introduction and Myatt's Fields area 'Survey of London': vol 26: Lambeth: Southern area (1956), pp. 141–5, <http://www.british-history.ac.uk/report>, accessed 1 August 2011.
2. HALS DE/X10/Z1, W. Minet, *Hadham Hall and the Manor of Bawdes alias Hadham Parva* (Wiles and Son, Colchester, 1914), with additional pages added in scrapbook form.
3. C. Walker, *Hadham Hall, Little Hadham Archaeological Excavation (West Side)*, Hertfordshire Archaeological Trust (unpublished report, June 1994): although previously believed to have been unoccupied during the Roman period, the excavations revealed evidence of a low-status farmstead on the site dating to the first century AD.
4. Minet can trace the name to 1634, but considers that the construction was much earlier: HALS DE/X10/ZI, Minet, p. 8.
5. A. Rowe, *Medieval Parks of Hertfordshire* (Hatfield, 2009), p. 169.
6. HALS D/P43/29/9, G. Tebby, *Parish History – 400 Years of Hadham Hall* (pamphlet published 1928), p. 9.
7. W. Page (ed.), *VCH Hertfordshire*, vol. iv (London, 1971), p. 52.
8. HALS D/P43/29/9, Tebby, p. 11. For the purpose of this chapter the spelling 'Capel' will be adopted.
9. HALS DE/X10/Z1, Minet, pp. 8–11.
10. H. Chauncy, *The Historical Antiquities of Hertfordshire*, vol. i (London, 1700), p. 307.
11. HALS DE/X10/Z1, Minet, p. 9.
12. J. Nichols, *Progresses and Public Processions of Queen Elizabeth*, vol. ii (London, 1823), p. 222.
13. Records of St Michael's Church, Bishop's Stortford, quoted in HALS DE/X10/Z1, Minet, p. 10.
14. HALS DE/X10/Z1, Minet, pp. 9–10.
15. HALS 64244, Steward's Account: Hadham Hall 1628–29, and HALS DE/X10/Z1, Minet, pp. 78–80.
16. P. Henderson, *The Tudor House and Garden* (New Haven, CT and London, 2005), p. 35.
17. Henderson, *Tudor House and Garden*, p. 71.
18. Both the gatehouse or 'Entry' and the Great Barn to its north-west are roughly aligned on the foundations of the earlier Baud house (*c.*1440), and they, together with the fishponds, must have already existed when Henry Capel built the new mansion: HALS DE/X10/Z1, Minet, pp. 78–80.
19. Capital letters refer to the key in Figure 3.1.
20. J.T. Smith, *Hertfordshire Houses – Selective Inventory* (Oxford, 1993), p. 120. One of the fluted pillars was thought to have been restyled as the font in Little Hadham Church, but Minet found it in the churchyard at the west end of the church – sadly it is no longer there: HALS DE/X10/Z1, Minet, pp. 65–6.
21. N. Pevsner, *The Buildings of England – Hertfordshire* (London, 1953, revised by B. Cherry, Harmondsworth, 1977), p. 241.
22. HALS DE/X10/Z1, Minet, p. 63. It is thought by Smith that the additional rooms incorporated into this cross wing were part of Capel's improvements in the 1630s.
23. At Woburn Abbey, the colonnaded grotto, originally thought to have been open to the elements, was glazed by the 1650s: D. Duggan, 'Isaac de Caus, Nicholas Stone, and the Woburn Abbey Grotto', *Apollo* (August 2003), p. 53, and Smith, *Hertfordshire Houses*, p. 121.
24. Minet makes the point that the foundations for the service area do not relate to the symmetry of the Capel house and that this building dates from the earlier Baud house:

HALS DE/X10/Z1, Minet, pp. 62–3.

25. It is likely that the 'bayley' was the porter's lodge in the outer wall of the walled garden: HALS DE/X10/Z1, Minet, p. 75, and HALS 64244, Steward's Account.

26. HALS DE/X10/Z1, Minet, p. 67.

27. HALS DE/X10/Z1, Minet, p. 66.

28. Smith, *Hertfordshire Houses,* p. 120.

29. Henderson, *Tudor House and Garden,* p. 19.

30. *Ibid.,* pp. 26–8.

31. Smith, *Hertfordshire Houses,* p. 120.

32. Chauncy, *Hertfordshire,* p. 308.

33. Page (ed.), *VCH Hertfordshire,* p. 52.

34. R. Strong, *The Renaissance Garden in England* (London, 1979), p. 103.

35. This was economically sound as food prices rose substantially during the period: Henderson, *Tudor House and Garden*, p. 12.

36. HALS 64244, Steward's Account.

37. HALS D/EGr/32, Undated pamphlet *The Life of Lord Capell*, p. 253.

38. Page (ed.), *VCH Hertfordshire*, p. 52, and R. Hutton, 'Capel, Arthur, first Baron Capel of Hadham (1604–1649)', *Oxford Dictionary of National Biography (ODNB)*, (Oxford, 2004), online edn, October 2006, <http://www.oxforddnb.com/view/article/4583>, accessed 13 February 2009, and a calculation of the modern equivalent calculated using <http://www.nationalarchives.gov.uk/currency>, accessed 7 August 2011.

39. *ODNB*, entry Arthur Capel.

40. The significance of the house is reflected in the hearth tax returns of 1663 – Hadham Hall had fifty-two fireplaces, when the next highest number in the parish was nine: HALS E 179/248/24/8, Hearth Tax reel 1.

41. Sir A. Van Dyck, *Charles I and Henrietta Maria with their two eldest children, Prince Charles and Princess Mary*, 1632, oil on canvas, dimensions 370.8 x 274.3cm (The Royal Collection).

42. Dutch and Flemish prints were admired and collected and often included images of fountains: Henderson, *Tudor House and Garden,* p. 191 and figure 119.

43. R. Strong, *The Artist and the Garden* (New Haven, CT and London, 2000), p. 55.

44. Henderson, *Tudor House and Garden*, figure 116, p. 95 and also the staircase at St Germain-en-Laye.

45. The three-dimensional drawing depicts these features as arbours, but it seems more likely that they are indeed gates: Strong, *Artist and the Garden*, p. 55.

46. Strong, *Artist and the Garden*, pp. 47–8, and figure 52.

47. Henderson, *Tudor House and Garden,* p. 68.

48. G. and S. Jellicoe, *et al.* (eds), *The Oxford Companion to Gardens* (Oxford, 1986), p. 567.

49. Henderson, *Tudor House and Garden,* p. 164.

50. D. Duggan, 'Isaac de Caus: Surveyor, Grotto and Garden Designer', *Studies in the History of Gardens and Designed Landscapes*, 29/3 (July–September 2009), pp. 152–68.

51. Parigi's classical designs emphasised perspective: Strong, *Artist and the Garden*, pp. 113–16 and figure 138.

52. J. Newman, 'Jones, Inigo (1573–1652)', *ODNB* (Oxford, 2004), online edn, September 2010, <http://www.oxforddnb.com/view/article/15017>, accessed 4 January 2012.

53. A. White, 'Stone, Nicholas (1585x8–1647)', *ODNB* (Oxford, 2004), <http://www. oxforddnb.com/view/article/26577>, accessed 2 August 2011.

54. W.L. Spiers, 'The Note-book and Account-book of Nicholas Stone', *Walpole Society,* vol. vii (1919), p. 60.

55. Stone's account book, quoted in Henderson, *Tudor House and Garden,* p. 198.

56. 'Frisketting' is probably a derivation of the Italian word *frescati*, a cool grotto: J.A. Repton, in J. Britton, *The Architectural Antiquities of Great Britain, represented and illustrated in a series of views, elevations, plans, sections, and details of various Ancient English Edifices: with historical and descriptive accounts of each*, vol. ii (1809), p. 98.

57. Duggan, *Studies in the History of Gardens,* pp. 152–68.
58. Strong considers that de Caus' style is too fussy to have been responsible for Hadham, but as this 'fussiness' would have only been evident in the grotto (whose existence is the subject of conjecture), this argument does not seem persuasive: Strong, *Renaissance Garden,* p. 185.
59. The term 'homestall' appears on tithe maps and generally means the area around the house which includes domestic gardens.
60. F. Bacon, 'Of Gardens' (1625) in J. Dixon Hunt and P. Willis (eds), *The Genius of the Place – The English Landscape Garden 1620–1820* (Cambridge, MA and London, 1988), p. 52.
61. E. Den Hartog and C. Teune, 'Gaspar Fagel (1633–88): His Garden and Plant Collection at Leeuwenhorst', *Garden History,* 30/2 (Winter 2002), p. 199 and figure 4.
62. Email correspondence between the author and Dr L. Albers, 29 June 2011.
63. W. Lawson, *A New Orchard and Garden* (London, 1623), p. 8.
64. J. Roberts, 'The Gardens of the Gentry in the Late Tudor period', *Garden History,* 27/1 (Summer 1999), p. 96.
65. Lawson, *A New Orchard,* section: 'A Country Housewife's Garden', p. 8.
66. C. Currie, 'Fishponds as Garden Features, *c.*1550–1750', *Garden History,* 18/1 (Spring 1990), pp. 22–46.
67. Minet discovered brick foundations in the Peninsular Pond (the largest fishpond). His drawing indicates that the pond was of a formal design with pipes connecting the two sections: Minet, 'Survey of Brick retaining Walls to Peninsular Pond', sheets 1 and 2, HALS D/X10/Z1.
68. *Biographia Britannica,* vol.ii (London, 1748), p. 1161.
69. A. Thomson (ed.), *The Impact of the First Civil War on Hertfordshire, 1642–47* (Rickmansworth, 2007), p. lxxii.
70. Page (ed.), *VCH Hertfordshire,* pp. 51–3.
71. Thomson, *The Impact of the First Civil War,* p. lxxiv.
72. HALS M212, Estate Management Delinquency Papers.
73. HALS M212, Estate Management Delinquency Papers, and William's expenses account in Thomson, *The Impact of the First Civil War,* pp. 176–7.
74. *Biographia Britannia,* vol. ii, pp. 1163–4.
75. Edward, Earl of Clarendon, *The History of the Rebellion and Civil Wars,* vol. iii (Oxford, 1704), p. 208.
76. G. Owen, (ed.), *Calendar of the Cecil Papers in Hatfield House* (London, 1971) vol. xxii: 1612–1668, <http://www.british-history.ac.uk>, accessed 22 August 2011, entry for 29 May 1631.
77. A. Capel, *Daily Observations or Meditations Divine, Morall. Written by a Person of Honour and Piety* (London, 1655), p. 51.
78. Henderson, *Tudor House and Garden,* p. 34.
79. Strong, *Renaissance Garden,* p. 92.
80. Henderson, *Tudor House and Garden,* p. 180.
81. Strong, *Renaissance Garden,* p. 82.
82. Capel, *Daily Observations,* pp. 93–4.
83. <http://www.cotswolds.info/famouspeople/baptist-hicks.shtml>, accessed 18 August 2011.
84. Capel, *Daily Observations,* p. 60.
85. R.L. Greaves, 'Capel, Arthur, first earl of Essex (*bap.* 1632, *d.* 1683)', *ODNB* (Oxford, 2004), online edn, May 2010, <http://www.oxforddnb.com/view/article/4584>, accessed 12 February 2009. Arthur was only successful in recovering his estates after petitioning Parliament in 1651.
86. L. Knyff and I. Kip, *Britannia Illustrata* (London, 1707).
87. M. Cook, *The Manner of Raising, Ordering, and Improving Forrest Trees* (London, 1676).
88. Cook, *Forrest Trees,* p. 21.

89. Cook, *Forrest Trees,* pp. 27–8.
90. *ODNB*, entry Arthur Capel, first earl of Essex.
91. HALS DE/X10/Z1, Minet, p. 75.
92. HALS DE/X10/Z1, Minet, p. 31.
93. HALS 10465, Capel Estate Account Books; and HALS DE/X10/Z1, additional manuscript notes by Minet.
94. HALS DE/X10/Z1, Minet, p. 33.
95. Ordnance Survey Map, 1st edn. (1878) 1:2500, Hertfordshire Sheet, XXII.4.
96. HALS 70899, Sale Particulars (1900).
97. HALS 70899, Sale Particulars (1900).
98. H. Cooper-Reade, *Hadham Hall, Little Hadham, Hertfordshire, an Initial Evaluation,* Hertfordshire Archaeological Society, unpublished report, September 1992.

Bibliography

Primary sources

Capel, A., *Daily Observations or Meditations Divine, Morall. Written by a Person of Honour and Piety* (London, 1655).

Cook, M., *The Manner of Raising, Ordering, and Improving Forrest Trees* (London, 1676).

Cooper-Reade, H., *Hadham Hall, Little Hadham, Hertfordshire, an Initial Evaluation*, Hertfordshire Archaeological Society, unpublished report, September 1992.

De Caus, I., *Wilton Garden* (London, 1645).

Lawson, W., *A New Orchard and Garden*, (London, 1623).

Ordnance Survey Drawing 1800, sheet number 141.

Ordnance Survey Map, 1st edn. 1878, 1:2500, Hertfordshire Sheet, XXII.4.

Van Dyck, Sir A., *Charles I and Henrietta Maria with their two eldest children, Prince Charles and Princess Mary*, 1632, oil on canvas, dimensions 370.8 x 274.3cm (The Royal Collection).

Walker, C., *Hadham Hall, Little Hadham Archaeological Excavation (West Side)*, Hertfordshire Archaeological Trust, unpublished report, June 1994.

Hertford Archives and Local Studies (HALS):

D/EGr/32, Undated pamphlet *The Life of Lord Capell*.

DE/X10/P1, Little Hadham Tithe Map, 1844 – Tracing on Linen, by W. Minet.

DE/X10/Z1, Minet, W., *Hadham Hall and the Manor of Bawdes alias Hadham Parva* (Wiles and Son, Colchester, 1914) with additional pages added in scrapbook form.

DE/X10/Z2/6, Loose items relating to Hadham Hall *c.*1900–31.

DE/X10/Z2/9, Layout of Hadham Hall, 1900.

DP43 29/1–4, Miscellaneous papers relating to memorials and the Capel tomb in Little Hadham Church, Parish registers, Hadham Hall and the Capel family.

D/P43/29/9, Tebby, G., *Parish History – 400 Years of Hadham Hall* (pamphlet published 1928).

E 179/248/24/8, Hearth Tax reel 1.

M/205, Capel Papers, Maldon, Income and expenditure accounts.

M/211, A note of my travel and charges for the Lady Capell 1644 May 25 to 1645 March 18.

M/212, Estate Management Delinquency Papers.

M/350, Extracts from Bishop's Stortford churchwarden's accounts 1578.

10447–69 Capel Estate Account Books.

64244, Steward's Account: Hadham Hall 1628–29.

64322A, Hadham Hall the Seat of Arthur Baron Capel, *c.*1648.

70899, Volume containing drawings, photographs, plans and printed matter relating to Hadham Hall.

Gerish Box 32, Little Hadham.

Secondary sources

Biographia Britannica, vol ii. (London, 1748).

Britton, J., *The Architectural Antiquities of Great Britain, represented and illustrated in a series of views, elevations, plans, sections, and details of various Ancient English Edifices: with historical and descriptive accounts of each*, vol ii. (1809).

Chauncy, H., *The Historical Antiquities of Hertfordshire*, vol. i (London, 1700).

Clarendon, E., Earl of, *The History of the Rebellion and Civil Wars*, vol. iii (Oxford, 1704).

Clutterbuck, R., *The History and Antiquities of The County of Hertford* (London, 1827).

Colvin, H., *A Biographical Dictionary of British Architects, 1600–1840* (London, 1978).

Dixon Hunt, J. and Willis, P. (eds), *The Genius of the Place – The English Landscape Garden 1620–1820* (Cambridge, MA and London, 1988).

Dury, A. and Andrews, J., *A Topographical Map of Hartfordshire* (London, 1766; reprinted by Hertfordshire Record Society, 2004).

Hadham Hall Management Company, Unpublished '*History of Hadham Hall*'.

Henderson, P., *The Tudor House and Garden* (New Haven, CT and London, 2005).

Jellicoe, G. and S. *et al.* (eds), *The Oxford Companion to Gardens* (Oxford, 1986).

Knyff, L. and Kip, I., *Britannia Illustrata* (London, 1707).

Nichols, J., *Progresses and Public Processions of Queen Elizabeth,* vol. ii (London, 1823).

Page, W. (ed.), *VCH Hertfordshire,* 4 vols (Folkestone, 1912; repr. London, 1971).

Pevsner, N., *The Buildings of England – Hertfordshire* (London, 1953, revised by B. Cherry, Harmondsworth, 1977).

Rowe, A., *Medieval Parks of Hertfordshire* (Hatfield, 2009).

Salmon, N., *The History of Hertfordshire* (London, 1728).

Smith, J.T., *English Houses 1200–1800 – The Hertfordshire Evidence* (London, 1992).

Smith, J.T., *Hertfordshire Houses – Selective Inventory* (Oxford, 1993).

Spiers, W.L., 'The Note-book and Account-book of Nicholas Stone', *Walpole Society,* vol. vii (1919).

Strong, R., *The Artist and the Garden* (New Haven, CT and London, 2000).

Strong, R., *The Renaissance Garden in England* (London, 1979, 1998).

Thomson, A. (ed.), *The Impact of the First Civil War on Hertfordshire, 1642–47* (Rickmansworth, 2007).

Journals

Currie, C., 'Fishponds as Garden Features, *c.*1550–1750', *Garden History,* 18/1 (Spring 1990), pp. 22–46.

Den Hartog, E. and Teune, C., 'Gaspar Fagel (1633–88): His Garden and Plant Collection at Leeuwenhorst', *Garden History,* 30/2 (Winter 2002), pp. 191–205.

Duggan, D., 'The Fourth Side of the Covent Garden Piazza: New Light on the History and Significance of Bedford House', *British Art Journal,* 3 (Autumn, 2002), pp. 53–65.

Duggan, D., 'Isaac de Caus, Nicholas Stone, and the Woburn Abbey Grotto', *Apollo* (August 2003), pp. 50–7.

Duggan, D., 'Isaac de Caus: Surveyor, Grotto and Garden Designer', *Studies in the History of Gardens and Designed Landscapes,* 29/3 (July–September, 2009), pp. 152–68.

Johnson, P., 'Proof of the Heavenly Iris: The Fountain of Three Rainbows at Wilton House, Wiltshire', *Garden History,* 35/1 (Summer 2007), pp. 51–67.

Roberts, J., 'The Gardens of the Gentry in the Late Tudor period', *Garden History,* 27/1 (Summer 1999), pp. 89–108.

Web sources

Cotswolds Tourist Information & Travel Guide England UK, <http://www.cotswolds.info/famouspeople/baptist-hicks.shtml>, accessed 18 August 2011.

Greaves, R.L., 'Capel, Arthur, first earl of Essex (*bap.* 1632, *d.* 1683)', *Oxford Dictionary of National Biography* (Oxford, 2004), online edn, May 2010, <http://www.oxforddnb.com/view/article/4584>, accessed 12 February 2009.

Hutton, R., 'Capel, Arthur, first Baron Capel of Hadham (1604–1649)', *Oxford Dictionary of National Biography* (Oxford, 2004), online edn, October 2006, <http://www.oxforddnb.com/view/article/4583>, accessed 13 February 2009, and a calculation of the modern equivalent calculated using <http://www.nationalarchives.gov.uk/currency>, accessed 7 August 2011.

Myatt's Fields, Denmark Hill and Herne Hill: Introduction and Myatt's Fields area 'Survey of London': vol. 26: Lambeth: Southern area (1956), pp. 141–5, <http://www.british-history.ac.uk/report.aspx?compid=49775>, accessed 1 August 2011.

National Archives: <http://www.nationalarchives.gov.uk/currency>, accessed 7 August 2011.

Newman, J., 'Jones, Inigo (1573–1652)', *Oxford Dictionary of National Biography* (Oxford, 2004), online edn, September 2010, <http://www.oxforddnb.com/view/article/15017>, accessed 4 January 2012.

Owen, G. (ed.), *Calendar of the Cecil Papers in Hatfield House* (London, 1971), vol. xxii: 1612–1668, <http://www.british-history.ac.uk>, accessed 22 August 2011.

White, A., 'Stone, Nicholas (1585x8–1647)', *Oxford Dictionary of National Biography* (Oxford, 2004), <http://www.oxforddnb.com/view/article/26577>, accessed 2 August 2011.

CHAPTER FOUR

Mr Lancelot Brown and his Hertfordshire clients

Helen Leiper

Introduction

Landscape gardener Lancelot (Capability) Brown (1716–83)[1] has been credited with a hand in making twelve Hertfordshire parks and gardens, but with the exception of Ashridge, Beechwood and Moor Park very little is known about them.[2] The reason for this is simple: the available evidence is patchy or entirely lacking and the work Brown did has been overlaid or lost completely. Brown's surviving personal papers comprise an account book and a collection of letters, with other plans and documents dispersed in private collections and county record offices.[3] Dorothy Stroud identified ten of the Hertfordshire sites in her comprehensive study of Brown's life and work, which, in addition to the three above, were Cole Green, Digswell, The Hoo, Littlegrove, Pishiobury, Wrotham and Youngsbury, with Porters Park a later addition.[4] Research into Brown's bank account has brought a greater understanding of his business arrangements and identified General William Keppel, of Durham Park, as another client.[5] This chapter will consider what these men may have had in common with each other. It will also present new research on the park and gardens made for Earl Cowper at Cole Green House, near Hertford, including the building of a temple and a menagerie, which had not previously been known about.

Lancelot Brown's name is inextricably linked with the 'English' landscape garden known throughout the world. Comparing the Drapentier view of The Hoo (Figure 4.1) with that in a later watercolour of the house and its setting (Figure 4.2), we can appreciate the radical changes that were taking place in landscape design during the eighteenth century, as a less axial design aesthetic became accepted.[6] German visitor Count Frederick Kielmansegge observed in 1761, '...English design, is

Figure 4.1 'The Hoo', drawn by J. Drapentier. Taken from H. Chauncy, *The Historical Antiquities of Hertfordshire* (1700). REPRODUCED BY KIND PERMISSION OF HALS.

Figure 4.2 Watercolour painting of 'The Hoo' by an unknown artist, n.d. KIM/9. REPRODUCED BY KIND PERMISSION OF HALS.

arranged according to modern ideas of an improvement on the beauty of Nature'.[7] As the most successful and well known of his generation of landscape gardeners, Brown was later blamed for the wholesale destruction of formal gardens and avenues, but we shall see that this was not necessarily the case.

Hertfordshire's location, close to London with good road connections, has always made it a convenient spot for a country retreat, especially for men with court, government or business interests in the capital. The location of the parks and gardens where Brown is thought to have advised is shown on the map in Figure 4.3. There is a bias towards the south of the county, with a particular cluster around Barnet in the far south – one of the closest and most accessible areas for travel to and from London. East Barnet was noted as having 'in its neighbourhood several handsome houses of the Londoners and which are the more pleasant by being so near the chase'.[8]

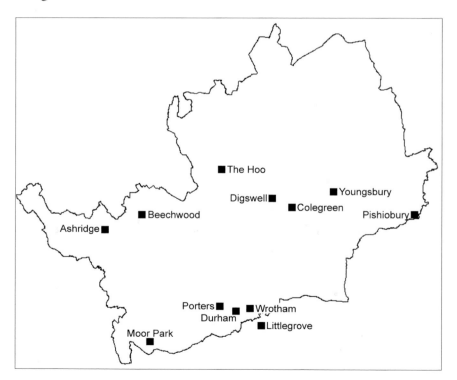

Figure 4.3 Map of Hertfordshire, showing the twelve Hertfordshire parks where Brown is thought to have been consulted. Boundary changes in 1965 transferred Littlegrove to the London Borough of Barnet.

Brown's Hertfordshire clients needed to be wealthy landowners to afford the kind of landscape design services he offered, but it is interesting to find that his earliest clients – Lord Anson, Sir Thomas Sebright, Earl Cowper and Thomas Brand – were all members of the Society of Dilettanti, a dining club for those who had been to Italy on a grand tour and who had an interest in the arts.[9] The Duke of Bridgewater was also a grand tourist, although not a member and he gave up his interest in art collecting until later in life.[10] Politics played an important part in all their lives, with a majority serving as Members of Parliament or sitting in the Lords.[11] Admiral Anson was First Lord of the Admiralty, and Admiral Howe and Generals Keppel and Byng knew each other from their service together.

Career gardener

The portrait by Sir Nathaniel Dance of Lancelot Brown (Plate 4.1) shows him dressed as a gentleman, a position he attained by working his way up from a manual labourer to become a wealthy man and landowner in his own right during his fifty-year career. Brown had trained as a gardener at Kirkharle Hall, north of Newcastle, before his appointment as head gardener to Richard Temple, first Viscount Cobham at Stowe in Buckinghamshire in 1741. Head gardeners were one of the most senior servants in a household and had regular contact with their employer. They were in charge of the day-to-day management of the gardens and staff, which at Stowe numbered thirty-five to forty.[12] Brown was only twenty-five when he was appointed on a wage of £25 per annum, plus an additional £9 on board.[13] Nevertheless, he seems to have satisfied Cobham's desire for someone 'able to converse instructively on his favourite pursuit, but free from the vanity and conceit which had made his former assistants disinclined to alterations upon which he had determined'.[14]

At Stowe, Brown practised gardening at the highest level and developed his skills by educating himself in architecture as well as landscape design. Brown's contribution to the gardens was to continue the naturalisation instigated by Lord Cobham, who ordered the removal of the grand parterre in 1742.[15] Lord Anson's sister-in-law, Jemima Yorke, took a keen interest in estate management and garden design.[16] She saw Brown working on the Grecian valley at Stowe in the summer of 1748, commenting somewhat unfavourably:

there are now going on Improvements in the 60 acres last enclos'd, which is a fall and Rise again of the Hill on the opposite Side ... but seems to have no Variety: the Slopes bare on the Other Side with Walks up or round them.[17]

In spite of this reservation, she and her husband would also employ Brown at Wrest Park for their own garden improvements, and recorded the 'professional assistance of Lancelot Brown, Esq. 1758–60' on a monument.[18] During the ten years Brown was employed at Stowe, he assisted other members of Cobham's circle with their garden projects, thereby making useful contacts and broadening his experience. Brown's character as well as his skill was integral to his success and he was known for his honesty and integrity. William Pitt the Elder commended him as 'an honest man, and of sentiments much above his birth'.[19]

In 1751 Brown moved close to London, where he set up in business on his own account at Hammersmith. In the first years of his new venture he continued to work for some of his earlier clients and importantly secured new work with Lord Coventry at Croome, Worcestershire, and Lord Egremont at Petworth, in Sussex. Brown's method of work was to meet the client and discuss the project.[20] He would obtain a survey of the site before preparing a plan with his proposals for the changes to be made. Clients could implement these proposals themselves, or, as at Petworth, Brown could make a contract laying out exactly what work was to be done, with staged payments. He also specified what he and the client would each provide in order to complete the work.[21] He did not remain on-site for the duration of the work, but left a foreman in charge and made periodic inspections of the progress, thus making possible the large number and wide distribution of his commissions.

Hertfordshire clients
In September 1753 Lord Anson (1697–1762) sent an invitation to Brown asking him to call at Moor Park, Rickmansworth.[22] Anson was First Lord of the Admiralty and a senior Whig politician. He had risen successfully through the ranks to become extremely rich, before marrying his young wife, Elizabeth, in April 1748.[23] After buying Moor Park, the Ansons divided their time between Hertfordshire and the Admiralty in London, also visiting Shugborough Hall in Staffordshire, the home of Anson's elder brother Thomas, who was a founder member of the Society of Dilettanti.[24]

Moor Park had been expensively updated and landscaped for the previous owner Benjamin Styles in the 1720s. According to Horace Walpole, Anson bought the house, park and a small estate with it for £14,000 and spent a further £6,000 on improving the grounds 'under the Direction of Brown'.[25] Records at Drummonds Bank, where Brown had his account, show regular yearly payments between 1754 and 1759. Over six years, £3,122 was paid out, to cover labour and materials, starting with £20 paid to Nathaniel Richmond.[26] The removal of the formal gardens and the re-contouring of the flat site at great expense did not impress Horace Walpole. Visiting in 1760, Walpole complained, 'I was not much struck with it after all the miracles I had heard that Brown had performed there' and made disparaging comments about the 'artificial molehills'.[27]

Lord Anson died at Moor Park in 1762.[28] Sir Laurence Dundas, who had made a fortune as an army contractor, before becoming MP for Newcastle under Lyme, bought Moor Park the following year.[29] He too was a member of the Society of Dilettanti. He may have continued some work in the gardens with a payment of £652 14s 7d to William Ireland, one of Brown's men, in 1765. Ireland appears to have been working independently at this time, although he later worked for Brown from 1768 to 1783.[30] The politician and garden commentator Thomas Whately visited Moor Park in the late 1760s and gave a fuller and more favourable appraisal of the work which Walpole had so roundly criticised, praising the grouping and disposition of the trees and the contouring of the land, summing up: 'a more varied, a more beautiful landskip, can hardly be desired in a garden'.[31]

A glimpse of the newly finished park was captured in a painting of Moor Park by Richard Wilson in c.1765–7 for Sir Laurence Dundas. Wilson's view of the west front shows the luxury of a space devoted to the comfort and relaxation of its prestigious owner, seen riding round his grounds (Plate 4.2). Wilson depicts the landscape park in use, with deer and sheep grazing and figures going about their daily business in the background. An indication of the labour involved in this apparently natural scene is given by a rolling stone, shown lying under the tree in the foreground, which would have been hauled by the gardeners. In another view showing Rickmansworth Church, Wilson hinted at a more contentious aspect of the park: its enclosure. Workmen and their dog are pictured taking a rest from the task of fencing the park, which will set it apart from the village just outside the pale.

Another early Hertfordshire commission was in prospect for Lancelot Brown, at Beechwood Park, Flamstead, when Sir Thomas Sebright had a survey made of his well-wooded park in 1753.[32] Sir Thomas was not just a simple country squire but belonged to a family with wealth and political ambition. He had inherited Beechwood Park from his father, MP for Hertfordshire, at the age of thirteen. His father had served twenty-one years in Parliament and his brother would also hold office for nineteen years.[33] In 1746 Thomas undertook a grand tour to Italy and he was proposed as a member of the Society of Dilettanti the same year.[34] Exactly how Sir Thomas was introduced to Brown is unknown but it may have been through his Dilettanti contacts or via a family connection to William Pitt, one of Lord Cobham's circle.[35]

The plan dated 1754 shows Brown's proposals.[36] He intended to modify the existing layout by curving the straight edges of the blocks of woodland, to vary and define their planting, and to introduce meandering walks. Clumps and scattered trees would soften the edges. The kitchen gardens were to be screened and a sunk fence, or ha-ha, would protect the gardens from the animals in the park, while keeping an open view. Small ponds were to be retained, with an object forming a focal point in the park in front of the house, and with the existing avenues also retained. On the garden front, decorative and practical items for the enjoyment of the park were a temple, a seat and a barn with an ornamental front. Plans were also included for matching wings for the house, a gothic bath house and an ice house.[37]

The Dury and Andrews map of 1766 shows little change to the features that had appeared on the survey of 1753, so it is unclear which, if any, of Brown's proposals had been implemented by Sir Thomas before he died in 1761, aged thirty-six.[38] His brother John, who succeeded him, must have done some planting, as there are records of payments to John Davenport, nurseryman, between 1772 and 1784.[39] Arthur Young noted that among the 'stately beeches' and other well-grown native tree specimens, 'the cedars are immense'.[40] Views of the early nineteenth-century park show the house still surrounded by large trees in undulating parkland and a pond remaining on the entrance front.[41]

'Beautifying Colegreen'[42]
During the period Brown was still working at Moor Park for George and Elizabeth Anson, William, second Earl Cowper (Figure 4.4), employed

Brown at Colegreen Park, near Hertford. William's father, the eminent Lord Chancellor and Whig politician, had built Cole Green House and made a deer park near Hertford at the beginning of the eighteenth century.[43] The second Earl attended Exeter College, Oxford, but did not follow his father into the law. A formative experience was his grand tour to Italy, begun in 1729. Shortly after his return to England, William married, although lack of money was a problem and he was obliged to reduce his spending to relieve his debts during his marriage.[44] He became a gentleman of the bedchamber to George II from 1733 to 1747 and as Lord Lieutenant and *custos rotulorum* [keeper of the rolls] he was the crown representative and principal justice of the peace in Hertfordshire from 1744.[45] The cost of maintaining the Earl's gardens in 1747 was put at £50 16s per annum.[46]A second marriage to Georgiana Caroline

Figure 4.4 Portrait of William, second Earl Cowper, attributed to Bartholomew Dandridge. Private Collection. SUPPLIED BY THE COURTAULD INSTITUTE OF ART. (Every effort has been made to trace the copyright holder and to obtain their permission for the use of this material. The publisher apologises for any errors or omissions and would be grateful if notified of any corrections that should be incorporated in future reprints or editions of this book.)

Spencer in May 1750 improved his finances and linked him with some of the wealthiest and most influential families in the country. Georgiana was the daughter of John Carteret, second Earl of Granville.[47] She was also the widow of the Hon. John Spencer, and her son, John, became the first Earl Spencer. Georgiana's sisters also married well and Brown was later employed by various members of the family, most notably at Bowood, Longleat and Blenheim.

There is no surviving survey or plan for Cole Green Park from the period of Brown's employment. An estate map dated 1703/4 shows the house at the time the first Earl bought the land, with its garden and embryonic park, surrounded by fields leading down to the river Mimram (Plate 4.3). The Cowper family bought up much of this land during the eighteenth century, which was incorporated into their Panshanger estate in the nineteenth century.[48] The evidence of Brown's work at Cole Green is in a ledger kept by the second Earl, which records household expenditure between 1755 and his death in 1764.[49] Among the many entries are seven payments to 'Mr Lancelot Brown' showing that over nine years Brown was paid £718 7s 6d, which is £100 more than was previously thought.[50] The ledger records not only the payments to Brown, but reveals the sequence of work, including some details of what that entailed. Thus we see that during the period of Brown's employment, first the garden and then the park were improved, as well as renovations in the house being carried out, with new plumbing and drains and including a new necessary (water closet), laundry and stables.

The exact dates of Brown's engagement cannot be established, since there is no contract or explicit note of their first meeting. It is possible that Brown was consulted in January 1752 before work started on a new kitchen garden at Cole Green and that notes recorded in the Earl's diaries could have formed part of a contractual agreement that has not survived. This kitchen garden had an octagonal design, and building had started in 1752. Trees and seeds were bought from John Williamson, a nurseryman often used by Brown and his clients.[51] By 1755 this garden was in production, with pine plants received from Philip Miller for the hothouse and a half a guinea tip to the gardener for the first pineapples.[52] Brown's employment had certainly begun by autumn 1755, since Earl Cowper received a letter from his brother hoping that 'Mr Brown and you may still go on with y[ou]r scheme for beautifying Colegreen', which indicates that work was already under way.[53]

Brown's first payment of £100 was recorded on 11 December 1755 but from midsummer 1755 Cowper was also paying for garden labour directly, via his head gardener, John Christi. Christi's wages were £9 per half year, plus board. This increased to £10 in summer 1756 when his successor, James Anderson, was hired on slightly better terms. Wages for 'sevts [servants] in Gardens' were usually paid every three weeks, although not for a fixed sum as that varied according to the men employed for the task in hand. It is difficult to assess exactly how many men were employed at a given time, as in most cases the rates of pay are not explicit and depend on the job. 'Henry Field Waggoner' is paid £8 8s per annum, while Wm. Mark 'Odd boy' gets only 3 shillings a week.[54] The sum of £15 12s was itemised for one year of 'board of ye Waggoners at 6d a week', making a total of twelve men employed on haulage.[55] Like Earl Egremont at Petworth, Earl Cowper provided carts and serviced them with grease and repairs.[56] Horses were not specifically mentioned but very regular visits were made by local blacksmith Jonas Thorogood. Wagons would have been needed for the heavy work of lifting and carrying the quantities of bricks, which were cleaned, presumably after removing walls in the gardens.[57] The sunk fence would also have had to be dug out, before work began on the brickwork in May 1756. Gravel was delivered for the 'south walk' in June 1756 and 3 shillings paid to stonemason John Cocks for a rolling stone. This would have been used by the gardeners to firm the path, perhaps in preparation for an inspection of the work in the garden by Brown, who received a payment in the same month.[58] Later another stone was bought for rolling the grass.[59]

Benjamin Read, 'Mr Brown's Head servant', was named and given a guinea in late June 1756, presumably as a tip at the end of his foremanship of this stage of the works.[60] They appear to have been preparing the ground for planting, since it is not until the following year that shrubs are sent from Charles Bridgeman and from John Williamson, with the accounts entry for the latter making it clear that they were sent 'to Colegreen by Mr Brown's order'.[61] Wages for 1757 also reveal an increased workforce, which peaked between March and the beginning of June. The work seemed to proceed smoothly, apart from a couple of occasions – one recorded in a letter from Spencer Cowper in October 1756, wherein he suggests a problem: 'As to Brown's Sauciness, I believe you have nothing to combat it with, but Patience', but sadly

no more details are given.[62] In June 1759 an unnamed man was also
given a guinea, with the terse comment, 'Given to Brown's man who
little deserved it'.[63] On a more positive note, a Mrs Wynner gave 'Mr
Brown's Gardiners' a guinea, although again the reason is unknown.[64]
George William Harris, Rector of Egglescliffe, visited Cole Green twice
in 1757, while staying with the Earl's brother, the Dean of Durham, at
Panshanger. The house is noted as standing in the centre of the park and
a number of pictures in the library are remarked upon, but even though
the supper party walked around the garden, only 'View' is recorded.[65]

Work continued in the gardens but from 1757 payments begin for
labourers in the park, for felling timber and then planting new hedges. In
1759 the account book tells us a menagerie was being made. Netting is
bought for it and it is given a lime wash.[66] 'Hens and Virginian Turkies'
are bought.[67] The following year Eli Aubrey is paid for 'Ironwork for
Menagery', at which point it is presumably finished.[68] In the spring of
1762 a temple was bought from Lord Albemarle's sale and a wagon
was sent to collect it.[69] It had a stone floor and was painted.[70] There is
visual evidence for it on the Dury and Andrews map, which shows trees
around a circle of dots in the park, south-west of the house (Figure 4.5).

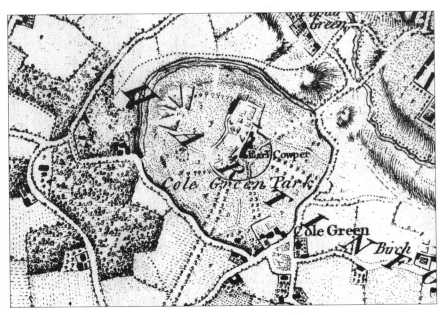

Figure 4.5 Detail of Dury and Andrews' map, 1766, showing the landscape features at Cole
Green Park. REPRODUCED BY KIND PERMISSION OF HALS.

This suggests the temple was a rotunda, backed by trees.[71] The map also places the menagerie at the far western side of the park where a number of straight lines radiate unevenly in a fan shape, with a small structure in the middle. In this position it would most likely be an ornamental feature, since it would have been visible from the house.

A comparison of the Dury and Andrews map with the survey map of 1703/4 (Plate 4.3) gives us some record of the changes at Cole Green in the intervening sixty-two years. The park has been enlarged with land bought by the second Earl, and paled with a curved boundary. The agricultural fields have been united into open parkland and a drive and paths cross it. The approach to the house is no longer directly to the east front but comes obliquely from left and right. The entrance court and formal gardens have been removed and a sunk fence or ha-ha encircles the house and gardens. The area behind the house, by the kitchen garden, is not entirely clear, but probably shows beds, with planting to screen the walls. The four acres of woodland have been thinned. Three avenues radiate from the house: one to the east front, following a line of trees marked in pencil on the 1703/4 estate map; one directed towards Cole Green; and one extended beyond the park boundary towards Holy Well. The menagerie and temple are also seen in the park, behind the house.

Marine artist John Charnock (1756–1807) made three views of Cole Green, which show the ha-ha and give an impression of the gardens in the late eighteenth century (Figure 4.6). A deep depression can still be seen at the site, even though the bricks were removed when the house was taken down in 1801.[72] Charnock shows a deciduous avenue to the east front of the house, but firs are present among trees framing the house, in the views of the south east and west fronts. This may indeed represent the actual planting, as Earl Cowper had a shopping list of trees in his diary for 1752, which included a number of firs, pines and larch, as well as tulip tree and magnolia.[73] In a rare comment on his design principals, Brown wrote of '… Beauty depending on the size of the trees and the colour of their leaves to produce the effect of light and shade so very essential to the perfecting a good plan'.[74] The avenue to the east front, photographed for *Country Life* in the 1930s, is still present in part today and contains some veteran oaks.[75] The account book also shows that Earl Cowper made three specific purchases of American seeds for Cole Green between 1758 and 1761.[76] Of the few named plants, the melons, pineapples and potatoes were obviously destined for the

Figure 4.6 View of Cole Green, by John Charnock. REPRODUCED BY KIND PERMISSION OF THE NATIONAL MARITIME MUSEUM.

kitchen garden. Different sorts of grass and clover seed were bought for the park and a large quantity of new turf was bought for the 'Lawn'.[77] The veteran trees remaining at the site are mainly deciduous broad-leafed species: oak, *Quercus robur*, sweet chestnut, *Castanea sativa*, and beech, *Fagus sylvatica*. Two more ornamental trees have been dated to the mid-eighteenth century.[78] A *Gingko biloba* is planted between the former gardener's cottage and the walls of the kitchen garden where it would have been in a prime position for special attention. This tree is of a similar age to one planted in Kew Gardens, which was also planted by a wall and trained 'like a fruit tree'.[79] The other specimen is an ancient acacia, *Robinia pseudoacacia*, which also has a counterpart at Kew. Although these trees are common today, in the eighteenth century they were exotic and rare, and Horace Walpole delighted in the 'odours beyond those of Araby'.[80]

Brown's final payment was 'on account', which indicates that work was still in progress when Earl Cowper died in September 1764. After William's death, his son, George, remained in Florence, where he had settled following his grand tour.[81] This was a matter of regret to the second Earl, who had arranged for George to be elected as MP for Hertford in 1759–61, probably as an inducement to him to return home and abandon an unsuitable liaison in Florence.[82] An unsigned and undated drawing in the Cowper archive gives an impression of the work Brown may have done in the park (Figure 4.7). Clumps of trees are scattered on mounds, and a small pond in the foreground chimes with one at Beechwood. Part of the avenue has been broken up, with the house in the background. George's sons eventually returned to take up their inheritance, but the fifth Earl decided to relocate the family seat to Panshanger, in a more picturesque position on the other side of the valley, with advice from Humphry Repton.[83] The park landscaped by Brown was largely returned to agricultural use and almost all trace of it has been lost.

An unsigned and undated eighteenth-century watercolour of workmen and their horses at Ashridge reminds us that Brown's major landscaping projects were executed with just picks and shovels, horses and carts and a lot of physical effort.[84] Not only was it a hard life for his workmen, but he himself travelled the length and breadth of the country

Figure 4.7 View of Colegreen House and park by an unknown artist. CV HERTING/39.
REPRODUCED BY KIND PERMISSION OF HALS.

to supervise the work on-site and to meet his clients. The distances involved meant that clients often had to wait until Brown was passing or visiting another client nearby. While Brown was still working at Cole Green, Francis Egerton, third Duke of Bridgewater, and Thomas Brand of The Hoo employed him for architectural and landscape work.

Bridgewater's nickname, 'the canal duke', came from his lifelong interest in the promotion and construction of canals.[85] He had been sent on a grand tour in 1753, attended by Robert Wood, an antiquarian and archaeologist. Bridgewater insisted on visiting the Languedoc Canal, and attended courses on science and engineering at Lyons Academy. They eventually went to Florence and then to Rome in 1754, where Bridgewater took lodgings at the same place as Robert Adam, whom he engaged to buy pictures for a proposed collection.[86] Bridgewater fell ill and by coincidence Thomas Brand of The Hoo, a family acquaintance, who happened to be in Rome at the same time, attended on him.

Bridgewater returned to England in 1755, still only nineteen years old, and settled into a life of gambling and horse racing.[87] In 1758 he unexpectedly became engaged to Elizabeth Gunning, a celebrated beauty. This may be the reason he wanted to make improvements at Ashridge, but the engagement was broken off in November the same year, and he never married.[88] Brown's account book shows that Bridgewater paid for several journeys in 1759–60 and for four plans and two elevations for the house with sums to Mr Holland for the architectural work.[89] Sums relating to work in the gardens are for the years 1761–8, and show that Bridgewater spent a total of £2,946 11s 7d. An estate map of 1762 shows the park a year or two after Brown had started work.[90] Established formal rides through the park remain clearly defined, but it is north of the house in the area called the 'Golden Valley' where it is thought he concentrated his efforts.[91]

Thomas Brand was a Member of Parliament as well as an active and leading member of the Society of Dilettanti, following his grand tour in 1738–9.[92] He returned to Italy in 1753, after the death of his wife, Lady Caroline Pierrepont, left him grief stricken, with two small children.[93] In Italy he collected art and bought a 'landskip' from 'an Englishman, one Wilson who is in such repute as to be employed by many of the Italians & I think he is really the best painter of that sort I have seen abroad'.[94] An undated eighteenth-century estate map shows The Hoo before the creation of the landscape park, with enclosed gardens and courts and a long avenue approaching the house from the river.[95] The only recorded payment by Thomas Brand to Brown is £150 in 1758.[96] This would have been enough to pay for a visit by Brown and some drawings, but not for landscaping work. Stroud notes this may have been done in 1760–2, with Brown's drawing for a bridge over the lake rejected in favour of one by William Chambers.[97] Horace Walpole described Brand as an old school friend and 'a very intimate friend of mine', but reveals nothing about The Hoo.[98] The Dury and Andrews map shows that significant landscape changes have been made by 1766, including the widening of the river. A watercolour (Figure 4.2) illustrates the informal planting of the park, with the mature trees in front of the house suggesting that a remnant of the avenue has been integrated in the design, although there are some reservations about the accuracy of the painting.[99]

Later clients

Several of Brown's later clients were relative newcomers to the county and did not remain very long. The manor of Durham Park (now named Dyrham Park), near Potters Bar, had been sold to the Keppel family in 1733 by John Austen, MP for Middlesex. William Keppel followed his father, second Earl of Albemarle, and eldest brother, George, into the army, while his older brother, Augustus, had joined the navy. All three brothers shared prize money for their part in the siege and capture of Havana in 1762, a campaign planned by Admiral Anson.[100] Garden historian David Brown identified seven payments in Brown's Drummonds bank account, amounting to £1,473 13s 6d, for work done for William Keppel at Durham Park, in 1765–72.[101] The Dury and Andrews map records the military arrangement of the gardens prior to their alteration, but Brown's work may have included the lake made by widening the Mimmshall Brook, the drive curving towards the house and the informal park landscape recorded by the Ordnance Survey at the turn of the century.[102] Certainly by 1779 it had been 'greatly beautified ... by laying most of the neighbouring fields belonging to the estate into a park, and turning and repairing the roads'.[103] However, Keppel sold Durham Park to Christopher Bethell, in 1773 – the year after Brown had finished the work – so further evidence is needed to establish what Brown's work comprised.

William Keppel's brother Augustus had sat at the court martial that led to the execution of Admiral John Byng, owner of neighbouring

Wrotham Park. Byng's success in the navy had won him a 'little fortune' and from about 1748 he had begun to look for a site for a country house, north of London, in addition to his London home.[104] Starting in 1750 Byng bought up land around Kitt's End and employed Isaac Ware to build the house. After his execution, his nephew, George Byng, MP for Middlesex, inherited Wrotham Park.[105] There is a note in Brown's account book of a couple of visits to Wrotham and a survey by Samuel Lapidge, in 1765 – perhaps in association with work at nearby Durham. A survey map of 1780 recorded the design: an apparently random arrangement of clumps and single trees scattered throughout the park, surrounded by a belt which may have been designed by Lapidge.[106]

Richard Howe had been on board one of the ships attempting to accompany Anson's circumnavigation of the globe in 1740. He gained considerable wealth in a long and distinguished career as an excellent commander, influential in bringing professionalism to the officer corps.[107] Admiral Howe bought Porters Lodge (also known as Porters Park), Shenley, from writer and gardener George Mason in 1772,[108] living there when not at sea or at his house in Grafton Street, London.[109] Howe wrote to Brown in 1773 asking him to visit, saying, 'my ambition is to benefit by your lights', although there is no record of further involvement by Brown.[110] Howe may have taken advice from Mason, who was no admirer of Brown's and lived close by at Aldenham.[111] Admiral Howe was 'almost pathologically secretive' and it is likely that any relevant papers have been destroyed.[112]

Littlegrove in East Barnet had extensive views, in this case south, towards London. The estate was bought by Justice Edward Willes in 1767 for £4,000. After Brown had been paid £700 for unspecified work in 1768–70, the estate was resold by Judge Willes' widow in 1794, for 8,000 guineas, making it a profitable investment.[113] Sales particulars in 1862 describe an estate 'laid out with the greatest possible taste' and 'ornamented with fine evergreens and American shrubs'.[114] On the coloured plan of the property, the grounds are shown with a belt along the road side, a walled kitchen garden, shrubbery walks, ponds and a circuit drive around the small park. The site was built over in the 1930s, with only fragments of the walled garden remaining.[115]

At Youngsbury, Mrs Jane Poole's coloured estate map of 1768 shows the estate bounded by the river Rib and a paddock crossed by footpaths, where the park would be made.[116] On the plan, 'proposed

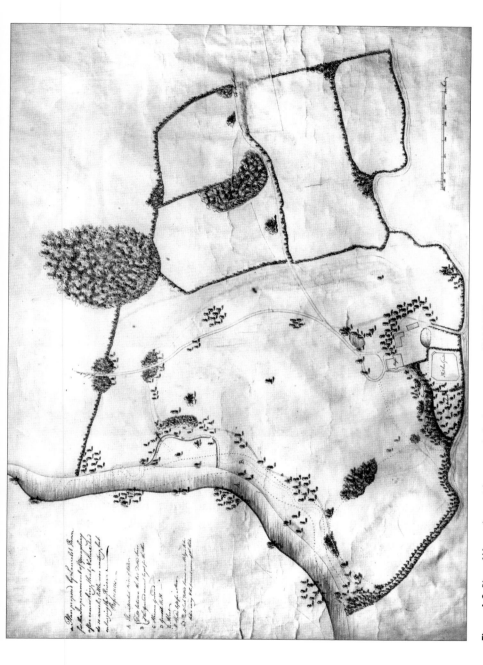

Figure 4.8 Plan of Youngsbury with proposals for improvements. HALS DE/A 2845. REPRODUCED BY KIND PERMISSION OF THE HON. C.A. SAVILE.

Figure 4.9 Portrait of David Barclay. REPRODUCED BY KIND PERMISSION OF BARCLAYS
GROUP ARCHIVES.

by Lancelot Brown', he had written that 'little was wanting but
enlarging the river', and a pleasure ground, a gravel walk, a stew, a seat
and hedges to be removed were shown (Figure 4.8). This plan has no
name or date inscribed, leaving the client's name open to speculation.
Mrs Poole or her son Josiah might have employed Brown, but David
Barclay, who bought Youngsbury in 1769[117] or a Colonel Monson,
who had been living at the house prior to the sale, seem more likely.[118]
Bank records have not revealed payments by any of them to Lancelot
Brown, although cash could have been paid.[119] Barclay (Figure 4.9) was
a member of a prominent Quaker family of merchants and bankers.[120]
He was involved with political and philanthropic causes and acted as an
intermediary between Benjamin Franklin and Lord North's government,

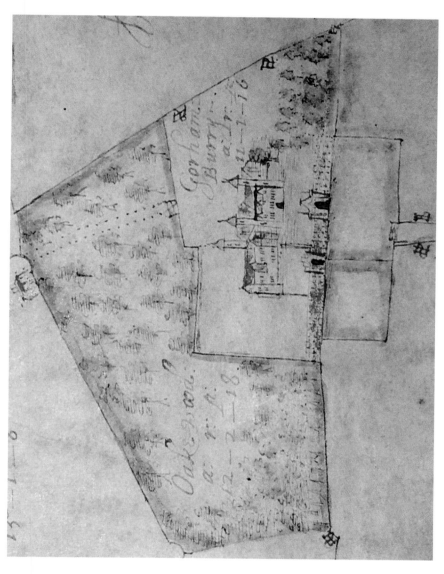

Plate 1.1 Detail of Gorhambury estate map of 1634. D/EV P1. REPRODUCED BY KIND PERMISSION OF HALS.

Plate 1.2 Lord Burghley on his mule in the gardens at Theobalds. Late eighteenth- or early nineteenth-century copy of a sixteenth-century original. REPRODUCED BY KIND PERMISSION OF THE MASTERS OF THE BENCH OF THE HONOURABLE SOCIETY OF GRAY'S INN.

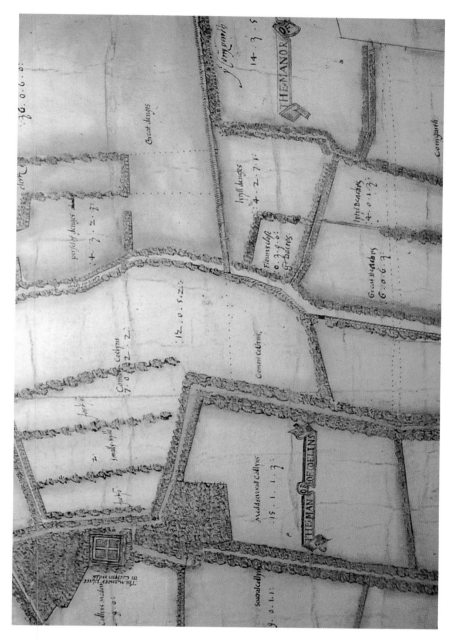

Plate 2.1 Detail of a map of c.1575 showing fields belonging to the manors of Theobalds (pink) and Cullings (green) which were soon to become part of Lord Burghley's new park. North is at the top. Note the double row of dots on the right-hand side marking a later tree-lined walk and the Cullings moat bottom left. MS Gough Drawings a.3. Fol. 27. REPRODUCED BY KIND PERMISSION OF THE BODLEIAN LIBRARY, UNIVERSITY OF OXFORD.

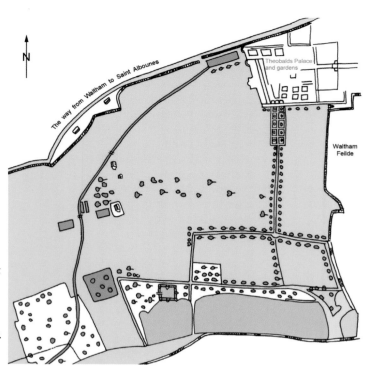

Plate 2.2
Digitised
tracing of part
of the plan
of Theobalds
by J. Thorpe
held in the
British Library.
Cotton MS
Aug.I.i.75.

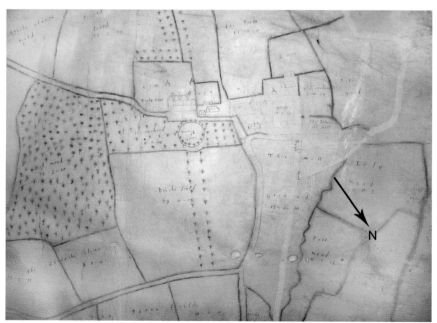

Plate 2.3 Detail of a plan of the Bushey Hall estate, 1685. Note the colours of the house and water have been added digitally for greater clarity. DE/Hx/P2.

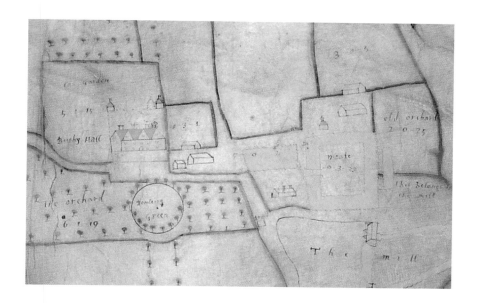

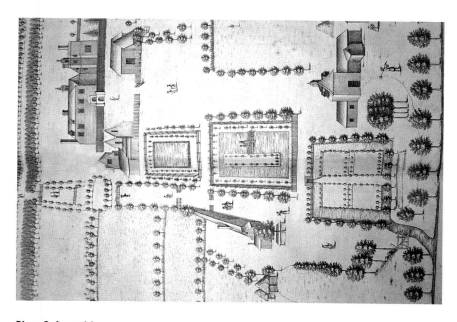

Plate 2.4a and b

A comparison of the water features depicted on the 1685 plan and the view of Bushey Hall from the west by J. Drapentier, 1700. Taken from H. Chauncy, *Historical Antiquities of Hertfordshire*, pp. 540–3. DE/Hx/P2. REPRODUCED BY KIND PERMISSION OF HALS.

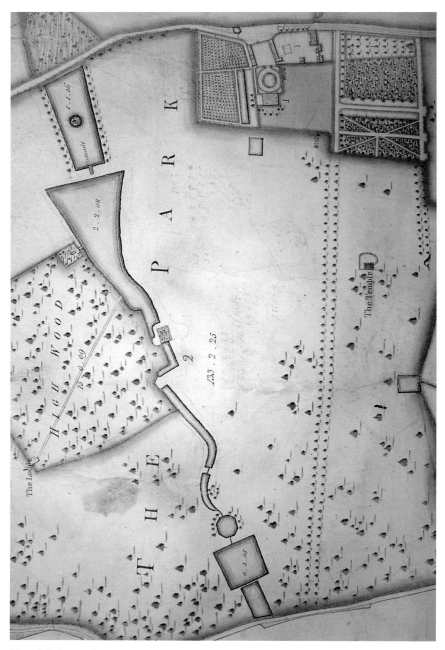

Plate 2.5 Detail of a 'Plan of the manor of Holbatches alias Popes ... belonging to Mrs Rebecca Asheton surveyed by Taylor and Chilcott in the year 1785'. North is to the left. CPM Supp 69.

Plate 2.6 Portrait of Sir Benjamin Truman by T. Gainsborough, *c.*1770–4. © Tate, London 2012. REPRODUCED BY KIND PERMISSION OF THE TATE GALLERY.

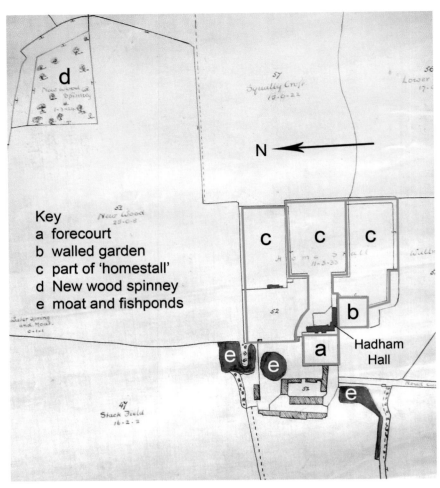

Key
a forecourt
b walled garden
c part of 'homestall'
d New wood spinney
e moat and fishponds

Hadham Hall

Plate 3.1 Detail of Little Hadham Tithe Map, 1844. Tracing on Linen by W. Minet with additional annotation by the author. DE/X10/P1. REPRODUCED BY KIND PERMISSION OF HALS.

Plate 3.2 Painting of Hadham Hall, East Wing, *c.*1640, artist unknown. REPRODUCED BY KIND PERMISSION OF HERTFORD MUSEUM.

Plate 3.3 Portrait of the Capel Family by C. Johnson, *c.*1641. REPRODUCED BY KIND PERMISSION OF THE NATIONAL PORTRAIT GALLERY.

Plate 4.1 Portrait of Lancelot Brown by Sir N. Dance, R.A., c.1769. REPRODUCED BY KIND PERMISSION OF THE BURGHLEY HOUSE COLLECTION.

Plate 4.2 'View of Moor Park', west front, by R. Wilson, *c*.1765. Photographed by Jerry Hardman-Jones. REPRODUCED BY KIND PERMISSION OF THE ZETLAND COLLECTION.

Plate 4.3 Detail of a survey map showing William Cowper's estate, drawn by J. Halsey, 1703/4. D/EP/P 4. REPRODUCED BY KIND PERMISSION OF HALS.

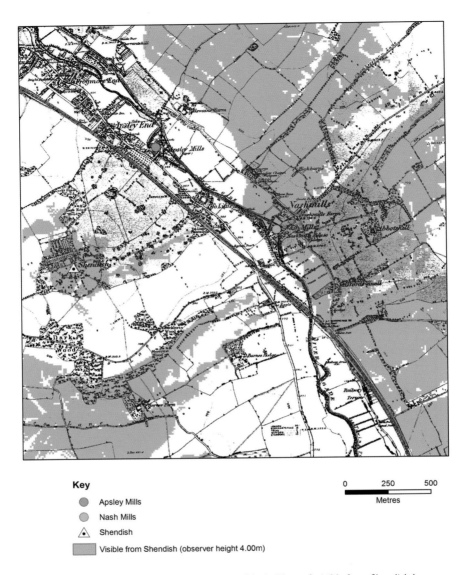

Plate 5.1 GIS-generated viewshed showing areas (shaded brown) visible from Shendish house.

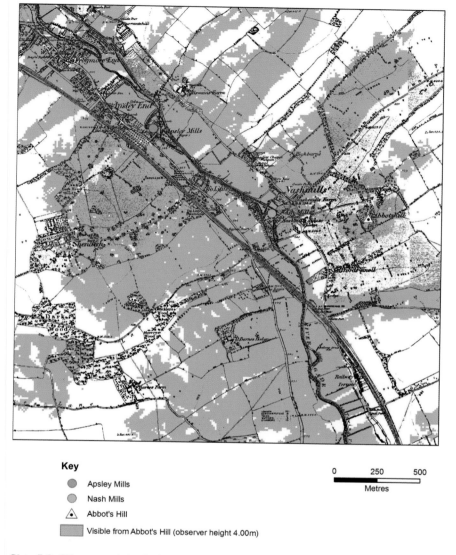

Apsley Mills

Nash Mills

Abbot's Hill

Visible from Abbot's Hill (observer height 4.00m)

0   250   500

Metres

Plate 5.2 GIS-generated viewshed showing areas (shaded brown) visible from Abbots Hill house.

Plate 6.1 Fanhams Hall Japanese gardens. PHOTOGRAPH BY KATE HARWOOD.

Early Transparent Gage.

Rivers' Early Prolific.

Plate 7.1 Rivers Early Prolific Plum painted by May Rivers, daughter of the nursery director, c.1890. REPRODUCED BY KIND PERMISSION OF THE RIVERS ARCHIVE.

Perpetual Moss.
Mauget.
See Group 31.

J. Andrews, Zinco.

Day & Son, Lith™ to the Queen

Plate 8.1 Lithograph of *Rosa centifolia Perpetuelle* Mauget by James Andrews. Plate 11 in *The Rose Garden* by William Paul.

negotiating for reconciliation in the impending American war.[121] The nature of his religious beliefs meant that wealth was not for ostentatious display, although Quakers did make gardens and Barclay's friend and fellow Quaker, John Scott, had built an elaborate grotto near Ware. This work gave employment to local labourers and may well have had a philanthropic motive.[122] Whoever paid for Brown's plan, which has remained at Youngsbury,[123] the 1793 estate map shows that Barclay had completed the landscape scheme in most respects when he sold it to William Cunliffe Shaw in 1793.[124]

Conclusion

During the 1750s Lancelot Brown's Hertfordshire clients came from an elite group of wealthy men who had travelled in Europe, or, in Admiral Anson's case, throughout the entire world. Their shared experience of the grand tour continued with membership of the Society of Dilettanti, which fostered the development of public taste, as well as their more infamous activities.[125] These men belonged to a circle of people who were knowledgeable about the arts and the latest developments in landscape design. Brown and his men had the skills and experience to advise or to implement the design as the client wished. George Mason called Brown's clients 'those, who consider nothing so much, as the having of trouble taken off their hands' but this may have been exactly the service Brown's patrons were looking for.[126] Brown was known for his good client relations and did what he was asked to do. Even if there was a problem it was sorted out and work continued. He used existing landscape features to best advantage, thinning or planting as required. Avenues were not routinely removed but modified to look less formal, and where water to make a lake was lacking, a river, ponds and pools were blended into the scheme.

After the mid-1760s clients came from a wider social group, including top lawyers like Judge Willes at Littlegrove, senior naval and military men, and possibly even the Quaker banker David Barclay. Land had always been seen as an investment but owners were increasingly looking to consolidate their holdings and manage their estates more effectively, while enjoying the benefits it offered.[127] Work in Hertfordshire formed only a fraction of the commissions tackled by Brown over his long career and consulting Brown did not always result in the work being done by him.[128] There are still many gaps in our knowledge, and further work is needed to establish the extent of Brown's involvement at Digswell and at Pishiobury, if any.[129]

Research into Brown's employment at Cole Green Park has revealed the most detailed account of his work in the county. The sequence of work, the costs and an idea of what the work entailed are contained within the accounts ledger. A previously unknown payment to Brown of £100 has been discovered, as well as a menagerie and temple built in the park. Earl Cowper's liking for American plants can be established, even though the planting details are only rudimentary. The £718 7s 6d paid to Brown by Cowper was a small amount in comparison with what was paid for work at Moor Park, Ashridge or Durham Park but it ensured that the landscape at Cole Green was as modern and as fashionable as he could afford. A landscape park, although expensive to create, was less costly and easier to maintain in the long term than formal gardens. As well as making a public statement of the owners' forward thinking and modern taste, a landscape park offered owners an exclusive and private setting for their country home, where they could rest, entertain or pursue healthy rural activities such as riding, hunting, shooting and fishing.

Acknowledgements
I would like to thank the staff at Hertfordshire Archives and Local Studies; Dr Gillian Gear, archivist at Barnet Museum; Charles Dace, archivist at Wrotham Park Estate; the Earl of Ronaldshay, the Hon. C.A. Savile; Anne Rowe and Jenny Milledge.

Notes

1. His nickname, 'Capability', is thought to have come from his frequent reference to the capabilities of a place; D. Stroud, *Capability Brown* (London, 1950; 1984), p. 37.
2. Hertfordshire Gardens Trust and T. Williamson, *The Parks and Gardens of West Hertfordshire* (2000).
3. Letters are at the British Library. The account book is at the Royal Horticultural Society Lindley Library, in London, which was unfortunately closed during the latter part of this study.
4. R. Turner, *Capability Brown and the Eighteenth Century English Landscape* (London, 1985), p. 186. Further accounts of Brown's life and work can be found in T. Hinde, *Capability Brown: The Story of a Master Gardener* (London, 1986); J. Phibbs, 'Brown, Lancelot [Capability Brown] (*bap.* 1716, *d.* 1783)', *Oxford Dictionary of National Biography (ODNB)*, (Oxford, 2004), online edn, May 2009, <http://www.oxforddnb.com/view/article/3635>, accessed 2 August 2011; and J. Brown, *The Omnipotent Magician: Lancelot 'Capability' Brown 1716–1783* (London, 2011).
5. Note 3, p. 8, D. Brown, 'Lancelot Brown and His Associates', *Garden History*, 29/1, issue on Lancelot Brown (1716–83) and the Landscape Park (Summer 2001), pp. 2–11; P. Willis 'Capability Brown's Account with Drummond's Bank, 1753–1783', *Architectural History*, vol. xxvii, issue on Design and Practice in British Architecture: Studies in Architectural History Presented to Howard Colvin (1984), pp. 382–91.
6. H. Chauncy, *The Historical Antiquities of Hertfordshire*, 2 vols (London, 1700; 2nd edn Bishops Stortford, 1826; repr. 1975), ii, p. 402, and Hertfordshire Archives and Local Studies (HALS) KIM/9.
7. Count Frederick Kielmansegge, *Diary of a Journey to England in the Years 1761–1762*, tr. Countess Kielmansegge (London, 1902), p. 55.
8. Enfield Chase. D. Defoe, *A Tour thro' the Whole Island of Great Britain divided into Circuits or Journies, originally begun by... Daniel De Foe, continued by ... Mr. Richardson*, 4 vols (9th edn, 1779), p. 138.
9. L. Cust, *History of the Society of Dilettanti*, ed. S. Colvin (London, 1898).
10. He was perhaps an exception because of his comparative youth, K.R. Fairclough, 'Egerton, Francis, third duke of Bridgewater (1736–1803)', *ODNB* (Oxford, 2004), online edn, October 2009, <http://www.oxforddnb.com/view/article/8584>, accessed 3 December 2011.
11. G.P. Judd, *Members of Parliament 1734–1832* (New Haven, CT, 1955).
12. Hinde, *Story of a Master Gardener*, p. 19.
13. Turner, *Capability Brown*, p. 55.
14. John Penn, quoted in Hinde, *Story of a Master Gardener*, p. 18.
15. National Trust, *Stowe Landscape Gardens* (London, 1997), p. 61.
16. J. Collett-White, 'Yorke Jemima, *suo jure* Marchioness Grey (1722–1797)', *ODNB* (Oxford, 2004), <http://www.oxforddnb.com/view/article/68351>, accessed 21 June 2011.
17. J. Brown, *The Omnipotent Magician*, p. 58, quoting from Dr George Clarke's *Descriptions of Lord Cobham's Garden at Stowe, 1700–1750*.
18. Stroud, *Capability Brown*, p. 80.
19. Turner, *Capability Brown*, p. 59.
20. E. Hall, '"Mr Brown's Directions": Capability Brown's Landscaping at Burton Constable (1767–82)', *Garden History*, 23/2 (1995).
21. West Sussex Record Office (WSRO), PHA 6623 Contracts for Petworth (1753, 1754).
22. British Library (BL), Add. Mss. 69795 Brown correspondence, f.1.

23. E.H. Chalus, 'Elizabeth, Lady Anson (1725–1760)', *ODNB* (Oxford, 2004), <http://www.oxforddnb.com/view/article/68350>, accessed 21 June 2011.

24. Cust, *Society of Dilettanti*, p. 8.

25. H. Walpole, *Horace Walpole's Journals of Visits to Country Seats Etc.*, ed. P.J. Toynbee (1927–8), XVI, p. 24.

26. Hertfordshire Gardens Trust and Williamson, *Parks and Gardens*, p. 42.

27. Stroud, *Capability Brown*, p. 70.

28. N.A.M. Rodger, 'Anson, George, Baron Anson (1697–1762)', *ODNB* (Oxford, 2004), online edn, May 2008, <http://www.oxforddnb.com/view/article/574>, accessed 25 August 2008.

29. R.P. Fereday, 'Dundas family of Fingask and Kerse', *ODNB* (Oxford, 2004); online edn, January 2008, <http://www.oxforddnb.com/view/article/64103>, accessed 5 August 2011.

30. D. Brown, 'Lancelot Brown and His Associates', *Garden History*, 29/1 (Summer 2001), p. 6.

31. T. Whately, *Observations on Modern Gardening, Illustrated by Descriptions* (London, 1770), pp. 4–5.

32. HALS Acc. 3898/4 Photocopies of the Beechwood plan and survey.

33. D.R. Fisher, 'Sebright, Sir John Saunders, seventh baronet (1767–1846)', *ODNB* (Oxford, 2004); online edn, January 2008, <http://www.oxforddnb.com/view/article/24997>, accessed 3 August 2011.

34. J. Ingamells, *A Dictionary of English and Irish Travellers in Italy, 1701–1800* (New Haven, CT, 1997), p. 845.

35. T. Rowe, *The Beechwood Companion: The Story of A House and its People* (n.p., 2006), p. 30.

36. HALS Acc. 3898/4.

37. Rowe, *Beechwood Companion*, p. 25.

38. A. Dury and J. Andrews, *A Topographical Map of Hartford-Shire, from an Actual Survey*, 1 mile: 1.95 inches (1766; repr. Hertford, 2004).

39. Hertfordshire Gardens Trust and Williamson, *Parks and Gardens*, p. 41.

40. A. Young, *General View of the Agriculture of the County of Hertfordshire* (London, 1804; 1971), p. 147.

41. HALS D/ECL ZIII 360 A–C, Buckler views of Beechwood Park.

42. H. Leiper, '"Beautifying Colegreen": The Eighteenth Century Park and Gardens of Colegreen House in Hertfordshire', MA dissertation, Birkbeck College, University of London, 2008. Note that both 'Colegreen' and 'Cole Green' were used during the eighteenth century.

43. HALS DE/P/P5, contract and plan for Cole Green House, 1704.

44. HALS DE/P/F249, letter from Joseph Atwell, 13 August 1733.

45. D. Warrand (ed.), *Hertfordshire Families* (London, 1907), p. 139.

46. HALS DE/P/A185, estimate of expenses, 1747.

47. J. Cannon, 'Carteret, John, second Earl Granville (1690–1763)', *ODNB* (Oxford, 2004), online edn, May 2006, <http://www.oxforddnb.com/view/article/4804>, accessed 21 May 2008.

48. H. Prince, 'The Changing Landscape of Panshanger', *Transactions of the East Herts Archaeological Society*, XIV, pt.1 (1955–7), pp. 42–58.

49. HALS DE/P/A8, Earl Cowper's accounts ledger, 1755–64.

50. Leiper, 'Beautifying Colegreen', appendix B.

51. HALS DE/P/F243–4, diaries, 1752–53.

52. *Ibid.*, 29 July 1755.

53. HALS DE/P/255, letter from Spencer Cowper, Dean of Durham, 31 October 1755.

54. HALS DE/P/A8, 29 December and 15 November 1756.

55. *Ibid.*, 6 November 1755.

56. WSRO, PHA 6623, Contract 1 May 1753: 'the Earl of Egremont does promise ... to find at his or their expence five able Horses with all sorts of Harness, Twelve Dutch Carts, Forty two wheelbarrows & keep the Same in Repair during the Execution of this work ...'.

57. HALS DE/P/A8, 14 March 1756.
58. *Ibid.*, 5 June 1756.
59. *Ibid.*, 12 May 1759.
60. *Ibid.*, 25 June 1756.
61. *Ibid.*, 19 May 1757.
62. HALS DE/P/F256, 8 October 1756.
63. HALS DE/P/A8, 13 June 1759.
64. *Ibid.*, 26 May 1756.
65. 2 and 4 June 1757. *Hertfordshire Heritage*, ed. C. Shearman, 'Diary of the Reverend George William Harris', 22 (1996), pp. 12–15.
66. HALS DE/P/A8, 25 April 1759.
67. *Ibid.*, 22 April 1759.
68. *Ibid.*, 12 April and 8 May 1760.
69. *Ibid.*, 9 April 1762, £36 0s 6d paid for the temple and pavement.
70. *Ibid.*, 1 June 1762, £5 19s to John Gockins for painting temple and £5 12s 6d to 'James Hill Stonemason in full of a bill for laying pavement in temple at Colegreen', 30 June 1762.
71. Humphry Repton shows such a rotunda in proposals for Tewin Water, HALS D/Z42/Z1, view IV.
72. HALS DE/P/EA23/2, account of materials recovered from Cole Green House.
73. HALS DE/P/F243.
74. Stroud, *Capability Brown*, p. 157.
75. C. Hussey, 'Panshanger Hertfordshire, A Seat of Lord and Lady Desborough', *Country Life*, 11 January 1936, p. 43.
76. HALS DE/P/A8, 19 April 1758, 27 March 1759, 25 April 1761.
77. *Ibid.*, 26 December 1762.
78. Information supplied by the owner. Site visit June 2008.
79. John Smith quoted in R. Desmond, *Kew: The History of the Royal Botanic Gardens* (London, 1995), p. 399.
80. Horace Walpole to George Montagu, quoted in M. Laird, *The Flowering of the Landscape Garden: English Pleasure Grounds 1720–1800* (Philadelphia, 1999), p. 139.
81. Although he did visit briefly in 1786 – H. Belsey, 'Cowper, George Nassau Clavering, third Earl Cowper (1738–1789)', *ODNB* (Oxford, 2004), online edn, January 2008, <http://www.oxforddnb.com/view/article/61668>, accessed 4 December 2011.
82. *Ibid.*
83. Repton put the arguments for the change of site in his Red Book for Panshanger – HALS DE/P/21.
84. HALS D/ECL ZIII 362 C.
85. H. Malet, *Bridgewater: The Canal Duke 1736–1803* (Manchester, 1977).
86. Ingamells, *Dictionary*, p. 125.
87. Malet, *Bridgewater*, p. 21.
88. *Ibid.*, pp. 21–4
89. Lindley Library, London.
90. HALS AH 2770, large scale estate map of Ashridge. Surveyed by George Grey of Lancaster (1762).
91. A. Bryant, K. Senecki and R. Wheeler, *The Garden at Ashridge* (Ashridge, 1989), p. 3.
92. Cust, *Society of Dilettanti*, pp. 16, 250.
93. Ingamells, *Dictionary*, p. 117.
94. *Ibid.*, Brand to second Earl of Strafford, 28 February 1755.
95. A. Constable, P. McManus and A. Rowe, 'The Hoo, Kimpton', Hertfordshire Gardens Trust Research Group Report (2005), p. 4.
96. P. Willis, 'Capability Brown's Account with Drummond's Bank, 1753–1783', *Architectural History*, 27 (1984), p. 385.
97. Stroud, *Capability Brown*, pp. 229–30.

98. W.S. Lewis, *Correspondence of Horace Walpole*, 36 vols (New Haven, CT, 1937–80), xx, pp. 434–5.

99. Constable, McManus and Rowe, 'The Hoo, Kimpton', p. 6.

100. R. Mackay, 'Keppel, Augustus, Viscount Keppel (1725–1786)', *ODNB* (Oxford, 2004), online edn, January 2010, <http://www.oxforddnb.com/view/article/15439>, accessed 5 August 2011.

101. D. Brown, 'Lancelot Brown and His Associates', *Garden History*, 29/1 (Summer 2001), pp. 8–9.

102. BL, Ordnance Survey drawings, surveyed 1799, published in 1805.

103. Defoe, *A Tour thro' the Whole Island of Great Britain*, p. 139.

104. D. Pope, *At 12 Mr Byng was Shot* (London, 1962; 2002), pp. 26–9.

105. D.A. Baugh, 'Byng, John (*bap.* 1704, *d.* 1757)', *ODNB* (Oxford, 2004), online edn, January 2008), <http://www.oxforddnb.com/view/article/4263>, accessed 23 November 2010.

106. A. Simpson, 'A History of the Estate and Garden at Wrotham Park', *The London Gardener or The Gardener's Intelligencer*, 7, Journal of London Historic Parks and Gardens Trust (2001–02), pp. 66–79.

107. R. Knight, 'Howe, Richard, Earl Howe (1726–1799)', *ODNB* (Oxford, 2004), online edn, October 2009, <http://www.oxforddnb.com/view/article/13963>, accessed 14 June 2011.

108. G. and S. Jellico, P. Goode and M. Lancaster, *The Oxford Companion to Gardens* (Oxford, 1991), p. 358.

109. D. Syrett, *Admiral Lord Howe: A Biography* (Stroud, 2006).

110. Letter to Brown from Porters Lodge, 18 December 1773, BL, Add. Mss. 69795.

111. J. Sambrook, 'Mason, George (1735–1806)', *ODNB* (Oxford, 2004), online edn, January 2008, <http://www.oxforddnb.com/view/article/18271>, accessed 10 January 2012.

112. Syrett, *Admiral Lord Howe*, pp. xv–xvi.

113. J.E. Cussans, *History of Hertfordshire*, 3 vols (Wakefield, 1870–81; repub. 1972), iii, p. 61.

114. BL, Plan of the Little Grove Estate, East Barnet (London, 1862).

115. G. Gear, 'Little Grove House and Grounds,' *Barnet & District Local History Society*, 42 (2006), pp. 1–12.

116. HALS DE/A/2831, estate map, Mrs Jane Poole (1768).

117. R. Clutterbuck, *The History and Antiquities of the County of Hertford*, 3 vols (London, 1821–7), iii, p. 231.

118. He may have been related to the Monsons at Broxbournebury, but his identity remains uncertain. T.H. Bowyer, 'Monson, George (1730–1776)', *ODNB* (Oxford, 2004), online edn, May 2006, <http://www.oxforddnb.com/view/article/18985>, accessed 3 August 2011.

119. I am grateful to Nicholas Webb at Barclays Bank for assisting my research of David Barclay's Gurney's Bank account and to Phillip Winterbottom and archivists at the Royal Bank of Scotland for information regarding the Drummonds Bank records.

120. C.W. Barclay, *A History of the Barclay Family, with Full Pedigree from 1066 to 1924* (London, 1924–33).

121. J.M. Price, 'Barclay, David (1729–1809)', rev. Leslie Hannah, *ODNB* (Oxford, 2004), <http://www.oxforddnb.com/view/article/37150>, accessed 14 June 2011.

122. D. Perman, *Scott of Amwell: Dr. Johnson's Quaker Critic* (Ware, 2001), p. 64.

123. Pictures were explicitly excluded from the sale when Barclay bought the house. HALS DE/A167, assignment of household goods and furniture at Youngsbury.

124. HALS DE/A/2830, estate map, Youngsbury, Sutes and Fabdens (1793).

125. J.M. Kelly, *The Society of Dilettanti: Archaeology and Identity in the British Enlightenment* (New Haven, CT, 2009).

126. G. Mason, *An Essay on Design in Gardening* (London, 1768; 1795), p. 126.

127. T. Williamson, *Polite Landscapes: Gardens & Society in Eighteenth Century England* (Stroud, 1995; repr. Sutton, 1998), p. 14.

128. Williamson estimates 170 major commissions; *ibid.*, p. 80.
129. John Phibbs, makes the case for Digswell in 'Digswell Place Digswell House and Digswell Place: A Survey of the Landscape', Debois Landscape Survey Group, for Hertfordshire Gardens Trust (1997). Pishiobury was attributed to Brown by Cussans, *History of Hertfordshire*, vol. i, p. 83, and N. Pevsner, *Hertfordshire, The Buildings of England* (London, 1953; rev. edn 1977), p. 271.

Bibliography

Primary sources
British Library (BL):
Add. Mss. 69795 Brown Correspondence.
Ordnance Survey Drawings, surveyed 1799 (1805).
Plan of the Little Grove Estate, East Barnet (London, 1862).

Hertfordshire Archives and Local Studies (HALS):
Acc. 3898, Hertfordshire Gardens Trust Research Group Notes.
AH 2770, large scale estate map of Ashridge. Surveyed by George Grey of Lancaster (1762).
DE/A/2830, estate map, Youngsbury, Sutes and Fabdens (1793).
DE/A/2831, estate map, Mrs Jane Poole (1768).
DE/A167, assignment of household goods and furniture at Youngsbury.
D/ECL ZIII 360 A–C, Buckler views of Beechwood Park.
DE/P/A8, Earl Cowper's accounts ledger (1755–64).
DE/P/A185, estimate of expenses (1747).
DE/P/EA23/2, account of materials recovered from Cole Green House.
DE/P/F243–4, diaries, 1752–53.
DE/P/F249, letter from Joseph Atwell (13 August 1733).
DE/P/F253– 6, letters from Spencer Cowper, Dean of Durham.
DE/P/P5, contract and plan for Cole Green House (1704).
DE/P/21 Humphry Repton, Red Book for Panshanger (n.d.).
D/Z42/ Z1, Humphry Repton, Red Book for Tewin Water (1799).
KIM/9, watercolour painting of The Hoo.

Hertfordshire Gardens Trust (HGT) Research Group Reports:
Constable, A., McManus, P., and Rowe, A., 'The Hoo, Kimpton' (2005).
Leiper, H., '"Beautifying Colegreen": The Eighteenth Century Park and Gardens of Colegreen House in Hertfordshire', unpublished MA dissertation, Birkbeck College, University of London, 2008.
Phibbs, J.L., 'Digswell Place Digswell House and Digswell Place: A Survey of the Landscape', Debois Landscape Survey Group, for Hertfordshire Gardens Trust (1997).

Lindley Library, London:
Lancelot Brown Account Book.

West Sussex Record Office (WSRO):
PHA 6623, Contracts for Petworth (1753, 1754).

Secondary sources
Barclay, C.W., *A History of the Barclay Family, with Full Pedigree from 1066 to 1924* (London, 1924–33).
Brown, J., *The Omnipotent Magician: Lancelot 'Capability' Brown 1716–1783* (London, 2011).
Bryant, A., Senecki, K. and Wheeler, R., *The Garden at Ashridge* (Ashridge, 1989).
Chauncy, H., *The Historical Antiquities of Hertfordshire,* 2 vols (London, 1700; 2nd edn Bishops Stortford, 1826; repr., 1975).
Clutterbuck, R., *The History and Antiquities of the County of Hertford,* 3 vols (London, 1821–7).
Cowell, F., *Richard Woods (1715–1793): Master of the Pleasure Garden* (Woodbridge, 2009).
Cussans, J.E., *History of Hertfordshire,* 3 vols (Wakefield, 1870–81; repub. 1972).
Cust, L., *History of the Society of Dilettanti*, ed. S. Colvin (London, 1898).
Defoe, D., *A Tour thro' the Whole Island of Great Britain divided into Circuits or Journies, originally begun by… Daniel De Foe, continued by … Mr. Richardson,* 4 vols (9th edn, 1779).

Desmond, R., *Kew: The History of the Royal Botanic Gardens* (London, 1995).

Dury, A. and Andrews, J., *A Topographical Map of Hartford-Shire, from an Actual Survey,* 1 mile: 1.95 inches (1766; repr. Hertford, 2004).

Gordon, C., *The Coventrys of Croome* (Chichester, 2000).

Hertfordshire Gardens Trust and T. Williamson, *The Parks and Gardens of West Hertfordshire* (2000).

Hertfordshire Heritage, ed. C. Shearman, 'Diary of the Reverend George William Harris,' 22 (1996), pp. 12–15.

Hinde, T., *Capability Brown: The Story of a Master Gardener* (London, 1986).

Ingamells, J., *A Dictionary of English and Irish Travellers in Italy, 1701–1800* (New Haven, CT, 1997).

Jellico, G. and S., Goode, P. and Lancaster, M., *The Oxford Companion to Gardens* (Oxford, 1991).

Judd, G.P., *Members of Parliament 1734–1832* (New Haven, CT, 1955).

Kelly, J.M., *The Society of Dilettanti: Archaeology and Identity in the British Enlightenment* (New Haven, CT, 2009).

Kielmansegge, Count F., *Diary of a Journey to England in the Years 1761–1762*, tr. Countess Kielmansegge (London, 1902).

Laird, M., *The Flowering of the Landscape Garden: English Pleasure Grounds 1720–1800* (Philadelphia, 1999).

Lewis, W.S., *Correspondence of Horace Walpole*, 36 vols (New Haven, CT, 1937–80).

Malet, H., *Bridgewater: The Canal Duke 1736–1803* (Manchester, 1977).

Mason, G., *Essay on Design in Gardening* (London, 1768; 1795).

Meir, J., *Sanderson Miller and his Landscapes* (Chichester, 2006).

National Trust, *Stowe Landscape Gardens* (London, 1997).

Page, W. (ed.), *VCH Hertfordshire*, 4 vols (Folkestone, 1912; repr. London, 1971).

Perman, D., *Scott of Amwell: Dr. Johnson's Quaker Critic* (Ware, 2001).

Pevsner, N., *Hertfordshire, The Buildings of England* (London, 1953; rev. edn 1977).

Pope, D., *At 12 Mr Byng was Shot* (London, 1962; 2002).

Rowe, T. *The Beechwood Companion: The Story of A House and its People* (n.p., 2006).

Stroud, D., *Capability Brown* (London, 1950; 1984).

Syrett, D., *Admiral Lord Howe: A Biography* (Stroud, 2006).

Turner, R., *Capability Brown and the Eighteenth Century English Landscape* (Chichester, 1999; repr. 2006).

Walpole, H., *Horace Walpole's Journals of Visits to Country Seats Etc.,* ed. P. J. Toynbee, (1927–8), p. XVI.

Warrand, D. (ed.), *Hertfordshire Families* (London, 1907).

Whately, T., *Observations on Modern Gardening, Illustrated by Descriptions* (London, 1770).

Williamson, T., *Polite Landscapes: Gardens & Society in Eighteenth Century England* (Stroud, 1995; repr. Sutton, 1998).

Young, A., *General View of the Agriculture of the County of Hertfordshire* (London, 1804; 1971).

Journals

Brown, D., 'Lancelot Brown and His Associates', *Garden History,* 29/1, issue on Lancelot Brown (1716–83) and the Landscape Park (Summer 2001), pp. 2–11.

Gear, G., 'Little Grove House and Grounds', *Barnet & District Local History Society,* 42 (2006), pp. 1–12.

Hall, E., '"Mr Brown's Directions": Capability Brown's Landscaping at Burton Constable (1767–82)', *Garden History,* 23/2 (1995).

Hussey, C., 'Panshanger Hertfordshire, A Sear of Lord and Lady Desborough', *Country Life,* 11 January 1936, pp. 38–44.

Prince, H., 'The Changing Landscape of Panshanger', *Transactions of the East Herts Archaeological Society,* XIV, pt.1, (1955–7), pp. 42–58.

Simpson, A., 'A History of the Estate and Garden at Wrotham Park', *The London Gardener or The Gardener's Intelligencer,* 7, Journal of London Historic Parks and Gardens Trust, (2001–02), pp. 66–79.

Willis, P., 'Capability Brown's Account with Drummond's Bank, 1753–1783', *Architectural History,* vol. xxvii, issue on Design and Practice in British Architecture: Studies in Architectural History Presented to Howard Colvin (1984), pp. 382–91.

Web sources

Baugh, D.A., 'Byng, John (*bap.* 1704, *d.* 1757)', *Oxford Dictionary of National Biography* (Oxford , 2004), online edn, January 2008, <http://www.oxforddnb.com/view/article/4263>, accessed 23 November 2010.

Belsey, H., 'Cowper, George Nassau Clavering, third Earl Cowper (1738–1789)', *Oxford Dictionary of National Biography* (Oxford, 2004), online edn, January 2008, <http://www.oxforddnb.com/view/article/61668>, accessed 4 December 2011.

Bowyer, T.H., 'Monson, George (1730–1776)', *Oxford Dictionary of National Biography* (Oxford, 2004), online edn, May 2006, <http://www.oxforddnb.com/view/article/18985>, accessed 3August 2011.

Cannon, J., 'Carteret, John, second Earl Granville (1690–1763)', *Oxford Dictionary of National Biography* (Oxford, 2004), online edn, May 2006, <http://www.oxforddnb.com/view/article/4804>, accessed 21 May 2008.

Chalus, E.H., 'Elizabeth, Lady Anson (1725–1760)', *Oxford Dictionary of National Biography* (Oxford, 2004), <http://www.oxforddnb.com/view/article/68350>, accessed 21 June 2011.

Collett-White, J., 'Yorke Jemima, *suo jure* Marchioness Grey (1722–1797)', *Oxford Dictionary of National Biography* (Oxford, 2004), <http://www.oxforddnb.com/view/article/68351>, accessed 21 June 2011.

Fairclough, K.R., 'Egerton, Francis, third duke of Bridgewater (1736–1803)', *Oxford Dictionary of National Biography* (Oxford, 2004), online edn, October 2009), <http://www.oxforddnb.com/view/article/8584>, accessed 3 December 2011.

Fereday, R.P., 'Dundas family of Fingask and Kerse', *Oxford Dictionary of National Biography* (Oxford, 2004), online edn, January 2008,<http://www.oxforddnb.com/view/article/64103>, accessed 5 August 2011.

Fisher, D.R., 'Sebright, Sir John Saunders, seventh baronet (1767–1846)', *Oxford Dictionary of National Biography* (Oxford, 2004), online edn, January 2008, <http://www.oxforddnb.com/view/article/24997>, accessed 3 August 2011.

Knight, R., 'Howe, Richard, Earl Howe (1726–1799)', *Oxford Dictionary of National Biography* (Oxford, 2004), online edn, October 2009, <http://www.oxforddnb.com/view/article/13963>, accessed 14 June 2011.

Mackay, R.,'Keppel, Augustus, Viscount Keppel (1725–1786)', *Oxford Dictionary of National Biography* (Oxford, 2004), online edn, January 2010, <http://www.oxforddnb.com/view/article/15439>, accessed 5 August 2011.

Phibbs, J., 'Brown, Lancelot [Capability Brown] (*bap.* 1716, *d.* 1783)', *Oxford Dictionary of National Biography* (Oxford, 2004), online edn, May 2009, <http://www.oxforddnb.com/view/article/3635>, accessed 2 August 2011.

Price, J.M., 'Barclay, David (1729–1809)', rev. Leslie Hannah, *Oxford Dictionary of National Biography* (Oxford, 2004), <http://www.oxforddnb.com/view/article/37150>, accessed 14 June 2011.

Rodger, N.A.M., 'Anson, George, Baron Anson (1697–1762)', *Oxford Dictionary of National Biography* (Oxford, 2004), online edn, May 2008, <http://www.oxforddnb.com/view/article/574>, accessed 25 August 2008.

Sambrook, J., 'Mason, George (1735–1806)', *Oxford Dictionary of National Biography* (Oxford, 2004), online edn, January 2008, <http://www.oxforddnb.com/view/article/18271>, accessed 10 January 2012.

CHAPTER FIVE

Gardens and industry: The landscape of the Gade Valley in the nineteenth century

Tom Williamson

Introduction

Garden historians and landscape historians often work in effective isolation, the former dealing with spaces that were consciously designed, the latter with the entire physical environment, as transformed by all kinds of economic, social and cultural activity. Each approach has its own important contribution to make, but in reality the creation of parks and gardens cannot be examined in isolation from the wider 'vernacular' landscape, which formed both the raw material and the setting for the design. Conversely, the presence of designed landscapes, and aspects of their particular form, often had a wider impact on the physical environment, both at the time of their creation and in subsequent periods. Indeed, the two kinds of landscape, 'designed' and 'vernacular', were never as distinct or as hermetically sealed from each other as historians sometimes assume. In this chapter I will examine some of these issues by looking briefly at the valley of the river Gade between Croxley and Hemel Hempstead, concentrating in particular on the parks and gardens created by Charles Longman and John Dickinson at Shendish in Kings Langley and Abbots Hill in Abbots Langley, but also examining other designed landscapes in the valley, and considering all within the wider context of local industrial expansion from the later eighteenth century.

The industrialisation of the Gade valley

Although historians are now often cautious about using the terms 'agricultural revolution' or 'industrial revolution', the later eighteenth and nineteenth centuries were unquestionably periods of phenomenal economic development. While Hertfordshire lacked the raw materials or adequate reserves of water power to fuel significant levels of industrialisation, the period from 1750 to 1870 did see an important expansion in some manufacturing and processing industries, and a substantial growth in the size of many of the county's towns, as well as major improvements in its communication systems.[1]

In the course of the eighteenth century the county's road network was systematically improved, largely through the activities of turnpike trusts.[2] These were established by individual acts of Parliament, and were empowered to establish tolls on specified roads and use the income so generated to maintain them to an adequate level. By 1770 there were fifteen trusts in Hertfordshire and all the principal roads were turnpiked.[3] The trusts included the Sparrows Herne Trust, established in 1762, which looked after what was later to become the A411 from Bushey, through Watford, to Tring and then Aylesbury, running on its course between Watford and Hemel Hempstead along the valley of the river Gade. As well as fuelling economic expansion, the relative ease of communication the improved roads provided further encouraged the erection of villas and small mansions, in the south of the county especially, by wealthy London businessmen, lawyers and politicians – something which was already being noted as a feature of the county in the seventeenth century.

Also of importance as a driver of economic development were a number of new canals and navigations which were constructed through the county in the eighteenth century. The most important of these was the Grand Junction, later the Grand Union, which linked London with the Midland canal system and which was authorised by a Parliamentary act of 1793 and completed as far as Tring in 1799.[4] This also followed the valley of the river Gade (and that of the Bulbourne) on its journey through the county. Indeed, many sections represent no more than stretches of the river, suitably improved. More dramatic in their impact than either turnpikes or canals, however, were the railways. The first of these to appear in Hertfordshire, George Stephenson's line from London to Birmingham, again followed for much of its course the valley of the Gade, reaching Boxmoor near Hemel Hempstead in 1837 and passing through Tring the following year.[5] The railway had an almost immediate effect upon the Grand Junction and the Sparrows Herne turnpike, the board of the latter reporting to the county magistrates in

1838 that as a consequence of the 'great reduction in the income of this road occasioned by the London and Birmingham Railway', they were no longer able to repair the principal bridges on the course of the road.[6] Nevertheless, the road remained one of the most important transport routes in the county, and the Grand Union continued to carry heavy traffic into the twentieth century. By the middle of the nineteenth century the Gade valley to the north of Watford thus represented the key transport corridor in Hertfordshire, with road, rail and canal following each other closely along much of its length.

The later eighteenth and nineteenth centuries also saw the expansion of industry in Hertfordshire. Much of this was concerned with processing the county's agricultural produce. Malting experienced phenomenal growth, mainly in the east of the county, where it was centred on Ware, Hertford and Bishop's Stortford; while most Hertfordshire corn mills were rebuilt in the eighteenth and nineteenth centuries, larger and more sophisticated than before.[7] One important industry, however, was unrelated to agriculture – paper-making, a speciality of Hertfordshire. Paper had been manufactured in the county on a small scale for centuries: at Sele Mill near Hertford as early as the late fifteenth century; and again in the seventeenth century at Sopwell near St Albans, and at Hatfield. But the eighteenth century saw a significant expansion of the industry, fuelled in part by London's insatiable desire for newspapers and in part by the inexorable growth of government bureaucracy. The new mills, initially located in converted corn mills, were concentrated in the south, along the valleys of the Gade and the Chess especially.[8] Here they were close to London, which provided both the principal market and a major source of the rags that were the industry's main raw material. The rivers, moreover, supplied the ready supply of water required both for the manufacturing process and to power the machinery which pulped rags into paper.

In 1801 the rights to employ a system of manufacture more rapid than existing processes, which had recently been developed in France, were acquired by the Foudrinier brothers, Henry and Sealy, who operated mills at Two Waters and Frogmore near Hemel Hempstead.[9] After initial difficulties, the system, which produced continuous sheets of paper, was functioning at Two Waters by 1803, but the brothers went bankrupt seven years later. By this time, however, John Dickinson had developed his own, more advanced, method of production and had established himself in 1809 at Apsley, a little downstream, acquiring nearby Nash Mills in 1811. By 1826 he had established a new works a little further down the Gade, at Home Park in Kings Langley; and in 1830 he opened another at Croxley, still further to the south, beyond Watford. All these premises were by this stage powered principally by steam.[10] By the 1870s, paper mills, owned by a variety of businesses, were closely spaced along the valleys of the river Chess (at Solesbridge in Chorleywood, Mill End and Scots Bridge in Rickmansworth); the Colne (at Batchworth in Rickmansworth and Hamper Mill in Watford); and especially the Gade (Frogmore, Apsley, Nash, Home Park and Croxley).

By the middle decades of the nineteenth century the lower Gade valley thus formed a kind of corridor of industrialisation within what was still, for the most part, a rural landscape. But not along its entire length. There was a marked diminution in the intensity of development between Croxley Mill, around a kilometre downstream from Cashio Bridge, and a point a little to the north of Hunton Bridge: a distance of some five kilometres (Figure 5.1). And this was because the valley here

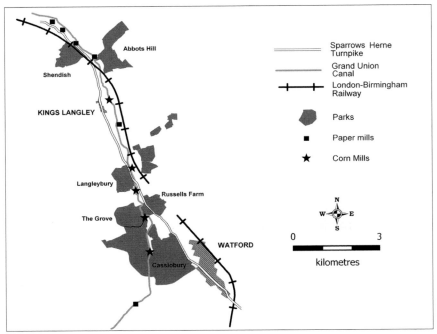

Figure 5.1 Parks and industry in the valley of the Gade in the second half of the nineteenth century.

had been occupied, since the mid-eighteenth century, by a number of important mansions and their associated designed landscapes.

Cassiobury, The Grove, Russells and Langleybury

Cassiobury, located beside the river Gade near Watford and the home of the Earls of Essex (Figure 5.1), was one of the great designed landscapes of Hertfordshire, and the only example to appear as an illustration in Kip and Knyff's *Britannia Illustrata* of 1707. This shows the mansion, largely rebuilt at the end of the seventeenth century, set within parkland and with a complex network of avenues cut through an extensive wilderness to the north-east of the house, which were planted by Moses Cook in the late seventeenth century. The landscape underwent numerous modifications in the course of the eighteenth century, with the establishment of additional avenues (including the surviving lime avenue, which now runs through the West Hertfordshire golf course) in the Upper Park, to the west of the river Gade. These were extended as rides through the adjacent area of ancient woodland called Whippendell Wood. Various alterations of an uncertain nature were also made to the grounds by Charles Bridgeman in the 1720s and by Thomas Wright of Durham in the late 1730s and early 1740s.[11] By 1798, when a fine map of the estate was produced, the open parkland covered an area of around 230 hectares, the 'wilderness' 37 hectares, and the semi-ornamental Whippendell Wood a further 46 hectares, over 3 square kilometres in all.[12]

The landscape laid out around Cassiobury originated as a deer park of sixteenth or seventeenth-century date. The park at The Grove, in contrast, which lay within the valley of the Gade a little to the north, was entirely a creation of the eighteenth century, laid out around a new house built (perhaps to designs by Matthew Brettingham) by Thomas Villiers, first Earl of Clarendon, in the 1750s. Dury and Andrews' county map, published in 1766, shows that this extended over an area of around 75 hectares and, unlike Cassiobury, lacked any avenues or other geometric planting, simply because by the time it was created such things had fallen entirely from fashion.[13] But the park contained a remarkable range of ornamental buildings, which are described in an anonymous poem of 1779 and in an account of the landscape written by Daniel Carless Webb in 1810, as well as being depicted in a series of sketches made by Thomas Baskerfield which survive in the British Library. They include a 'Temple of Pan', the 'Praeneste' or 'Temple of Fortune', the Mausoleum, the 'Scotch Hut', a 'Tuscan Seat', a Ruined Tower, a pyramid, an ornamental hoggery, various 'druidical seats' and a rustic seat.[14] The mansion stood on the western side of the park with the land falling away to the east towards the Gade, which ran through the middle. When Dury and Andrews' map was surveyed, the park abutted on Whippendell Wood to the south-west but was otherwise separated from the grounds of Cassiobury by an area of farmland. To the east, however, immediately across the main road from Hemel Hempstead to Watford (the Sparrows Herne turnpike) lay another small park, associated with the house called Russell or Russells Farm or Russells – the home of Lady Essex and part of the Cassiobury estate. Dury and Andrews' map shows that this also, like the park around The Grove, entirely lacked formal, geometric features like avenues, presumably because it was laid out when the house itself was first built in the middle of the eighteenth century.[15]

A tight cluster of parks, some owned for a time by related individuals, thus existed in and around the valley of the Gade to the north of the town of Watford by the time that Dury and Andrews' map was surveyed in the early 1760s. But in addition the map shows another major residence lying within the valley, a little apart from these, some 1.5 kilometres to the north of The Grove. Langleybury, which had been built in the early eighteenth century by Sir Robert Raymond (leading lawyer and friend and ally of Robert Walpole), lacked a true park at this time, although one was apparently provided with extensive gardens and pleasure grounds. But a park had probably been created here by the 1790s, to judge from an illustration of the house by Oldfield; and certainly by 1810, when grounds of around sixteen hectares are shown on the draft 2": one mile Ordnance Survey map. These were subsequently extended in the course of the nineteenth century and by the 1870s covered over fifty hectares.

By the middle decades of the nineteenth century the park at Cassiobury had been extended to the north, and now abutted directly on that laid out around The Grove. The Grove, as noted, was separated by only the main road from Watford to Hemel Hempstead (the Sparrows Herne Turnpike) from the grounds of Russells Farm. There was an area of farmland between Cassiobury and Russells Farm and another (a rather larger one) between The Grove and Langleybury. But these were not the property of other proprietors; nor were they even, for the most part, in the hands of tenants. Instead they comprised fields kept in hand as part of the home farms of the respective estates, interspersed with plantations. The farmland associated with The Grove was of particular importance in the eighteenth century as the Earl of Clarendon was a prominent agricultural improver whose activities were noted by Arthur Young:[16] there were a number of semi-ornamental farm buildings on the estate, including a hoggery. To judge from the Ordnance Survey First Edition 6" map, the fields lying between the parks were crossed by a number of drives which, in the case of Cassiobury, led to ornamental lodges lying some way beyond the bounds of the park,

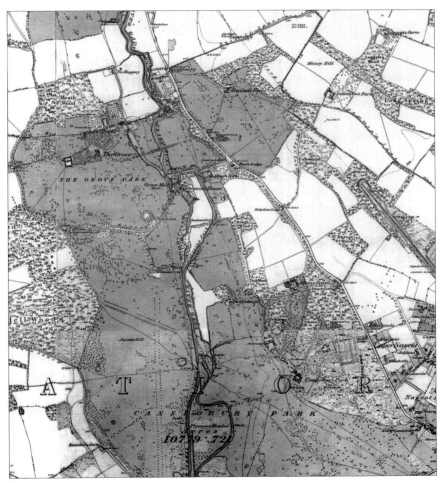

Figure 5.2 Cassiobury, The Grove and Russells Farm, as depicted on the First Edition OS map, 6 inches to the mile, 1877.

sensu stricto (Beech Lodge and Ridgeway Lodge; Figure 5.2). In short, the interstices of the four designed landscapes had something of the character of the *ferme ornée*, rather than being functional agricultural land. Indeed, by the start of the nineteenth century – and probably earlier – much of this area was in effect being treated as a single designed landscape, for the area between The Grove and Cassiobury was ornamented with a range of garden buildings by the second Earl of Clarendon, including a Malayan hut and a domed temple called the Eggshell.[17] A walk ran along the river from The Grove, through an area called Charlotte's Vale, and into Cassiobury Park. By the middle of the nineteenth century another ornamental route existed on the eastern side of the river. Williams described in the 1880s how:

> There is a wide plantation called the Woodwalks, commencing at Cashio Hamlet and continuing past the mansion to Grove Mill, the timber in which is of a great height, and being closely planted, affords a delightful shade to the drive through it, which commences just above Little Cassiobury, and terminates near Beech Lodge, on the road to Hunton Bridge. Here the daffodil, snowdrop, primrose, fern, wood anemone, and violet abound, with the campion and foxglove towering above their lowly neighbours; and the place is rendered more charming by the delightful songs of many thrushes and blackbirds, the cooing of wood-pigeons, and the sweet and clear notes of the nightingale in its song at early morn and at the close of the day.[18]

Ornament and industry

The emerging industrial landscape of the Gade valley was firmly excluded from this ornamental and consciously rural landscape in the valley immediately to the north and west of Watford. The most striking expression of this was the revisions made to the original route of the London to Birmingham railway. As finally constructed, the line, coming north from London, entered the county near Oxhey and ran across the low ground lying to the west of Carpender's Park before joining the valley of the river Colne at the bottom of Chalk Hill in Bushey. This it followed before turning north-west, towards Watford Junction, eventually reaching the valley of the Gade more than three kilometres further along the same alignment (Figure 5.1). It would, however, have made more sense to run the line directly to the north-west of Carpender's Park, and thus to the west of the town of Watford, cutting through the fairly narrow (*c*.1.5 kilometre) neck of land separating the valley of the Colne from that of the Gade, which it could then have followed northwards. Any such route was vehemently opposed by the Earl of Essex and the Earl of Clarendon, and the present course was adopted: but at some cost.[19] To the north-west of Watford Junction the ground rises to a height of over 100 metres OD, necessitating not only a large cutting but also the construction of the Watford Tunnel, some 1.6 kilometres in length.

> Unfortunately it was not accomplished without any accident, for a terrible one occurred by the falling of a large mass of earth that smothered a number of labourers, killing eleven of them. Very great difficulty occurred in recovering the bodies of the unfortunate men, and the excitement that prevailed while the earth was being removed was very great. Thousands of people collected daily ... near the scene of the accident, which might be likened more to a fair than anything else; booths for the sale of beer and refreshments were erected ...[20]

Yet it was not only the railway that was excluded from this section of the Gade valley. To the north of Hunton Bridge and Langleybury there were, by the middle of the nineteenth century, paper and pulp mills beside the river at Two Waters (just to the south of Hemel Hempstead) and Frogmore, as well as Dickinson's establishments of Apsley Mill, Nash Mills and Home Park Mill. There was then a gap in industrial development, corresponding to the cluster of parks and the block of ornamented estate land flanking the Gade (just described), which extended for over five kilometres before the landscape of industry returned, with Dickinson's Croxley Mills and, a little further downstream, the various industrial establishments around the town of Rickmansworth (Figure 5.1). Most of the mills were, by the 1840s, powered by steam, and most comprised large clusters of buildings: John Hassell described Apsley Mill in 1819 as 'occupying a large space of ground, and rather resembling a village than a manufactory'.[21] These were not the kinds of features which established landowners would welcome in the view from their homes, and, if they controlled that view, such intrusions were understandably excluded. If they did not control it, and could not find other ways in which to prevent the intrusion, landowners sometimes prevailed on local industrialists (who were themselves usually keen to be accepted into local county 'society') to take

Figure 5.3 Apsley Mill, with decorative planting of Lombardy poplar and conifers. Undated sketch, early nineteenth century, by Harriet Dickinson. REPRODUCED BY KIND PERMISSION OF APSLEY PAPER TRAIL.

actions to improve the appearance of their premises. John Dickinson's new paper mill at Batchworth, erected in the late 1820s, could be seen from Lord Ebury's mansion at Moor Park, and for this reason was provided with an 'Egyptian front' facing the house, featuring massive columns and an entablature of painted stucco.[22] A watercolour sketch by Harriet Dickinson showing a panorama of the Gade valley and drawn up before the construction of the railway, suggests that some attempt was made to improve the appearance of Apsley Mill with decorative planting, perhaps for the benefit of the owner of Shendish, an up-market farmhouse to the west (Figure 5.3).[23] But if at all possible, industrial plant was simply excluded from the prospect altogether.

By the end of the nineteenth century, to judge from the Ordnance Survey 6" maps, the Gade valley, both to the north of Langleybury and to the south of Cassiobury, was replete with other traces of modernity which were entirely absent from the intervening five or six kilometres: gas works, small terraces of houses, canal wharfs, nonconformist chapels, even (to the south of Cashio Bridge) an electric telegraph running beside the canal. The extent of incipient industrialisation in the valley, even in the 1870s, should not of course be exaggerated. This was still a largely rural landscape, even on the valley floor. But the way in which the valley had been pervaded by modernity was made more noticeable by the marked absence of all these structures and facilities from the area around Cassiobury, The Grove, Russells and Langleybury.

It is equally important to note the kinds of economic activity which *were* allowed to intrude on this largely ornamental landscape. Firstly, and most obviously, there was the Grand Junction Canal itself, which was constructed in the 1790s when the parks, except Langleybury, were already long-established. Both here, and elsewhere in England, landowners appear to have accepted canals crossing their land as a necessary inconvenience from which their estates would benefit economically. There was usually, as in this case, little opportunity for their diversion along some more amenable route, for they were generally tied to the course of an existing river (although there was scope for minor adjustments: the towpath of the Grand Union crossed to the side of the canal away from the mansion as it passed The Grove). In addition, although canals were busy thoroughfares, they were bodies of water broadly similar to the kinds of lakes and widened rivers that had long been major features of designed landscapes. The early nineteenth-century bridge (Figure 5.4) which carries the main drive to The Grove across the canal – brick covered in stucco, with elegant balustrades and side arches – is reflected in the mirror of the water as assuredly as (for

Figure 5.4 The ornamental bridge carrying the main drive to The Grove across the Grand Union Canal.

example) James Paine's bridge at Chatsworth. And passing longboats, glimpsed in the distance, provided the kind of lively element in the prospect which, especially under the influence of late eighteenth-century 'picturesque' ideas, polite taste found appealing. In the 1880s Henry Williams, describing the view from Cassiobury's Upper Park, began with the words: 'The eye first catches the heavily laden boat, as it glides silently along the canal'.[24] Canals were thus rather different to railways, which were characterised by their cuttings and embankments, their noisy and dirty trains.

More interesting, perhaps, is the continued location of water mills along this section of the Gade. The antipathy which these landowners evidently shared towards paper and pulp mills was not extended to traditional corn mills. There were three between Hunton Bridge and Cashio Bridge. Langleybury Mill and Grove Mill were positioned on the edge of these two parks, while that at Cassiobury stood near the centre of the park. They were located only 700, 500 and 600 metres from their respective mansions. Grove Mill appears to have stood in full view of the house; those at Langleybury and Cassiobury probably were, the latter located close to some of the main drives running through the park and occupying a pivotal position beside the bridge that joined the Upper Park – to the west of the Gade – to the Home Park, lying to the east. It is possible that, to some extent, mills were tolerated within the landscapes of gentility because they, or their predecessors, pre-dated the parks and gardens laid out around them. But they could nevertheless have been relocated, or removed, had the owners of these designed landscapes (who in all cases also owned the mills in question) chosen so to do. The mill by The Grove, described by Williams in the 1880s as 'a picturesque building', actually burnt down in the 1870s, but was almost immediately replaced, and on precisely the same site.[25] The mill at Cassiobury, similarly described by Williams as 'a picturesque old building', was no longer being used to grind flour by the time he was writing, in the 1880s, but instead housed the gear for pumping water to the hall.

> A beautiful cascade by the side of the mill pours its pellucid water into the trout
> stream below, and adjoining are the bridge over the canal, the locks and lock
> cottage forming, together with a number of beech and other trees growing near,
> a piece of rich scenery that has on many occasions attracted the notice of artists
> visiting Watford.[26]

in prominent lines, having been incorporated – with remarkably little thinning – from the boundaries of the earlier fields, the entire layout of which is thus still clearly visible on the map. The house now stood back from the public road, which had been diverted to the east, although there does not appear to be a surviving Road Order relating to this change: the replacement route still passed within 150 metres of the house.[35] The only area of the park in which the planting was relatively complex and sophisticated lay in the immediate vicinity of the house, to the east and, in particular, to the west, where the ground sloped away towards the valley of the Gade. The main approach to the house ran through this section of the park, from a lodge on the road to Nash Mills. There were a number of small clumps here, and a dense scatter of specimen trees, mainly conifers, loosely mirrored by another to the north-east of the house. Surviving examples indicate that these were principally cedars of Lebanon.[36] The drive passed to the north of the house and then, joining a second drive which ran in from an entrance on Bunkers Lane to the north, turned south and proceeded to an entrance on the east front.

By 1877 the west front looked out across an area of formal gardens, with a panorama of the Gade valley as a backdrop. These gardens lay immediately below the low terrace on which the house stood and comprised a rectangle divided into four by straight paths which met at a central pond. They were flanked by geometric beds set into the lawn and were still formally planted, to judge from surviving photographs, in 1897.[37] The path forming the western side of this area was extended, linear fashion, some way to the south, providing a promenade from which to enjoy the view across the valley. From its end a more curvilinear walk threaded through an area planted with shrubs and specimen trees, including (again to judge from surviving specimens) beech, oak and yew. Other areas of shrubbery, and more conifers, could be found to the east, beyond the drive, while in the far north – beyond the rectangular formal garden – were areas of irregular planting, probably shrubberies, set into the lawn. The entire area of gardens was bounded by a light iron fence. We do not know for certain that all of these features existed when Dickinson was alive, but on stylistic grounds they would appear to have been additions of the 1850s or 1860s.

The grounds of Abbots Hill, like the mansion itself, appear unremarkable in stylistic terms, although competent enough in execution, and it is a shame that their designer or designers remain unknown.

Shendish, in contrast, the house erected in 1853 by Charles Longman, had both a more remarkable garden, and a better documented one. Aside from the fact that the owners of both mansions were involved in the local paper business, there were numerous other parallels between the two sites. Shendish was designed by the architect John Griffith and, like Abbots Hill, was in a broadly 'Elizabethan' style, although built of white brick rather than stone.[38] Again like Abbots Hill it occupied the site of an earlier farmhouse, although one which had once had manorial pretensions; and it was likewise situated above the valley of the Gade, in a park which by 1877 (to judge once again from the First Edition Ordnance Survey) extended across an area of approximately sixty hectares, mainly downslope from the house, but which – to judge from the pattern of woods and boundaries to the west – probably originally covered a further thirty-five hectares on the more level ground behind it. As in the park at Abbots Hill, the majority of trees were clearly incorporated wholesale from the previous field boundaries, and again ghosted in a striking way the earlier pattern of fields, as shown on the Kings Langley Tithe Award map of 1838.[39] Earlier woods were incorporated too – Cocks Head Wood and Hens Head Wood to the north of the house – but there were also a number of small clumps and plantations strung around the park's perimeter. Once again the more ornamental sections of the park were close to the house, and flanking the main drive, which approached from the east. They contained small clumps, loose groups of trees and numerous free-standing specimens. (There was another drive, probably a service entrance, which came in from the north, passing close to the kitchen garden.) And, as in the case of Abbots Hill, public rights of way ran close to (within 150 metres of) the house.

There were thus a number of broad similarities between the two sites, born in part of the fact that both were laid out, on what were effectively virgin sites, in the middle decades of the nineteenth century and inherited nothing from earlier phases of design. But there were also significant differences. In particular, whereas Abbots Hill was provided with an architectural and geometric garden lying across its main front, and forming a foreground to the view across the Gade valley, the Ordnance Survey shows that at Shendish the main fronts of the house looked out across areas of informal and irregular planting – lawns scattered with specimen trees – although we also know that geometric beds were cut into these in a number of places. This is because we have a description of the grounds at Shendish soon after they were completed, which was included by their designer Edward Kemp in his popular book *How to Lay Out a Garden*, published in 1864. Kemp was an important writer and landscape gardener who had trained with Joseph Paxton at Chatsworth and who was for several years superintendent of Birkenhead park.[40] But he was also influenced by Loudon's 'gardenesque' notions, in which plants were exhibited for their own beauty rather than simply being used as part of a formal design – as they were, for example, in parterres featuring bedding-out plants.

Kemp discusses Shendish on two occasions in his book. In the first he describes the layout of the 'core' area of parkland near the house, which he calls the 'Home Pasture' and which covered around eight hectares, and the layout of the pleasure grounds in the mansion's immediate vicinity, as well as the main approach, which began at a new bridge across the railway line.[41] He describes how, when the house was first built, a footpath had to be diverted, although interestingly this was achieved without going through the usual legal processes involving the county magistrates and a Road Order: '... when the improvement in the line or in the character of the path is unquestionable, and no other proprietor's interests are compromised, a change of line can usually be effected without any legal process'. The path was diverted around the edge of the 'Home Pasture' and sunk below the level of the ground at the base of a kind of ha-ha, so that 'the persons using the footpath are not observed from the house'.[42] It passed beneath the main drive via a low bridge (the ha-ha survives in degraded, tumbled form: the bridge has gone). Both the pleasure grounds and the 'Home Pasture' beyond it contained numerous small clumps and their design was coordinated 'to compose a series of openings, through which the best views of the country are obtained from the house'.[43] On the south-western edge of the 'Home Pasture', and connected to the main area of pleasure grounds by a path, was an earlier chalk pit which was now made a feature of the grounds, 'the medium of displaying rugged masses of natural vegetation' of which 'wild Clematis (common here) will be a conspicuous feature'.[44] The pit, which lay within a small wood at the time that the Tithe Award map was surveyed in 1838, still remains, with some of its original rockwork but no trace of ornamental planting.

In the second discussion of Shendish, Kemp provides more information about the gardens, kitchen gardens, orchards and offices.

We learn that the pleasure grounds were largely laid to lawn and planted with Scots and Austrian pine, spruce, and 'deciduous trees ranging from five to twenty five feet in height, which Mr Longman has been most successful in transplanting from a property in the same district'.[45] The oldest trees in the pleasure grounds today are oak, beech, holm oak, red oak, lime and cedar, several examples of which would appear to be of the mid-nineteenth century.[46] It is here that Kemp tells us that the lawn had flower beds or 'scattered flower gardens' cut into it, some near the house but mostly ranged along the south side of the kitchen garden wall, a short distance to the north-east. The wall also had a border running along it which was 'filled with rows of striking summer flowers, and has a few evergreens in it, such as Irish Yews and Arbor-Vitae'. At the end of the wall there was an octagonal summer house, which still survives, complete with fine gothic detailing. 'From its great length, and the amplitude of the grass spaces among the flower-beds, these being diversified with choice evergreen shrubs, the general effect of the wall and the flower-garden is stately and imposing'.[47]

The gardens were still being developed when Kemp described them – they had evidently been laid out following the completion of the new house, rather than the two being conceived together as part of a single scheme – and his plan shows only a single greenhouse and some small forcing-houses in the kitchen garden, although it marks 'the site at which vineries and other fruit-houses may hereinafter be built'[48]: among the glass subsequently erected was a substantial display house manufactured by Sanders Frewer and Co. of Bury St Edmunds in Suffolk.[49] Indeed, in the Dickinson archive at Frogmore there is another version of Kemp's plan for the grounds, hand-drawn by Kemp himself in 1866 – two years after the publication of *How to Lay Out a Garden* – which differs in a number of details from the published versions (Figure 5.7), especially in respect to the layout of paths to the south and south-west of the house.[50] Interestingly, the First Edition 25" Ordnance Survey shows a pattern which differs from both the published and unpublished plans, suggesting that there may have been further revisions to the design.

Because Kemp, as well as being influenced by Paxton's ideas, was also an enthusiast for 'gardenesque' ideas, he was a particularly appropriate choice for Longman, who had long been interested in both geology and botany. In the words of Longman's obituary:

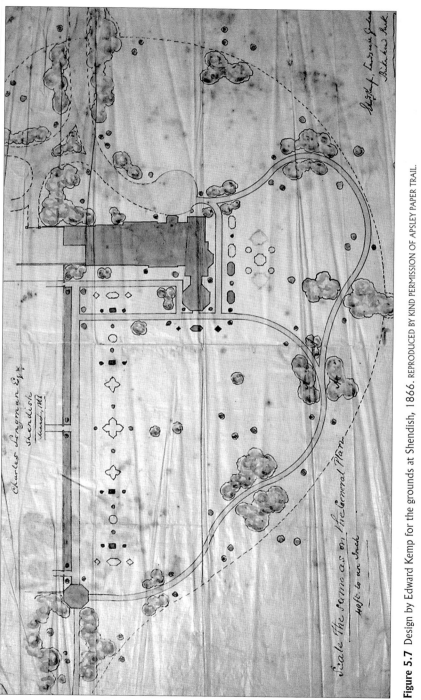

Figure 5.7 Design by Edward Kemp for the grounds at Shendish, 1866. REPRODUCED BY KIND PERMISSION OF APSLEY PAPER TRAIL.

> His gardens at Shendish, where he had erected a country house, are particularly
> mentioned by Mr Kemp, by whom the gardens were laid out, in his work on
> Landscape Gardening. They attest his love for botany, and the skill with which
> he practically applied his knowledge.[51]

He died, appropriately enough, 'while walking in his park', having
returned from a business meeting at Nash Mills.

Old parks and new

In some respects it is a relatively easy matter to compare and contrast
the styles of the landscapes laid out by Longman and Dickinson around
their houses at Shendish and Abbots Hill with those established around
the mansions further south in the Gade valley, The Grove, Langleybury,
Russells and Cassiobury, as these appeared in the late nineteenth century.
The most obvious difference was that the former were then relatively
new landscapes, and entirely mid-nineteenth century in design and
execution. It is true that their gardens (as opposed to their parks)
differed in important respects, largely because they were influenced by
slightly different fashions in Victorian garden design, with Shendish
displaying more adherence to 'gardenesque' principles while Abbots Hill,
eventually at least, opted for a mainstream formal approach (something
which may well reflect the differing interests of their owners, Longman
being an individual with a greater interest than Dickinson in botany and
related matters). But the landscapes further south were very different
in character, being more complex, multi-period creations. Cassiobury
incorporated elements of seventeenth-, eighteenth- and nineteenth-
century fashions; The Grove and Russells were essentially mid-/late
eighteenth-century landscapes, although altered and amended in the
course of the nineteenth century. Even Langleybury had an eighteenth-
and early nineteenth-century core to its parkland.

However, some of the differences between Shendish and Abbots
Hill, and the other landscapes, are hard to explain in terms of variations
in complexity resulting from differences in age, and are of more interest.
In particular, the mansions erected by Dickinson and Longman display
a very different attitude to the manifestations of modernity in the
local landscape than that evinced by Cassiobury and the other long-
established sites. It is noteworthy – symbolic even – that Abbots Hill
was completed the same year that the London to Birmingham railway

was opened: the passing trains were in full view of the house, as were the Grand Junction Canal and the main Watford–Hemel Hempstead road. At Shendish, the railway was hidden from view by a cutting (and anyway invisible from the house because of the lie of the land) but it is noteworthy that the park, rather than using it as its north-eastern boundary, was extended beyond it in such a way that a narrow slither of parkland existed between the line and the main road: the park, in other words, was laid out so that the railway line was included within it. Railways were transforming British life in this period, accelerating patterns of elite mobility that had already been encouraged by improvements in road transport. As Kemp noted in the opening section of *How to Lay Out a Garden*, the houses of businessmen were no longer restricted to the suburbs of towns and cities:

> Railways ... with their annual contracts for conveyance, and the rapidity, ease and certainty of transit, are now gradually bringing other parts of the country within the range of selection, and enabling the town merchant or man of business to locate himself from ten to twenty, or even thirty miles from the town, and thus get the benefits of country air and rural pleasures.[52]

The station at Hemel Hempstead (originally Boxmoor) lay only three kilometres by road from Shendish, and four from Abbots Hill. It is clear, however, that the embrace of the railways in the landscapes created for these two captains of industry expresses an approval born of something more than the enjoyment of convenience.

This easy proximity to a railway station would have met with Kemp's approval; so too would other aspects of the location of the two mansions, such as their elevated position and prospects of 'fields and gardens, and cultivated or unassisted Nature'.[53] But one important feature of the view he would not have found acceptable, for he was averse to any that featured an 'atmosphere darkened by smoke, and polluted by the gases of large manufactories'.[54] Shendish, it is true, enjoyed (because its site was determined by that of an earlier house) no direct prospect of Apsley Mill: but the latter lay, nevertheless, on the park's north-eastern boundary, immediately across the main road from Watford to Hemel Hempstead (the former turnpike). In the case of Abbots Hill, Nash Mills was not only the main object to be seen from the house and immediate grounds (Plates 5.1 and 5.2), it also lay just 100 metres from the main entrance to the park. These arrangements were not the result of chance. The two parks could have been extended less far, or in other directions; the mills could have been screened by plantations; or sites more distant from them could have been selected for the two mansions. Evidently, Dickinson and Longman embraced the modern world in a way that the Earls and other well-established neighbours, dwelling further south along the valley, did not. But this is hardly surprising, given that it was the source of their wealth.

Conclusion

The contrast between the different sections of the Gade valley in some ways lives on. In spite of the demolition of Cassiobury and the development of large sections of its estate in the early twentieth century, and the expansion of Watford more generally, the stretch of the Gade between Cashio Bridge and Hunton Bridge remains remarkably rural. Although only patches of farmland remain, the river's course is flanked by woods, golf courses (occupying the park at The Grove, and much of that at Cassiobury), playing fields and the public park at Cassiobury (created out of a large portion of the old park surrounding the mansion). The valley above Hunton Bridge, although running through what is in general a more rural environment sandwiched between the towns of Watford and Hemel Hempstead, seems in contrast more crowded, with the river and canal accompanied by the railway line, and with housing (much of it originally built for mill workers) extending in many places close to the river. Paper-making declined in the valley in the second half of the twentieth century and the last working mill, Nash Mills, ceased production in 2006. Nevertheless, Frogmore Mill survives reasonably intact (now a heritage centre devoted to the history of the local paper industry) and numerous traces of the industry can still be detected in the landscape, although most of the mill sites have been converted to other commercial or residential uses. Abbots Hill is now a private school; Shendish, having served for much of the twentieth century as a social club for Dickinson employees, is a hotel and golf course.

Acknowledgements
I would like to thank Mike Stanyon and the Apsley Paper Trail at Frogmore Mill, Apsley, for much help and advice, and for permission to reproduce Figures 5.3 and 5.7; HALS, for permission to reproduce Figure 5.5; and Jon Gregory, for preparing the 'viewshed' diagrams.

Notes
1. W. Branch Johnson, *The Industrial Archaeology of Hertfordshire* (Newton Abbot, 1970); T. Crosby, 'The Impact of Industry on the Market Towns of East Hertfordshire', in T. Slater and N. Goose (eds), *A County of Small Towns: The Development of Hertfordshire's Urban Landscape to 1800* (Hatfield, 2008), pp. 362–84.
2. W. Albert, *The Turnpike Road System in England 1663–1840* (Cambridge, 1972).
3. Branch Johnson, *Industrial Archaeology*, pp. 102–11; P. Plumb, 'Turnpike Roads', in D. Short (ed.), *An Historical Atlas of Hertfordshire* (Hatfield, 2011), pp. 40–1.
4. Branch Johnson, *Industrial Archaeology*, pp. 102–11; T. Manning, 'Rivers and Navigations', in Short (ed.), *Historical Atlas*, pp. 46–7.
5. Branch Johnson, *Industrial Archaeology*, pp. 122–33; G. Boseley, 'Railways', in Short (ed.), *Historical Atlas*, pp. 48–9; F.G. Cockman, *Railways of Hertfordshire* (Stevenage, 1983).
6. HALS TP4/5.
7. D. Perman, 'Malting and Brewing', in Short (ed.) *Historical Atlas*, pp. 88–9; Branch Johnson, *Industrial Archaeology*, pp. 28–54.
8. Branch Johnson, *Industrial Archaeology*, pp. 55–61; M. Stanyon, 'Papermaking', in Short (ed.), *Historical Atlas*, pp. 80–1.
9. A.J. Ward, *The Early History of Papermaking at Frogmore Mill and Two Waters Mill, Hertfordshire* (Berkhamsted, 2003).
10. J. Evans, *The Endless Web: John Dickinson and Co. Ltd 1804–54* (London, 1955).
11. Hertfordshire Gardens Trust and T. Williamson, *The Parks and Gardens of West Hertfordshire* (2000), pp. 16–18, 30–2.
12. HALS D/Ex 736/E2.
13. Hertfordshire Gardens Trust and Williamson, *Parks and Gardens*, p. 46.
14. D.C. Webb, *Observations and Remarks during Four Excursions made to Various Parts of Great Britain* (London, 1812), pp. 162–7; BL Add Mss 9063 f224: Thomas Baskerfield sketches.
15. Russells Farm is described as 'Lady Essex's new house' on a map of 1754: HALS D/P117 25/7.
16. A. Young, *General View of the Agriculture of Hertfordshire* (London, 1804), pp. 23, 83, 109, 114, 146, 191, 206, 224.
17. Hertfordshire Gardens Trust and Williamson, *Parks and Gardens*, pp. 69–70
18. H. Williams, *A History of Watford* (London, 1884), pp. 15–16.
19. L. Munby, *The Hertfordshire Landscape* (London, 1977), p. 217.
20. Williams, *History of Watford*, p. 112.
21. J. Hassell, *A Tour of the Grand Junction*, p. 30.
22. Evans, *Endless Web*, p. 52; Branch Johnson, *Industrial Archaeology*, p. 173.
23. Apsley Paper Trail, Frogmore Mill.
24. Williams, *History of Watford*, p. 16.
25. *Ibid.*, p. 34.
26. *Ibid.*, p. 16
27. J. Barnatt and T. Williamson, *Chatsworth: a Landscape History* (Macclesfield, 2005), p. 108.
28. T. Williamson, *The Origins of Hertfordshire* (2nd edn, Hatfield, 2010), pp. 182–3.
29. S. Hastie and D. Spain, *A Hertfordshire Valley* (Kings Langley, 1996), p. 96.
30. Evans, *Endless Web*, pp. 1–87.
31. *Ibid.*, p. 58.

32. *Ibid.*, p. 90

33. *Ibid.*, pp. 58–60.

34. HALS DSA4/63/1.

35. There are two Road Orders from the nineteenth century affecting roads in the vicinity of Abbots Hill – HALS QS3/Pc3: 277–9 (1869) and 280–90 (1850) – but neither appears to relate to this diversion.

36. M. Stanyon, 'Nash House, Abbots Hill and Shendish', unpublished report for the Hertfordshire Gardens Trust and Hemel Hempstead Local History Society, 1999, Section 7.

37. Hastie and Spain, *Hertfordshire Valley*, p. 133.

38. E. Kemp, *How to Lay Out a Garden* (London, 1864), p. 367.

39. HALS DP 64A.

40. J. Waymark, 'Kemp, Edward (1817–1891)', *Oxford Dictionary of National Biography* (Oxford, 2004).

41. Kemp, *How to Lay Out a Garden*, pp. 233–8.

42. *Ibid.*, pp. 235–6.

43. *Ibid.*, p. 236.

44. *Ibid.*, p. 237.

45. *Ibid.*, pp. 367–70.

46. J. Pavey, 'Shendish: a Victorian Landscape', unpublished dissertation, University of East Anglia, 1999.

47. Kemp, *How to Lay Out a Garden*, p. 369.

48. *Ibid.*, p. 368.

49. *Bury and Norwich Post*, 25 September 1867.

50. Apsley Paper Trail/documents/444.

51. *Pall Mall Gazette*, 25 June 1873. Longman was elected a fellow of the Geological Society in 1862. *Quarterly Journal of the Geological Society* (2 April 1862).

52. Kemp, *How to Lay Out a Garden*, p. 1.

53. *Ibid.*

54. *Ibid.*, p. 2.

Bibliography

Primary sources
Apsley Paper Trail:
Documents/444, architects' drawings for Shendish, and garden plan by Edward Kemp.

British Library (BL):
BL Add Mss 9063 f224, Thomas Baskerfield sketches.

Hertfordshire Archives and Local Studies (HALS):
D/Ex 736/E2, survey of Cassiobury Park and land in hand, 1798.
DP 64A, Kings Langley Tithe Award map, 1838.
D/P117/25/7, A Map of Three Fields (the Church-Lands) in Watford, 1754.
DSA4/63/1 and 2, Abbots Langley Tithe Award and Map, 1839.
QS3/Pc3, Quarter Sessions Road Closures.
TP 4/5, Minutes of meetings of trustees of the Sparrows Herne Turnpike Trust, 1823-40.

Secondary sources
Albert, W., *The Turnpike Road System in England 1663-1840* (Cambridge, 1972).
Barnatt, J. and Williamson, T., *Chatsworth: A Landscape History* (Macclesfield, 2005).
Boseley, G., 'Railways', in D. Short (ed.), *An Historical Atlas of Hertfordshire* (Hatfield, 2011), pp. 48–9.
Branch Johnson, W., *The Industrial Archaeology of Hertfordshire* (Newton Abbot, 1970)
Cockman, F.G., *Railways of Hertfordshire* (Stevenage, 1983).
Crosby, T., 'The Impact of Industry on the Market Towns of East Hertfordshire', in Slater, T. and Goose, N. (eds), *A County of Small Towns: The Development of Hertfordshire's Urban Landscape to 1800* (Hatfield, 2008), pp. 362–84.
Evans, J., *The Endless Web: John Dickinson and Co. Ltd 1804–54* (London, 1955).
Hassell, J., *A Tour of the Grand Junction* (London, 1819).
Hastie, S. and Spain, D., *A Hertfordshire Valley* (Kings Langley, 1996).
Hertfordshire Gardens Trust and Williamson, T., *The Parks and Gardens of West Hertfordshire* (2000).
Kemp, E., *How to Lay Out a Garden* (London, 1864).
Kip, J. and Knyff, L., *Britannia Illustrata* (London, 1707).
Manning, T., 'Rivers and Navigations', in D. Short (ed.), *An Historical Atlas of Hertfordshire* (Hatfield, 2011), 46–7.
Munby, L., *The Hertfordshire Landscape* (London, 1977).
Pavey, J., 'Shendish: a Victorian Landscape', unpublished dissertation, University of East Anglia, 1999.
Perman, D., 'Malting and Brewing', in D. Short (ed.), *An Historical Atlas of Hertfordshire* (Hatfield, 2011), pp. 88–9.
Plumb, P., 'Turnpike Roads', in D. Short (ed.), *An Historical Atlas of Hertfordshire* (Hatfield, 2011), pp. 40–1.
Stanyon, M., 'Nash House, Abbots Hill and Shendish', unpublished report for the Hertfordshire Gardens Trust and Hemel Hempstead Local History Society, 1999.
Stanyon, M., 'Papermaking', in D. Short (ed.) *Historical Atlas of Hertfordshire* (Hatfield, 2011), pp. 80–1.
Ward, A.J., *The Early History of Papermaking at Frogmore Mill and Two Waters Mill, Hertfordshire* (Berkhamsted, 2003).
Waymark, J., 'Kemp, Edward (1817–1891)', *Oxford Dictionary of National Biography* (Oxford, 2004).
Webb, D.C., *Observations and Remarks during Four Excursions made to Various Parts of Great Britain* (London, 1812).
Williams, H., *A History of Watford* (London, 1884).
Williamson, T., *The Origins of Hertfordshire* (2nd edn, Hatfield, 2010).
Young, A., *General View of the Agriculture of Hertfordshire* (London, 1804).

CHAPTER SIX

Some Arts and Crafts gardens in Hertfordshire

Kate Harwood

We moderns have the inestimable advantage of being able to make the best of both worlds, and work in town while we live in the country.[1]

The Arts and Crafts movement grew from the reaction of John Ruskin and William Morris to the mass-produced, often badly designed and shoddy goods of the new industrial workplaces. Not only were these offensive to the eye but also morally degenerate. The solution was well-designed hand-crafted goods that were of appropriate local materials, the making of which not only enhanced the lives of the users but gave the maker pride in his achievement. Of course, this involved looking back to a Golden Age when hand-made was the norm and all workmen had a pride in their work.

For garden design and planting, this was interpreted as a return to small cottage gardens with yew hedges or walls of local stone, hand-cut paving or old bricks, luxuriant planting, pergolas, dovecotes, wrought-iron work, and away from formal bedding schemes and garish colours. For larger gardens, this meant dividing one's plot into smaller garden rooms, often with distinct characters, such as a Tank Garden or a Spring Garden. As with all Arts and Crafts artefacts, they were expensive; a fact that militated against the poor possessing them. In Hertfordshire, it was the middle class and the new commuter class who laid out these gardens.

However, the self-same industrial revolution had provided that most useful of objects: the locomotive. In tandem with the revolt against machine-made, there was an increase in the number of towns and villages which had a reliable enough train service to encourage commuting. Hertfordshire was ideally placed to benefit and, indeed, has had a succession of owners of property from London, many of whom did not stay for more than a generation or two before selling up.

As Tom Williamson has said,[2] by the late nineteenth century people were looking for a house in the country rather than a country house with bothersome estate attached. Commuting to one of the leafy Hertfordshire towns for one's country evenings and weekends in an Arts and Crafts house with matching garden grew steadily through the first quarter of the twentieth century.

Those areas of Hertfordshire which had railway lines laid early tended to have Arts and Crafts houses and gardens before the First World War. This accounts for the cluster around Boxmoor, where the London to Birmingham railway was opened in 1837; around Berkhamsted, which it reached in 1838; and around Cheshunt and Broxbourne, where the Northern and Eastern railway opened in 1840. By 1883 building land in Broxbourne was being offered for sale for 'erection of small villa residences with good gardens within 500 yards of Broxbourne a first-class station on the main Line of the Great Eastern Railway, 30 minutes from Town by Express trains'.[3] These were Victorian houses between the New River and the railway with frontages of only twenty feet for each of the thirty-two plots. The Arts and Crafts houses of St Catherine's estate were only four years later. Even those houses of an earlier date were bought by commuters. Robert McVitie purchased Woodcock Hill in 1907, it being close to the direct line from Berkhamsted to Willesden where his biscuit factory was sited.[4] Later railway expansion across the county led to the Brookmans Park estate, laid out following the arrival of Great Northern Railway's station in 1926.[5] The first plan for this site was too ambitious. This was revised down to 2,500 houses and, although progress was slow, by the 1930s the building boom and the new golf course ensured its success.[6]

The choicest residential district in Metroland

The Metropolitan Railway arrived in Rickmansworth in 1887 and in Watford and Chesham by 1889. An annual guide, also called *Metro-land*, was published by the company from 1915 to 1932. This replaced the *Guide to the Extension Line*, which first appeared in 1904. *Metro-land* encouraged leisure travel and also published facts and figures for the would-be resident. Some stations, such as Croxley Green (1925) and Stanmore (1932), were designed by Charles W. Clark in an Arts & Crafts 'villa' style to indicate the attractiveness of the surrounding area. Early developments, as at Ruislip, were laid out on Arts and Crafts principles with Ruislip Manor Cottage Society Ltd using Michael Bunney and Clifford C. Makins as architects in 1912. Here some of the houses had hand-made roof-tiles, Tring bricks and oak and plaster half-timber work. These were let for sixteen shillings per week in 1912.

In Watford, Cassiobury house had been sold in 1922, demolished and its materials sold off in 1927, following the sale of parts of the estate from 1908.[7] The proximity of the Metropolitan Line station, opened in 1926, encouraged the developers William King & Co. to build the Cassiobury estate and Charles Brightman the Cassiobury Station estate.

Cedars estate covered 450 acres, with 30 houses being built on it by 1919 on plots of half an acre upwards. Building continued apace through the 1920s. It extended from the east side of Chorleywood Common to Rickmansworth either side of the Metropolitan Line. Village greens and open spaces were to be provided with what *Metroland* called 'unusual stretches of wide and well-made roads' and a 'Market-square'. The advertising described the estate as the 'choicest residential district in Metroland'.

By the 1930s the availability of mortgages with an average rate of interest of 4.25 per cent meant that private housing was now affordable for middle-class and many working-class pockets. The ease of commuting for these aspirational owners sealed the estate's success. It can be seen that the development of railway routes and the establishment of stations went hand-in-hand with the sale of large estates such as Cassiobury and Brookmans Park. A similar fate attended Moor Park at Rickmansworth, where the newly laid-out approach to the station is included in the sales brochure for the housing estate, as is a map of the area with the stations and railway lines clearly displayed.

Even in places which did not yet boast a railway station, as in Letchworth Garden City,[8] the proximity of the railway station at Hitchin was advanced as a selling point: 'Many Express trains reach it [Hitchin] in 39 and 42 minutes. There are cheap bookings on two days a week to London.'[9]

Not all occupants of Arts and Crafts houses were commuters. For example, Lt Col SR Timpson V.D.[10] of Berkhamsted worked in the town for Cooper's, the famous sheep-dip company; and Lt Benyon Croft at Fanhams had malting interests in nearby Ware. Many fairly wealthy landowners laid out an Arts and Crafts section or two. Cheverells near Markyate was one of a number of properties being extended and reworked at the turn of the century. Yew hedges enclosed small gardens with holm oak or a pond; formal lawns and a summer house led to an orchard and walled garden in a symmetrical arrangement.[11] Another such property was The Node, at Codicote, where Charles Nall-Cain and his wife (later Lord and Lady Brocket) gardened enthusiastically from the early 1900s until 1926, laying out, with the help of Pulham & Co., a formal sunken garden, pergola and balustraded terrace. Some laid out their entire garden in an Arts and Crafts manner, as at Temple Dinsley (Princess Helena College), where Edwin Lutyens put in one of the finest Arts and Crafts gardens in Hertfordshire for H.G. Fenwick, together with extensions to the house.

The artists' colony at Bushey was well known and, although not served by the railway until 1913 (and the village centre still has no station of its own), the inhabitants were sufficiently discerning for a clutch of gardens and houses by eminent designers and architects such as Voysey and Mawson to be built.

Another cluster of Arts and Crafts gardens is found around Knebworth, where Edwin Lutyens simplified the gardens at Knebworth House in 1908, Homewood (the dower house) for Lady Lytton in 1900–01 and maybe at Hillcroft where he designed a house in 1901/4 for Earl Lytton. At Knebworth House, Lutyens replaced the lower parterre with a lawn with central pool surrounded by pollarded limes. He used 180 yews along the line of the old moat to make it look more symmetrical and he turned the former box garden beyond the moat into two flower gardens, one containing yellow roses. By 1912 he had added a pergola, and orders for plants included swans and peacocks, which must have been of topiary.

Late nineteenth-century gardens

Philip Webb is well known as the architect who designed William Morris's ground-breaking Red House in 1860 but his early important garden commission was for Wycham Flower at Great Tangley Manor in Surrey, in 1880. Here he extended the house, much to Morris's approval, and laid out the garden in a naturalistic manner rather than with the usual Victorian bedding schemes, respecting the old fabric of walls and house. For his brother, a doctor in Welwyn, Webb designed the house

Figure 6.1 New Place, Welwyn. PHOTOGRAPH BY KATE HARWOOD.

and gardens at New Place (Figure 6.1). Built in 1879–80, the house was clothed in wisteria and vines with a backdrop of elms and the garden divided up with balustrades and yew hedges together with specimen trees, such as the headache tree, *Umbellularia californica*, and a Cedar of Lebanon.[12] Much of the garden has now disappeared under modern housing, although the remnant has been sympathetically managed.

William Richard Lethaby was a disciple of Ruskin and worked with Morris and Webb. An intermediate figure between the pioneers and those more pragmatic about the industrial society that followed, he designed little but was one of the most influential teachers and architects of the Arts and Crafts movement. He provided the frontispiece of a composite Arts and Crafts garden for J.D. Seddon's *Garden-Craft Old & New* (1891), and worked on two well-known houses and gardens: Melsetter in Orkney and Avon Tyrrell in Yorkshire. However, Little Court at Buntingford was extended in the 'style of Lethaby'.[13] If this was indeed by Lethaby, was the garden also altered, and was it influenced, as Avon Tyrrell was, by Webb's ideas?

William Robinson is best known as 'The Wild Gardener' for his championing of natural planting using perennials and sculptural plants such as Japanese Knotweed and bamboos, and for his intense detestation of architects and their garden designs reminiscent of railway embankments and pie-crusts. He particularly loathed the bedding-out regimen, which left one's garden full of 'new dug graves twice a year' while the planting schemes were changed.[14] The squabble in print between him and Reginald Blomfield over whether gardeners or architects were best fitted to design gardens eventually petered out. At North Mymms, Robinson was called in to lay out the gardens while Ernest George and Harold Peto were updating the Elizabethan house for Walter Burns and his wife, Mary Lyman Morgan, in 1893.[15] Robinson is credited with the design of the rose garden and pergola, and George with the rest of the garden. By 1900 the *Gardeners' Chronicle* could report that the garden '… bids fair to become in time one of the finest gardens in the Kingdom. Mrs Burns has great gardening tastes, and is gradually developing here all those fine horticultural associations we are likely to find'.[16]

Robinsonian characteristics found at North Mymms included a large pool for aquatics and nymphaeas, thousands of roses, pergolas and wired fruit walls in the kitchen garden. Of course, these are features one would expect in any good garden of the period, Robinsonian or otherwise. Although the pergola garden retains much of the original atmosphere, with detailed hard landscaping and profuse planting, the rose garden has lost much of the underplanting it once had. In Robinson's own garden at Gravetye Manor in Sussex, the roses were surrounded by violas and forget-me-nots, aubrietia and primulas, with clematis on trellises. Here each bed contained just one variety of rose, with many grey-foliaged plants such as pinks, catmint, dwarf artemisias, edelweiss and cotton lavender. *Country Life* in 1934 attributed the large shrub plantings on the church walk to the Burns' son-in-law, Lewis Harcourt, first Viscount Harcourt, from Nuneham Courtenay in Oxfordshire.[17] Harcourt was keenly interested in gardens and started redesigning his own when he moved there in 1904.[18] Following his experience at North Mymms, he gave Nuneham Courtenay rose gardens, a nymphaea garden and herbaceous gardens.

The other protagonist in the squabble was Reginald Blomfield, who designed houses at Broxbourne and various buildings for Haileybury School. At Lockleys near Welwyn, in about 1912, he laid out terraces, banks and lawns on the steep slope behind the house, with formal yew-hedged gardens to the east and west of the house and wilder, more natural planting in the areas near the river Mimram and on the island.[19]

Another early foray into Arts and Crafts was the St Catherine's estate at Broxbourne.[20] This was laid out as a leafy suburb, with architects Reginald Blomfield (five houses here between 1887 and 1892), Wood Bethel, Vincent Wing and Dudley Newman designing houses in the Richard Norman Shaw idiom with spacious gardens. The lanes were lined with horse chestnut and lime, and there were pollarded willow avenues. Spital Brook was equipped with handsome bridges and the estate was guarded by two picturesque Victorian lodges. Some fortunate owners had gardens running down to the New River with views of the Lea marshes beyond. Overall landscaping was by the prominent Broxbourne nurseryman George Paul and the effect was similar to the pioneering Bedford Park estate at Chiswick laid out in 1875, also a suburb for commuters into London.

Twentieth-century gardens
The most prolific garden designers of the time were Thomas Hayton Mawson and Edwin Lutyens/Gertrude Jekyll and they are well represented in Hertfordshire.

Thomas Hayton Mawson
Only one of Mawson's gardens in Hertfordshire survives, although designs or descriptions survive for ten others:[21] Kilfillan, Staghurst, Heather Cottage, The Kraal,[22] Stocks (all around Berkhamsted); Roebuck in Bushey; Thatched Rest at Welwyn;[23] Russell Park at Watford; Moor Park, and a house for M. Thompson at Moor Park.[24]

The surviving garden, Bushey Rose Garden, has recently been refurbished with a Heritage Lottery Fund grant, aided by research undertaken by Hertfordshire Gardens Trust.[25] Built on the site of Sir Hubert von Herkomer's Art School, Mawson tells the story of his commission in his autobiography.[26] According to Mawson, he was seeking larger premises for his expanding practice and was told of the empty art school at Bushey, which Herkomer had recently closed down. He made enquiries but

> Sir Hubert replied that I was just too late, as he had demolished the studios and had decided to convert the site into a rose garden. To assist him in the preparation of his designs, he had instructed his bookseller to send him the most authoritative work on the subject, and as a result he had just received a copy of 'The Art and

Craft of Garden Making', of which he thought I must be the author. Now that we
had come into touch with each other, he proceeded, he would like me to visit him
the following weekend to advise him. This I arranged to do.[27]

The garden which Mawson laid out for Herkomer has a sunken
court with a Bavarian tufa fountain, surrounded by rose gardens edged
with low box hedges with rose poles for climbing roses.[28] A summer
house, pergola, circular arbour and curved benches complete the picture.
Herkomer struck a bargain with Mawson similar to the one he had
struck with H.H. Richardson for the design of his house, Lululaund;
Herkomer would get a garden design and Mawson would have his
portrait painted by Herkomer, an eminent society painter. Herkomer
thought that the price of the portrait, 600 guineas, would be equivalent
to Mawson's fee. Mawson thought it a great bargain.

Staghurst gardens were described in *The Garden* in December 1917
in an article by Mawson.[29] Here he worked with Charles Henry Rew, the
Berkhamsted architect who designed the house for Mr Charles J. Gilbert,
a geologist.[30] He laid out the usual carriage-court, terrace, tennis court,
pergola laden with roses and jasmine, and formal garden containing a
sundial. As the garden was on a hill overlooking Berkhamsted, there
were sheltering fences of *Cotoneaster macrophylla*. A prominent feature
separating the sundial garden from the tennis lawn was a 'Rose fence' of
Penzance briars.[31]

Another Berkhamsted site where both Mawson and Rew worked
was Kilfillan for Harold de Haven Boyd. Here too we find Dan Gibson,
an architect and expert ironwork designer.[32, 33] Again there was a pergola
– this one stepped down to a long double herbaceous border, 'The Long
Walk', separating the tennis lawn from the orchard. Again the pergola
was covered with roses, and underplanted with irises. The cross beams
of the pergola were laid in a series of shallow hoops giving a wavy
appearance like that at Bushey, and Mawson thought that 'it was the
climbers which gave it its crowning glory', so much so that he illustrated
it in the *Art and Craft of Garden Making*.[34, 35] The usual kitchen garden
and rose garden were here supplemented by a garden which became
known, after its conversion to a school, as the Joggery, where a rusticated
portal smothered with honeysuckle and clematis led to a rock garden
of weathered limestone pavement planted with alpine plants including
alpine strawberries, and a lily pond.[36]

The fourth Mawson garden with enough details to picture it is The Kraal, on Whitehill, for Lt Col Timson, General Manager of Cooper's of Berkhamsted, who travelled widely through the colonies in connection with their famous sheep dip for scab. The Kraal was probably a reminder of his South African travels.[37] Here Mawson worked again with Dan Gibson, who designed the house. Mawson gives plans, illustrations and description in the *Art and Craft of Garden Making*.[38] As with his other sites, he is careful to separate the domestic offices, utility gardens and tradesmen's entrances from the pleasure gardens and terraces enjoyed by the family and their guests.

> ... the garden scheme on the South front of the house is centred on the main gable with its verandah and balcony. This allows of a full-sized tennis lawn backed up by a summer-house, with apsidal hedges on either side and a semi-circular arrangement of flower beds. As these features come to one side of the ground, there is room on the other for a nicely proportioned panel garden with a sundial in the centre, which is invaluable in adding interest to the scheme. Beyond this arrangement is a kitchen garden, and to give greater seclusion to it, pergolas are constructed over the walks connecting it with the pleasure grounds.

This garden, now renamed White Lodge, was illustrated in the *Ideal Home* magazine of July 1924 as 'a delightful example of the modern home at its best' and which commends it for its 'admirably planned garden' and its picturesqueness suited to a small garden (of one and a half acres). It is essentially the same garden as illustrated in *The Studio* in 1903.[39]

Other Mawson gardens are not as well documented and, as his business grew, some of these may have been taken on by his son.[40] There is a planting plan for Roebuck (11 Belmont Road) in Bushey laid out for Wilmot Ernest Lane.[41] It has the usual pergola, terrace, lawn, rose beds and clothed walls, with quite a modest list of everyday plants. At Stocks at Aldbury, in 1909, Humphrey Ward called him in to redesign the garden but, 'although many of the improvements I desired could not be carried out, owing to prohibitive cost, within restricted limits most of my plans were realised'.[42] This included a rose garden and a summer house, similar to that at Little Onn Hall in Staffordshire. Following the site's progress through Playboy Club, golf course and now private home, it is not surprising that nothing is left at all.

Elsewhere in Hertfordshire, Mawson designed the garden Thatched Rest at Welwyn for S. Glass and Heather Cottage in 1924, possibly at Potten End, near Amersfort.[43, 44] At present very little is known about these.

Mawson was admired by the Maharajah of Baroda, who bought five copies of his book to send to India. The maharajah invited Mawson to lunch at Russell Park, which he found 'a very pleasant one (Indian curries notwithstanding)', and Mawson produced a design for the gardens, which was implemented apart from a 'new drive planned as a safer route to Watford station and a new range of glasshouses'.[45] The maharajah also asked him for designs for his other house at Aldworth in Haslemere.

William Lever, later Viscount Leverhulme, was one of the longest lasting of Mawson's patrons. Mawson laid out Lever's country house garden at Thornton Manor on the Wirral, as well as his hillside garden at Rivington in Lancashire and the Hill House Garden, Hampstead. Hill House was purchased in 1904 and the first phase of Mawson's work there was completed in 1906, when Lever was elected MP for Wirral. There is an intriguing reference to plans for 'Moor Park Layout at Moor Park for Moor Park Estate' in the Cumbria Record Office[46] dated about 1910. At this time, the estate was owned by Lord Ebury, which begs the question as to whether Ebury commissioned Mawson or whether they are for another Moor Park estate.[47] Following the purchase of the 3,000 acres of Moor Park from Lord Ebury in 1919, Lever's plan for three golf courses and a country club on the estate was drawn up by Mawson (March 1921),[48] who by this time had extensive experience in town planning.[49] The plan shows two golf courses over the immediate grounds, and housing and another golf course covering the rest of the Charles Bridgeman and Capability Brown landscape, with the railway station (on the proposed extension of the railway) at the heart of the plan, rather like Jerusalem on medieval maps.

Edwin Lutyens and Gertrude Jekyll

Both Gertrude Jekyll and Edwin Lutyens laid out a number of gardens in Hertfordshire. They both worked on only one, Ashwell Bury, where Lutyens remodelled the house in 1922–6, years after Jekyll had worked on the gardens in 1908–09. Her plans show an informal lawn north of the entrance drive, which still exists. The lower lawn was to be approached from the bowling green to the south, from whence steps, flanked by a herbaceous border, led to a hedged central square, also with

borders and a walk westwards to a hedged circle, then on to steps down
to an inlet of the infant river Rhee. From here a walk along the riverside
led back to the central square. *County Life*[50] illustrations show a garden
in which the planting has been much reduced but still is exuberant. They
also show a witchert wall with a thatched capping. Witchert (clay and
straw) was one of the few materials available after the First World War
for non-essential building. This useful fact was realised by John St Loe
Strachey, editor of *The Spectator* (and father-in-law of Clough Williams-
Ellis), and was soon taken up in gardens across the country.

Temple Dinsley, laid out for H.G. (Bertie) Fenwick by Lutyens in
1908, was until recently considered to have Jekyll plantings but doubts
have recently been expressed as to whether she did have any involvement.[51]
Lutyens had worked for Fenwick's cousin Mark at Abbotswood, having
been introduced by Jekyll. The Lutyens balustrading to the pool garden
with the rose garden in the background appears in *Gardens for Small
Country Houses*.[52] The Lutyens layout incorporates two rose gardens,

Figure 6.2 Diamond Court, Temple Dinsley. A side gate
to the garden with its carefully manipulated shadows and
varied and detailed paving. PHOTOGRAPH BY KATE HARWOOD.

magnolia steps, herbaceous borders, orchards, pergolas, a pool garden and a two-storey summer house, the Belvedere, where the window looks out eastwards, giving the only external view in the whole garden; unfortunately, this now comprises the Lister Hospital at Stevenage. Plans of the gardens show the strong axiality of the design but on the ground the changes in level and placing of walls and gates render this unobtrusive, although, as in the best gardens, the visitor is enticed from one area to another. One of the many surprises in this garden is that the lack of external vistas is not noticed until the viewer is given what was a perfect picture of rolling hills and woods. The care taken over details is painstaking, as shown in the treatment of a side entrance (Figure 6.2).

Although the hedges remain, the garden's tree- and herbaceous planting has almost disappeared, with one of the rose gardens now grassed over. Plans are afoot to reinstate one of the orchards and Hertfordshire Gardens Trust planted the first tree in 2010.

Fenwick also commissioned Lutyens to design buildings at Hill (now Langley) End including cottages, barns and the house known as Hill End[53] for his wife. Here he laid out balustrades as at Temple Dinsley but also retained a seventeenth-century dovecote as part of the garden design, converting it into a summer house[54] – perhaps an echo of the piggery[55] he put in the Temple Dinsley park.

At Homewood, Fenwick's mother-in-law, Lady Lytton, laid out the gardens with Jekyllian motifs such as planting in pockets on the garden steps and drifts of flowers in the borders as evidenced in the webpages of *Country Life*.[56] The house and garden plan by Lutyens (1901[57]) 'arrange[d] both the main room to the southeast and the staircase hall facing southwest so that each aligns with large but simply planned lawns'.[58] Although Lutyens had proposed that the formal forecourt be surrounded by a low yew hedge to separate it from the adjacent woodland, rhododendrons were planted instead.

A Jekyll design was prepared for a quincunx herb garden at Knebworth House in 1907 but it was not executed until the plan was found in a drawer many years later and laid out in 1982.[59] It may have been intended as a present from Emily Lutyens to her brother Earl Lytton. We do know Jekyll produced plans in 1908/09 for Putteridge Bury near Luton for a rose garden and a pool garden. Although these were planted up by Hertfordshire Gardens Trust, it is now thought they were not executed at the time. The rose garden (Figure 6.3) was enclosed

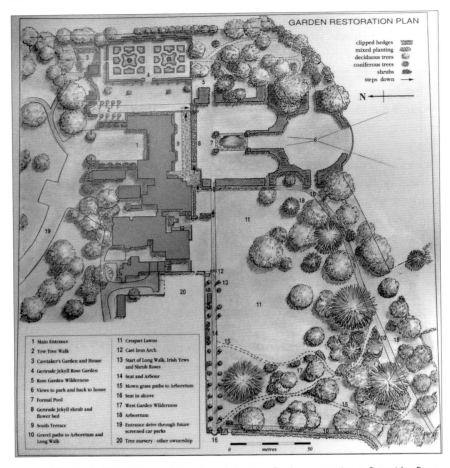

Figure 6.3 Hertfordshire Gardens Trust plan of the Rose Garden restoration at Putteridge Bury.

by yew hedges with small beds edged with *Stachys lanate,* and with a centre arrangement of, probably, lavender. The roses were grouped into yellow/salmon or pinks with a red and white combination in the centre. All these roses were supplied by Harkness of Hitchin. According to Jane Brown, it was important that no magenta roses were included.[60]

Similarly, Jekyll's planting plans of 1928 for two borders at Hitchin Priory may not have been completely implemented.[61]

Jekyll's planting plans for Amersfort, Potten End, survive and were implemented at the time. The hard landscaping was by Ernest Willmott, and Jekyll was asked for planting advice by the owner W.S. Cohen on the double flower borders, Monk's Walk, lawn borders, Rose Garden, trellis (Green Court) and Pergola. She also supplied plants for the short borders as requested:

> it would be a great help if you could manage at least to send off borders 2 & 3 on Saterday [*sic*] so that we could start putting in the wall plants we have – apart from this 1 is the most urgent as it is all ready for planting.[62]

The ground falls away from the house over a valley and Willmott designed two walks terminating in bastions to take advantage of the views. The other gardens were arranged around the house in a series of rooms and walks with lush planting.[63]

George Dillistone, of R.Wallace and Co., landscaped the grounds at Markyate Cell for Mr and Mrs Macleod in about 1910. He had worked with Lutyens at Castle Drogo for Julius Drewe, and at Goddards,[64] which was built as a 'Home of Rest for Ladies of Small Means' by Lutyens for Sir Frederick Mirrielees in 1899. In her book, Jekyll likens the Markyate Cell garden to Owlpen Manor and praises it as 'an example of what can be done to improve an old garden by judicious changes'.[65] Dillistone's chief task was to unite the different parts of the garden and this he did by cutting a vista via a new stairway, up the steep hill to the east, and enclosing it by purple beech to distinguish it from the general woodland at the boundary. This axial layout stretches from the forecourt of the house up through a series of grassy banks and balustraded terraces to a rose garden at the top. The pre-existing yew hedge was retained and other features such as a pergola leading to the kitchen garden added. The rose garden was to be furnished with roses and lavender, pinks and hollyhocks.

Robert Lorimer, the pioneering Scottish Arts and Crafts architect, was called in to extend Balls Park[66] at Hertford in 1924–5 for Sir Benjamin Faudel-Phillips. Three small gardens around that wing were laid out with yew hedges, a small fountain and walls clothed with climbers. No evidence has been discovered to link them to Lorimer, who was considered the 'Scottish Lutyens',[67] but they will be restored in the Arts and Crafts style, following advice from Hertfordshire Gardens Trust. Within the grounds of the mansion is a small eighteenth-century cottage surrounded by yew hedges forming small garden rooms. One of these enclosures contains the sunken 'Ben's Garden'.[68] *Country Life*[69] in 1912 shows the yew hedges newly planted around a rectangular garden with two terraces leading by steps on all four sides down to a grass plat, crossed by cruciform stone paths with a fountain and pool at the centre. Generous flower borders and flower-filled urns complete the picture. After years of dereliction this garden has been restored by the current owners.

Charles Voysey, H.M. Baillie Scott, Geoffry [sic] Lucas

Charles Annesley Voysey, who designed the houses Myholme, Tilehurst and Hollybank in Bushey as well as The Orchard in Chorleywood for himself around the turn of the century, may have had a hand in their gardens, as he did at 48 Storey's Way in Cambridge. No evidence for this has yet been uncovered, although we know he did design a bootscraper for Myholme. In 1898, *Country Life* championed Voysey's unpretentious weekend retreats as the 'ideal cottage in modern garb ... [which] ... manages to make utility the basis for aesthetic expression'.[70] His gardens were in the Arts and Crafts idiom with distinctive buttressed summer houses of harled walls under tiled roofs and with a concern for the way they would be enjoyed, with plenty of sun and shade in the appropriate places and all in proportion to the house.

Hugh Mackay Baillie Scott wrote a delightful book which explains the areas needed in any garden: rose garden, flower borders, orchard, vegetable garden and tennis or croquet lawn.[71] The illustrations in his book include pools, pergolas and lavish planting, but of a kind that respected the local soils and topography. He designed several houses in Hertfordshire – Corrie Wood in Letchworth being his most sophisticated. Again no information regarding his involvement in the design of any of the gardens has been discovered as yet.

Geoffry [sic] Lucas, an architect from Hitchin who was involved with the Garden City movement in Letchworth, Hampstead Garden Suburb and Gidea Park, was also responsible for houses at Hoddesdon. Among these is Yewlands, illustrated in *Modern Cottage Architecture* in 1904.[72] As is usual with architects of this period, an effort is made to depict the garden around the house. This garden was partially realised with terraces, hedge-enclosed garden rooms and a drive leading down to the New River. Lucas's detailed Italianate balustrading and double stair leading down to the lawn were never built, perhaps because the fall of the ground is so slight that the grassy bank installed looked more appropriate.

There are many small gardens for which there is little archival information but they are delightful echoes of the period. Many can be seen in the pages of publications such as *The Builder*, where the houses appear surrounded by hedged rooms and are set upon a small platform with steps down to a tennis lawn or a rose garden. Books of the period such as those by Jekyll and by Weaver, or *Recent Domestic Architecture* by Mervyn MacCartney, are an invaluable source of photographs for many sites. In volume v of his work, MacCartney describes the alterations to Morton House and garden carried out under the direction of Mr A. Winter Rose in about 1911. MacCartney describes the garden thus:

> At this house some interesting restoration work, with reconstruction and additions, has been carried out for Mr. F. W. Speaight, under the direction of Mr. A. Winter Rose, architect. Morton House is a small but interesting example of domestic architecture, chiefly of the Queen Anne period. The house practically adjoins Old Hatfield Palace, which was built by Bishop Merton in the reign of Edward IV., after whom it derives its name ... On the west of the sunk rose garden the old stables have been converted into an open-air dining loggia, the niche in the wall on the east side having been filled in with a skilfully-carved figure in stone of St. Etheldreda, the patron saint of the parish church. This figure was executed by Mr. Brooke Hirch.[73]

The illustration of this garden in *Gardens for Small Country Houses* shows a loggia with Tuscan order columns, similar to one at Rodmarton Manor. The courtyard garden is paved with a central circular pool and corner grass plats. The back wall, of some considerable height, is trellised and covered with climbing plants framing the gothic niche of St Etheldreda. Interestingly, Winter Rose designed another garden containing a similar statue, also illustrated in the book. In addition, he designed the gardens for Goodrich House[74] on Fore Street in Hatfield, home of Mr F.W. Speaight, mentioned above, where the scheme, although complicated by a right-of-way across the garden, was laid out in a series of rooms.[75]

Several gardens lack even such scanty archival details. One such is at Rothamsted where a small courtyard area was equipped with the elements of an Arts and Crafts garden in the late 1920s and early 1930s. The rectangular pool garden (Figure 6.4) with wall fountain, detailed paving, open loggia and clothed walls, including an ancient *Hydrangea petiolaris*, was used by the workers at the laboratory. A typical Arts and Crafts gate led through to the Director's Garden (now an executive housing estate).

Figure 6.4 Rothamsted garden. PHOTOGRAPH BY KATE HARWOOD.

A plan of the garden survives – as do designs for paving, fencing and water tanks – in the Rothamsted Archive, but these appear to have been largely unexecuted except for the layout and perhaps a wrought-iron gate,[76] although the one now in situ does not resemble this.

An Arts and Crafts house designed by Frank Salisbury, the well-known local artist, lies close to the Rothamsted Courtyard.[77] Red Gables has a beautifully detailed ironwork gate, and photographs of the garden to be found in the book *Ocean Devil*[78] show it to have been an Arts and Crafts garden, with rose arches and walls clothed in creepers. Salisbury himself commissioned designs for a pair of semi-detached villas in Harpenden.[79]

Another undocumented garden is at Presdales, where a small sunken garden with rustic stone steps contains a semi-circular pool with remains of a water spout over it, the surrounding gardens on two levels and a ruined pergola around two sides. Such evidence as there is suggests it was installed by Albert Sandeman, of the port and sherry importers, who was living in the house in 1902 when the *Gardeners' Chronicle*[80] described the house walls as covered with magnolias, ivies,

Ampelopsis veitchii, Jasmines, Clematis and other plants. Most of the gardens were laid to spring bulbs followed by summer bedding with roses and shrubs in the borders. No mention is made either of the sunken garden or of the artificial rockwork water gardens in the woods to the east of the house. The sunken garden appears on the Second edition, but not the First, of the Ordnance Survey, which suggests a late nineteenth-century date for installation.

Japanese and Italian gardens

The turn-of-the-century fashion for Italian and Japanese gardens resulted in these being added to many established sites, often in one of the garden rooms. One such was Wall Hall in Aldenham where, in about 1910, J.P. Morgan is thought to have installed three small rooms surrounded by clipped yew hedges including a formal Italian garden.[81] This is entered by a flight of semi-circular steps which led to a path across the garden to another gate leading to the orchard. A cross path led from the Loggia around the central square pool to the other side. The garden slid into dereliction after the war and has now been 'restored'[82] as part of the housing development covering Repton's landscape.

Another Italian garden, this time by Wood Bethel in 1900 for Lt Richard Benyon Croft (originally of Croft Castle) and a maltster in his father-in-law's Ware firm (Henry Page), was installed at Fanhams Hall in Ware.[83] Bethel's plan shows an Italian-style garden with steps and balustrades but there are also several garden rooms, one with a quincunx of trees, another with a bowling green, and beautifully detailed paving. The fall of the ground is not sufficient to give the authentic Italian atmosphere evoked by Harold Peto at Iford Manor or George Dillistone at Markyate Cell, but an effort has been made to lay out a terrace garden surrounding a rectangular pool with central fountain. Many of the clipped topiary pyramids and balls were replaced during restoration but some of the older ones survive. A similar arrangement of shallow terraces and parterres is shown at Presdales on the east front of the house, and at other sites around the county. From their planting style, these seem to be more a function of topography and Victorian formality rather than beautifully crafted and luxuriantly planted Arts and Crafts styles.

Fanhams Hall has also one of the finest Japanese gardens in the county.[84] Set in an arboretum, the design was by Mr Inaka and Professor Suzuki, and Japanese gardeners both laid it out and maintained it for some years. It was based on a Hill Garden design, incorporating a genuine Japanese tea house, a shrine, Japanese bridges and seventeen different patterns of lantern as well as a 'Mount Fuji', which was originally planted with white azaleas to replicate snow. The garden is approached by a sinuous wisteria pergola leading to the water garden with ingenious baffles in the stream to animate the flowing water. Japanese maples and pines are planted liberally (Plate 6.1). Although it was laid out in the Edwardian period, Lady Brocket returned to her childhood home from Brocket Hall when she was widowed in 1934 and carried out further work in the garden.

Japanese gardens became popular in the late nineteenth century, fuelled by Josiah Conder's book *Landscape Gardening in Japan* (1893) which not only illustrated examples of artefacts such as lanterns and tea houses, but also detailed annotated plans of layouts for various types of garden: hill, flat, lake, and tea in several styles.

In 1905 the Anglo-Japanese Alliance promoted an exhibition in London to foster closer trade and cultural links. Held at the White City in 1910, the Japanese section included two Japanese gardens created by Japanese designers and workmen, which attracted over eight million people, many for the evening fireworks, in the five months they were open. There was an outpouring of publications on all aspects of Japanese culture, and Japanese gardens were the new fashion. Some enthusiasts visited Japan, and on their return re-created the scenery as the Levers did at Rivington where Mawson had to blast out the hillside to produce a dramatic Japanese landscape. Here in Hertfordshire, it was Herbert Cooke (1865–1937) who visited Japan. On his return, in about 1905, he set about laying out a small Japanese garden at Cottered. After several years of development, Seyomon Kusumoto completed the design, taking from 1923 to 1926 to do so.[85] This garden has been called 'the most impressive example of a Japanese garden in England'.[86]

Relic Japanese gardens can be found across the county, often water gardens abandoned for new fashions and less outlay. Some have planting and hard landscaping left, such as at Ponsbourne Park at Newgate Street, where Pulham & Co. laid out a rockwork to the stream at about the time Edward Hildred Carlile, JP, MP and philanthropist, inherited in 1906. Even in the twenty-first century some of the planting – Japanese Maples and dwarf conifers – was still visible. Pulham & Co. also appear to have laid out a Japanese garden at The Node.[87] Carl Holmes, the

Figure 6.5 Sparrows Herne Hall. REPRODUCED BY KIND PERMISSION OF HALS.

American purchaser in 1926, enhanced the gardens and, it is reputed that the Japanese garden was installed for his Japanese wife, again using a Japanese designer and gardeners. The stone bridge and water courses (now dry), complete with rocky mounts as well as stands of bamboo, still exist but the Japanese Rest House and arched wooden bridge, the lanterns and crane statue have disappeared.[88] Other gardens have only luxuriant planting, including Japanese knotweed. Acers and a *Parotia persica* still exist in the abandoned water garden in the woods further east in Broxbourne. A third category we know only from archival sources, such as Sparrows Herne Hall at Bushey, which has, in its sales particulars of 1905,[89] mention of a lily pond. The undated (but before 1919) photograph[90] (Figure 6.5) of this lily pond shows a miniature Japanese garden. No other information has come to light and the garden itself has long disappeared.

Garden Cities
The social and humanitarian reasons behind the Garden City movement have been well documented elsewhere,[91] but the garden design elements of these pioneering settlements are within the purlieu of the Arts and Crafts garden.

Ebenezer Howard and his planners, Barry Parker and Raymond Unwin, recognised that the interconnection of gardens and landscape with houses was of vital importance not just for individual homes but for towns. Further, they realised that well-designed green spaces, be they gardens or parks, verges or allotments, contributed to the kind of cooperative civic society they wished to foster. In 1904 Unwin drew up the Building Regulations for the Garden City Pioneer Company of Letchworth, which were in themselves pioneering. For the first time, these included aesthetic as well as the usual technical standards. The 'Hertfordshire vernacular' was to be invoked with rough-cast painted walls, thatched or tiled roofs with nary a slate to be seen, nor indeed the 'ugly'[92] local Arlesey bricks. For the layout of the town itself, there were precedents: Parker and Unwin's New Earswick for the Rowntrees from 1902; Bournville for the Cadburys from 1895; Port Sunlight for Lord Lever from 1888. These, however, were all estate settlements, although the estates were not those of the landed gentry but of factories producing cocoa, chocolate and soap. Another nearby contemporaneous development was Hampstead Garden Suburb, which was not self-sustaining nor was it designed to be egalitarian. In 1903 the Letchworth Garden City Master Plan was drawn up with low-density housing of about twelve plots per acre. Importantly, industry was zoned but local so commuting to work was unnecessary. Further out, farms would supply the foodstuffs needed by the town and in return the town would supply night soil and a ready market close at hand. Provision was made for all classes of people, from inebriates to orphans, from brick makers to the blind and deaf.

Several things made the Garden Cities special. One was the emphasis on light and air being good for the health, both physical and spiritual. Houses were set around quasi-village greens (now alas sometimes used as car parks) or cul-de-sacs. Houses at the entrance of roads were set back to provide a welcoming gateway. Vistas and sight lines were calculated across road junctions (Figure 6.6).[93] The roads had pavements with grass verges planted with trees, and some of the first photographs of Letchworth show trees planted before houses were completed. Houses were called cottages and designed as detached and, later, semi-detached or short terraces, with no sign of the Bye-law terrace in sight. Although this could be construed as looking back to the Golden Age, it is in fact well in keeping with Howard's *Garden Cities of Tomorrow*[94] and a way to

Figure 6.6 Letchworth Garden City. PHOTOGRAPH BY KATE HARWOOD.

reform society by reforming the way people live and the environments they live in: 'Town and country must be married, and out of this joyous union will spring a new hope, a new life, a new civilization'.[95]

Mr John St Loe Strachey[96] was behind the cheap cottage movement which found its home in Letchworth. These detached cottages were designed, with varying degrees of success, by different architects or companies. The Bourneville Village Trust considered that 'the cost limit of £150 entails the most severe external treatment, but we have found that a few years' growth of creepers and shrubs quite eclipses man's efforts at decorating exteriors'.[97] Another architect, Herbert Stanley-Barrett, of Stanley-Barrett and Driver, claimed to have lived with a labourer for some time, 'to study his requirements'. So there was a separate parlour; if the vicar called unexpectedly he would escape the wet undergarments hanging up to dry. Stanley-Barrett also included a wooden porch, where the husband might smoke his pipe in peace of an evening. This, according to Mr Driver, also of Stanley-Barrett and Driver, would prevent the temptation to seek solace in the public house. Moreover, his wife, 'after she has cleared up and put the children to bed, may join him'. The front of the house overlooked the garden, not the road, as an inducement to keep the garden in trim.[98]

Unlike New Earswick and Bourneville, gardens were not provided with fruit trees, probably due to the housing being provided by a variety of societies and co-operatives, rather than a benevolent employer. The gardens were, however, spacious and there was ample provision of parks, allotments and other green space.

This ethos was taken into the Modern age in the development of Welwyn Garden City with its cul-de-sacs, beaux-arts town centre landscaping and tree-lined avenues. Other settlements that nodded towards this ethos, such as Knebworth village, were never completed. Lutyens produced a plan in 1910 for a village around the railway, which had arrived in 1884. This is an interesting mixture of ideas seemingly derived from Hampstead Garden Suburb and Letchworth, with a grand central square with radiating avenues. Although work started, progress was slow and was interrupted by the First World War. However, both here and in other places such as Harebreak estate in Watford, from the 1920s, the spacious, villagey, tree-lined legacy of the early Garden Cities is still apparent.

Summary

Hertfordshire, then, was ideally placed to have one's Arts and Crafts house and garden, often funded by commerce or the professions. It was also the site of the two earliest Garden Cities which spread the ethos of the Arts and Crafts garden to town planning and was echoed in Metroland in the southern part of the county. Far too many of these gardens have been lost to development, changes in garden fashions partly fuelled by changing economic circumstances, and neglect. Those which have been restored, such as the Rose Garden at Bushey and 'Ben's Garden' at Hertford, are rare now in Hertfordshire and a glimpse of the county's Golden Age.

Acknowledgements
My thanks go to the staff of Hertfordshire Archives and Local Studies, to Isobel Aptaker of Dacorum Heritage Trust, and Jennifer Potter, Jenny Sherwood, Margaret Harcourt Williams, Kate Banister and Mary de Soyres.

Notes

1. HALS D/EX 623/22 Advertising Brochure for Moor Park, n.d.
2. Hertfordshire Gardens Trust and T. Williamson, *The Parks and Gardens of West Hertfordshire* (2000), p. 91.
3. HALS DE/Hx/E92.
4. HALS ACC3898 Report on Woodcock Hill for Hertfordshire Gardens Trust (HGT).
5. The land was requisitioned by the Great Northern Railway from Gaussen of Brookmans Park in 1847 – HALS DEGA/34570.
6. Peter Kingsford, *A Modern History of Brookmans Park 1700–1950*, Chapter 4: <http://www.brookmans.com/history/kingsford/chfour.shtml>, accessed 22 August 2011.
7. HALS ACC3898 Report on Cassiobury by M. Thompson from HGT.
8. The first station was 1905, necessitated by the success of the Cheap Cottages Exhibition.
9. HALS D/EX 623 First Garden City Estate Office, November 1907.
10. 'V.D.' was Volunteer Decoration for officers of the Volunteer Force who had served for more than twenty years. It had been introduced in 1892 and in 1894 was applied to those who had served in India and the Colonies. It was replaced in 1908 by the Territorial Decoration.
11. Report by Debois Landscapes for SARBIR Developments.
12. Mary de Soyres, personal communication; and 'The Lesser Country Houses of To-Day: New Place, Welwyn, Herts, designed by Mr Philip Webb', *Country Life*, 23 July 1910, pp. 7–9.
13. English Heritage Building Listing No. 1174663.
14. W. Robinson, *The Wild Garden* (1870; London, 4th edn, 1894).
15. She was a sister to J.P. Morgan, the American banker and thus aunt to J.P. Morgan Jnr, who bought Wall Hall at Aldenham in 1910.
16. *Gardeners' Chronicle,* ii (1900), pp. 254–5.
17. Harcourt married the Burns' daughter, Mary Ethel, in 1899.
18. Harcourt paid for some of the expenses of the garden at North Mymms (Birmingham University Archive: CFGM/1/2/54. Letter of ?2 February 1910, stating L. Harcourt had paid £5 to cover the North Mymms Park budget).
19. H. Avray Tipping in 'Lockleys, Hertfordshire', *Country Life*, 10 July 1920, vol. xlviii., pp. 48–51.
20. Kate Harwood for HGT, *Broxbourne Local List*, 2011.
21. Cumbria Record Office. There may be other gardens.
22. Cumbria Record Office WDB69/51 Plan of Summer House for S.R. Numon [*sic*] Esq., and WDB86/10/308 Glass Lantern Slide of The Kraal, Report by Berkhamsted Local History Society *White Lodge* (2000) in HALS ACC3898.
23. Cumbria Record Office WDB/86/L.64: Garden of Thatched Rest, Welwyn for S Glass, ?1936.
24. Cumbria Record Office WDB86/A59/2, n.d.
25. See report for Liz Lake Associates by Kate Harwood 2006.
26. T.H. Mawson, *The Life and Work of an English Landscape Architect* (London, 1927).
27. *Ibid.*, p. 212.
28. Herkomer imported tufa from his homeland in Bavaria for the house Lululaund.
29. T.H. Marson, 'The Gardens at Staghurst, Berhamsted [*sic*]', *The Garden*, vol. lxxxi (29 December 1917), p. 212.
30. Jenny Sherwood, personal communication.

31. Penzance briars are vigorous briar roses, apt to become bare at the base and requiring drastic pruning. They may be developed from *Rosa ruginosa* and are named after Lord and Lady Penzance (or their gardener); personal communication – Jennifer Potter. Lord and Lady Penzance lived at Earshing Park, Godalming, and bred roses (Lord Penzance, Lady Penzance and others named after Walter Scott characters) as a hobby.
32. Dan Gibson was Mawson's business partner from 1898 until 1900 when he left to set up his own business. They continued to collaborate on many projects after 1900.
33. See Graythwaite Hall, Cumbria, for gate overthrows.
34. Mawson, *Life and Work*, p. 158.
35. T.H. Mawson, *The Art and Craft of Garden Making* (London, 4th edn, 1912), p. 150.
36. Information from Mawson, *Life and Work*, and material deposited by J. Hunn (HALS ACC3433).
37. Although an Afrikaans word meaning a cattle enclosure, it is often used to refer to the entire homestead.
38. Mawson, *Art and Craft of Garden Making*, pp. 336–8.
39. Dan Gibson exhibited three photographs at the Arts and Crafts Exhibition, including one of The Kraal. *The Studio*, 1903, reflects that exhibition.
40. Edward Prentice Mawson joined his father as a senior partner in 1911.
41. Cumbria Record Office WBD76/54, 1924.
42. Quoted in *Thomas H. Mawson: A Northern Landscape Architect* (Lancaster, 1976). Catalogue for an Exhibition held between October and December 1976 at the University of Lancaster.
43. Cumbria Record Office WDB86/L64, ?1936.
44. Cumbria Record Office WDB86/A23, 1924.
45. Mawson, *Life and Work*, p. 336.
46. Cumbria Record Office WDB86/M 67, *c*.1910.
47. Janet Waymark notes that the design of ?1910 is for Lord Leverhulme at Moor Park, Hertfordshire.
48. Cumbria Record Office WDB86/4/67/2.
49. By 1921 he had worked in Canada (British Columbia, Calgary and Vancouver), Greece (Athens and Salonika), The Hague, Stepney and Port Sunlight on town planning. He became President of the Town Planning Institute in 1923.
50. 'Ashwell Bury, Hertfordshire, The home of Mrs. Wolverley Fordham', *Country Life*, 2 May 1947, vol. ci, pp. 810–13.
51. Diana Kingham, personal communication.
52. G. Jekyll and L. Weaver, *Gardens for Small Country Houses* (London 1912, 1920), figure 153, p. 103.
53. Now three houses: Langley End House, Bathgate House and Clifton House. English Heritage Listed Building 162853, Grade II.
54. English Heritage Listed Building 162854, Grade II.
55. Now Grade II listed.
56. *Country Life* suggest these were taken for Weaver's *Small Country Houses of Today* (1919).
57. Plan in Knebworth House Archives. Report on Homewood by Mia Cooper for HGT, September 2003.
58. D. Dunster, *Key Buildings of the Twentieth Century Volume 1: Houses 1900–1944* (New York, 1985), pp. 5–6.
59. J. Brown, *Gardens of a Golden Afternoon* (London, 1982), p. 65
60. *Ibid.*, p. 130
61. Bridget Howlett, pers. com. *Country Life*, 17 October, pp. 592–8, 24 October, pp. 632–9, 1925.
62. From The Reef Point Collection File IV, Folder 94, in report by Debois Landscape Survey Group for HGT 1996. Letter 12 October 1911 from W.S. Cohen, Fairhill, Berkhamsted.
63. Further details can be found in Hertfordshire Gardens Trust and Williamson, *Parks and Gardens*, pp. 94–6.

64. The garden terraces at Goddards were laid out by Gertrude Jekyll.
65. *Gardens for Small Country Houses*, pp. xx–xxviii.
66. English Heritage Listed Building Record No. 1269013.
67. Jekyll commented that 'the difference between working with Ned and Lorimer was as between quicksilver and suet' quoted in Francis Jekyll *Gertrude Jekyll: a memoir*, p. 19.
68. English Heritage, *Register of Gardens of Special Historic Interest in England*, Record Number 1000523.
69. *Country Life*, 6 January 1912, vol. xxxi, p. 578.
70. 'Great British Architects: CFA Voysey (1857–1941)', *Country Life*, 16 May 2010, <http://www.countrylife.co.uk/culture/article/461887/Great-British-Architects-C-F-A-Voysey-1857-1941-.html>, accessed 13 September 2011.
71. H.M. Baillie Scott, *Houses and Gardens; Arts and Crafts Interiors* (London, 1906).
72. M.B. Adams (ed.), *Modern Cottage Architecture* (London, 1904), Plate 40.
73. M. MacCartney, *Recent Domestic Architecture*, vol. v, pp. 197–9.
74. English Heritage Listed Building 158382 Grade II*.
75. G. Jekyll & L. Weaver, *Gardens for Small Country Houses* (1912 edn), p. 70–1.
76. Designs for three wrought-iron gates entitled *Designs for Gates – Sir John Russell Dr. Sc. F.R.S.* and dated November 1928.
77. HALS D/EX 623/9.
78. J. MacManus's biography of George Hogg.
79. Plans in the Supplement to *The Builders Journal and Architectural Record*, 1902.
80. *Gardeners' Chronicle*, vol. ii (1902), p. 229.
81. Elizabeth Banks Associates, *Wall Hall, Aldenham Landscape History* (unpublished, 1999).
82. It has won a national 'Best Development' award; see <http://www.bell-cornwell.co.uk/green-belt-use-conversion.htm>.
83. Barr's Nursery of Lancaster may have planted the Italian Garden but this is not proven.
84. S. Rutherford, *Fanhams Hall, Ware: Framework Conservation Plan*, vol. i, unpublished, 2006, p. 5.
85. H. Goode, *The Japanese Garden at Cottered, Herts 1905–33* (n.p., 1933) and English Heritage *Register*.
86. D. Ottewill, *The Edwardian Garden* (New Haven, CT, 1989), pp. 56–7.
87. Claude Hitching <www.pulham.org.uk> and the *Gardeners' Magazine*, 10 February 1912.
88. Photograph of the Japanese Rest House from the Codicote Local History Society.
89. HALS DE/Hx/E108 Sales Particulars. Sparrows Herne Hall.
90. HALS Photograph Collection under Bushey.
91. M. Miller, *Letchworth: The First Garden City* (Chichester, 1989); English Heritage, *English Garden Cities* (Swindon, 2010); Hertfordshire Publications (ed.), *Garden Cities and New Towns* (Hertford, 1989).
92. Deemed ugly by Unwin who preferred red brick.
93. R. Unwin, *Town Planning in Practice* (London, 1911).
94. 1902 reprint of his 1898 *Tomorrow: A Peaceful Path to Real Reform*.
95. Ebenezer Howard, *Garden Cities of Tomorrow* (n.p., 1902), Introduction, p. 48.
96. Owner of *The Country Gentleman Land and Water Magazine* and editor of *The Spectator*.
97. <http://www.gardencitymuseum.org/exhibitions/cheap_cottages_exhibition>, 6 and 8 The Quadrant.
98. First Garden City Museum. Online Exhibition of Cheap Cottages 1905, 1 The Quadrant; <http://www.gardencitymuseum.org/exhibitions/cheap_cottages_exhibition>.

Bibliography

Primary sources
Birmingham University Archive:
North Mymms: CFGM/1/2/54 Letter of ?2 February 1910 from L Harcourt, Gillingham Street.

Cumbria Record Office:
Berkhamsted: Proposed house at Berkhamsted for F.J. Harvey, WDB86/A24, 1925.
Heather Cottage: Alterations to Heather Cottage, Berkhamsted, WDB86/A23, 1924 Photograph, WDB/86/9/81, c.1924.
The Kraal: Plan of Summer House for S.R Numon [sic] Esq., WDB69/51, n.d.
Moor Park: Proposed house at Moor Park for M Thompson, WDB86/A59/2, n.d.
Moor Park: Layout at Moor Park for Moor Park Estate, WDB86/M67, c.1910.
Moor Park: Layout of Moor Park for Lord Leverhulme, WDB86/4/67/2 and WDB86/3/26, 1921.
Roebuck, Bushey: Layout of Garden for 54 Bushley [sic] client W.E. Lane, WDB76/54, 1924.
Stocks: Gateway at Stocks in Tring for Mrs Humphrey Ward Photograph, WDB86/9/1, n.d.
Thatched Rest, Welwyn: Garden of Thatched Rest, Welwyn for S. Glass, WDB86/L64, ?1936.

Hertfordshire Archives and Local Studies (HALS):
Brookmans Park: DEGA/34570 Requisitions on title to lands required by Great Northern Railway 27 August 1847.
DEGA/34567-69 Printed plans of land required by Great Northern Railway February 1847
Broxbourne: DE/Hx/E92 Advertisement for erection of small villa residences on 3a, 1r, 0p 1883.
Cassiobury: ACC3898 Report for HGT by Thompson, M.
Kilfillan: ACC3433 Material deposited by J. Hunn.
Moor Park Sales: D/EX 623/22 and 623/23.
Salisbury Villas: D/EX 623/9 *The Builders Journal and Architectural Record*: Supplement, Plan and elevation of semi-detached villas for Frank O Salisbury, Esq.; J Percy Hall, ARIBA, 6 Victoria Grove, London, architect (The Builders' Journal and Architectural Record) DE/X623/9, July 1902.
Sparrows Herne Hall: Photograph of Lily Pond, n.d. DE/Ex/E108 Sales Particulars. Sparrows Herne Hall, Bushey heath, 1905.
Woodcock Hill: ACC3898 Report for HGT.

Rothamsted Archive:
Designs for Gates – Sir John Russell, D^r. S^c. F.R.S., November 1928.
Design for Metal tank by Cashmore Art Workers, Battersea (1932 on return panel of tank).

Railway timetables:
Bradshaw's General Railway and Steam Navigation Guide, for Great Britain and Ireland, January 1859.
Topham's Railway Time-table and Guide, July 1848.

Secondary sources
Adams, M.B. (ed.), *Modern Cottage Architecture* (London, 1904).
Baillie Scott, H.M., *Houses and Gardens; Arts and Crafts Interiors* (London, 1906).
Bisgrove, R., *William Robinson: The Wild Gardener* (London, 2008).
Brown, J., *Gardens of a Golden Afternoon* (London, 1982).
Conder, J., *Landscape Gardening in Japan* (London, 1893).
Debois Landscape Survey Group, Liz Lake Assocs., *Haresfoot Senior School (Amersfort House), Berkhamsted*, unpublished report for HGT, 1996.

Dillistone, G., *The Planning and Planting of Little Gardens* (London, 1920).

Dunster, D., *Key Buildings of the Twentieth Century Volume 1: Houses 1900–1944* (New York, 1985).

Elizabeth Banks Associates, *Wall Hall, Aldenham Landscape History*, unpublished, 1999.

English Heritage, *English Garden Cities* (Swindon, 2010).

Goode, H., *The Japanese Garden at Cottered, Herts 1905–33* (n.p., 1933).

Harwood, K., 'Bushey Rose Garden', report for Heritage Lottery Fund Application, unpublished, 2006.

Hertfordshire Gardens Trust, *List of Gardens of Local Importance for Dacorum*, unpublished, 2007.

Hertfordshire Gardens Trust, *List of Gardens of Local Importance for Broxbourne*, unpublished, 2011.

Hertfordshire Gardens Trust and Williamson, T., *The Parks and Gardens of West Hertfordshire* (n.p., 2000).

Hertfordshire Publications (ed.), *Garden Cities and New Towns* (Hertford, 1989).

Hitchmough, W., *Arts and Crafts Gardens* (London, 1997).

Howard, E., *Garden Cities of Tomorrow* (n.p., 1902).

Jekyll, F., *Gertrude Jekyll: a Memoir* (London, 1934).

Jekyll, G. and Weaver, L., *Gardens for Small Country Houses* (London, 1st edn, 1912; 4th edn, 1920).

Kirk, S., *Philip Webb: Pioneer of Arts & Crafts Architecture* (Chichester, 2005).

MacManus, J., *Ocean Devil* (London, 2008).

Mawson, T.H., *The Art and Craft of Garden Making* (London, 4th edn, 1912).

Mawson, T.H., *The Life and Work of an English Landscape Architect* (London, 1927).

Metroland, British Empire Exhibition Number (1924)

Mikes, D. and Hands, R. (eds), *Railways of Dacorum* (Berkhamsted, 2000).

Miller, M., *Letchworth: The First Garden City* (Chichester, 1989).

Miller, M., *English Garden Cities: An Introduction* (Swindon, 2010).

Ottewill, D., *The Edwardian Garden* (New Haven CT, 1989).

Potter, J., *The Rose* (London, 2010).

Purdom, C.B., *The Letchworth Achievement* (London, 1963).

Robinson, W., *The Wild Garden* (1870, London, 4th edn, 1894).

Rook, T., *Welwyn Garden City Past* (Chichester, 2001).

Rutherford, S., *Fanhams Hall, Ware: Framework Conservation Plan*, unpublished, 2006.

Unwin, R., *Town Planning in Practice* (London, 1911).

Waymark, J., *Thomas Mawson: Life, Gardens and Landscapes* (London, 2009).

Weaver, L., *Cottages: Their Planning, Design and Materials* (London, 1926).

Williams-Ellis, C., *England and the Octopus* (London, 1928).

Willmott, E., *English House Design: A Review* (London, 1911).

Thomas H. Mawson: A Northern Landscape Architect. (Lancaster, 1976). Catalogue for an Exhibition held between October and December 1976 at the University of Lancaster.

Journals

Le Lievre, A., 'An Account of the Garden at Aldenham House and of its Makers: Henry Hucks Gibbs, Vicary Gibbs and Edwin Beckett', *Garden History*, 14/2 (Autumn 1986), pp. 173–93.

Mawson, T.H., 'The Gardens at Staghurst, Berkamsted [*sic*]', *The Garden*, vol lxxxi, 29 December 1917.

Country Life:

Aldenham House: *Country Homes; Garden Old & New, Aldenham House, Herts, the residence of Lord Aldenham*, 12 January 1901, pp. 48–53.

Country Homes; Garden Old & New, Aldenham House – II, Herts, the residence of Lord Aldenham, 19 January 1901, pp. 80–5.

Ashwell Bury: *Ashwell Bury, Hertfordshire, The home of Mrs. Wolverley Fordham*, vol. ci, 2 May 1947, pp. 810–13.

Balls Park: vol xxxi, 6 January 1912, p. 578.

Felden Orchard, Boxmoor: Randal Phillips, R., *The Lesser Country Houses of To-Day; Felden Orchard, Felden, Boxmoor, Herts, designed by Messrs. Forsyth & Maule*, 25 August 1923, pp. 263–4.

Knebworth House: vol. xix, p. 486, vol cxlix, p. 68 and vol. clxxvii, pp. 244, 302, 374.

Lockleys: Avray Tipping, H., *Lockleys, Hertfordshire*, vol. xlviii, 10 July 1920, pp. 48–51.

New Place, Welwyn: *The Lesser Country Houses of To-Day: New Place, Welwyn, Herts, designed by Mr Philip Webb*, 23 July 1910, pp. 7–9.

North Mymms: vol. lxxxiv, p. 323; and vol. xcv, 30 June 1944, p. 1130.

Three Fields, Boxmoor: Randal Phillips, R., *The Lesser Country Houses of To-Day; Three Fields, Boxmoor, Herts, additions and alterations by Messrs. Forsyth & Maule*, 20 October 1923, pp. 539–40.

Gardeners' Chronicle:

North Mymms: vol. XXVIII, 3rd series (1900), p. 229.

Presdales: vol. II (1902).

The Studio:

The Kraal: *Recent Designs for Domestic Architecture*, vol. xxxiii, issue 140 (November 1904), p. 128.

Recent Designs for Domestic Architecture, vol. xlvii, issue 106 (July 1909), p. 45.

Web sources

First Garden City Museum, <http://www.gardencitymuseum.org/exhibtions/cheap_cottages_exhibition>.

Kingsford, P., *A Modern History of Brookmans Park 1700–1950*, <www.brookmans.com.history/kingsford/chfour/shtml>.

Voysey, C.F.A., <http://www.countrylife.co.uk/culture/article/461887/Great-British-Architects-C-F-A-Voysey-1857-1941-.html>, accessed 13 September 2011

CHAPTER SEVEN

Planting the gardens:
The nursery trade
in Hertfordshire

Elizabeth Waugh

Much is written of the design of great gardens and the evolution of garden style, of garden designers and the ambitious owners who commissioned their work. Far less is recorded about the suppliers of planting materials – those who produced the quantities of trees, shrubs and flowers required to flesh out the design, who took the tender plants discovered in faraway places and developed the conditions they required to flourish, who experimented with the technology needed to preserve and exploit them, and who themselves came eventually to develop new varieties. Nurseries do not figure large in garden history, yet their contributions are a significant part of the whole. Though businessmen working in commercial enterprises, for the great nurserymen the profit motive seems subordinate to the excitement of discovery, the scholarship of plant lineage, the beauty of form and colour, the stimulating and satisfying of garden fashions.

Over time from beginnings such as 'nursery' areas fostering young and special plants within great gardens, nurseries developed into independent businesses, some of which were great commercial empires. Head gardeners with all their unique skills became directors of nursery firms separate from the gardens they were employed in. In Hertfordshire the history of notable nurseries and the great gardens they serviced can be followed over the centuries from the early period of the Tradescants to the present day. However, attempts to follow this connection are frustrated by a lack of business records either preserved by the nurseries or held with the accounts of households they serviced. Listings of plant materials and who grew them, who ordered them, their cost, how they were used in or influenced garden designs and so on are scarce, as from year to year such papers were not considered interesting or essential enough to preserve, just as successive generations in the nurseries themselves faced with volumes of paper accounts found it best to dispose of them. However, it is possible, from the few catalogues and household accounts and the like that do survive, to try to sketch a larger picture of the general process.

A discussion of the planting of gardens in Hertfordshire offers insights for a view of the evolution of the nursery trade in England from the sixteenth to the twentieth centuries. Although the British Isles, scraped by glaciers and cut off from larger land masses by sea, have relatively limited native flora, the temperate climate proved hospitable to many new introductions and skilled gardeners improved their status by being able to find methods of providing what was needed to keep tender introductions safe. A focus on a few individual gardeners and nurserymen of Hertfordshire from consecutive periods models the trends in what was available to be purchased to stock the show gardens and how and where such stocks were held.

As the world had opened out to British explorers, the sixteenth- and seventeenth-century enthusiasm for collecting rare, new and exotic plants, and for bringing them home to adorn competing gardens and enhance prestige, was manifested by the Cecil family at Hatfield House as its famous gardens were established. John Tradescant the Elder came to Hatfield in 1610 to work as a head gardener but spent much of his time travelling, sent by his employer Lord Salisbury to follow up connections that must have been established earlier in his life. He collected new plants to fill the designs being developed by Lord Salisbury with the help of his gardeners and directed the culture and acclimatising of this new flora. Tradescant became a nurseryman – although not selling his plants and so not running a plant business – when he opened his own showground for the plants he had collected for himself and built on by exchanges with other gardeners at home and abroad, in London. That the grounds were in Lambeth rather than in the country areas where Tradescant had worked indicates the importance of London as the centre of cultivated taste and fashion in plants as in all things. London's dominance as the centre of the nursery trade continued until the late eighteenth century when nurseries began to appear in the provinces and gain prominence as transport became easier and London's once sparsely inhabited land areas gave way to housing.

Moses Cook in the later seventeenth century worked with three partners to open an early, very successful commercial nursery in Brompton Park, London, although he too had established his reputation and personal wealth in Hertfordshire, working for the Capel family as head gardener at Hadham Hall and later at Cassiobury. Like other nurserymen to follow, Cook wrote a book, well received in his time, which must have helped enable him to have the authority to commend plants and methods of planting to customers later on. He and his partners struggled with the identification and naming of plants, a necessity for nurserymen which continued to be problematic for the following generations.

William Malcolm – proprietor of a famous eighteenth-century London nursery, Malcolm's of Kennington – traded in Hertfordshire, as references to buying Malcolm's plants in some of the preserved accounts testify. Wealthy estate owners of the time in Hertfordshire continued to look to high-class London nurseries for a supply of the best plants, while relying on local suppliers for vegetable seeds and more ordinary garden needs. Since Hertfordshire estate owners had continuing London connections, such as houses or work in the city, it was not too distant to look there for bulky plant materials and the roads sufficed for their transportation. In a rare surviving plant catalogue, Malcolm leads the way in tying his plant names to the new Linnaean system, enabling firmer identification. The grandiose frontispiece to this catalogue depicts in allegorical form all that important nurseries of the time sought to offer: a wide range of plants and trees from around the known world, a scientific knowledge of plant requirements, skilled rare plant culture through engineering of special shelters and growing areas, and the tools and materials to carry out cultivation.

By the nineteenth century, at the heyday of the Hertfordshire nursery of Thomas Rivers and sons of Sawbridgeworth, many such commercial enterprises had opened in the provinces supplying locally and, if their reputation warranted, much further away too. The railway age had begun and efficient wide-ranging transport was easier. The local developing middle classes started to become customers and their needs were met not only by the supply of plants but through books, in Rivers' case a continuing supply of texts to help in the cultivation of plants such as roses (much in demand at the time), fruit varieties for glasshouse orchards and more. By this time, although the collecting of unusual species continued, if no longer at such a pace as for earlier nurserymen, plantsmen did not hesitate to experiment in order to develop new varieties – to pollinate for vigour, taste and timeliness of production of fruit, for example – despite the restrictions of established faith. Darwin was using these nurserymen's findings to support new theories of development. The established order of creation, which might be sought but not tampered with, was being questioned.

In the twentieth century, after the World Wars had brought about great social changes, many of the family-owned traditional nurseries declined and were closed. The loss of the great estates as customers, the increase in labour costs and the dispersal of the newly mobile local working population were factors in their decline. The spread of land required for growing on young plants disappeared under new housing. New kinds of nurseries grew up to supply the still voracious appetite for gardening; garden centres with their impersonal serve-yourself attitudes, stocked with plants grown elsewhere, became successful. Other models were council nurseries. Digswell Nursery in Welwyn Garden City is an interesting example of a nursery that was established to supply the needs of a new town. Central to the town design were ideas of planting, and a steady supply of plant materials of different kinds was required as well as the manpower to produce and set out what was grown. Digswell Nursery supplied that need through the period of the corporation and later as the council nursery.

What follows is a closer look at some notable nursery figures and their businesses and, as far as possible given the scarcity of good records, at the gardens they worked in.

John Tradescant at Hatfield House: Collector of exotic plants

John Tradescant the Elder is one of the great gardening names of the sixteenth and early seventeenth centuries. His reputation was established at Hatfield House in Hertfordshire where his activities can be traced through household accounts still preserved.[1] His achievements are an early example of what came to be foundation skills for later commercial nurserymen. His early development of gardening expertise resulted in his becoming a head gardener working for a noble and influential patron, initially at Hatfield. In addition to his accomplishments within the grand garden in planting and design, he was sent travelling to discover and bring back exotics. Having been sought out to work in other notable gardens, he amassed enough of a personal fortune and a great enough collection of his own plants to set up his own nursery garden in London next to his home in Lambeth. The garden of Tradescant's Ark, as his house where he displayed the odd objects he had picked up on his travels was known, was a showground. It was also a place in which to experiment with unfamiliar or delicate plants and to establish suitable conditions for their propagation, enabling him to exchange plants with some of the great gardeners in England and abroad of his time. His collections and his trade he passed on to his son who worked with him and carried on the enterprise. Tradescant the Elder's nursery was not a commercial one; that is, he did not propagate to sell.[2] Other aspects of his nursery – as a place to collect the new from every corner of the world as it became accessible to the British traveller, and as a showground for

Figure 7.1 John Tradescant depicted on a carved newel post at Hatfield House. REPRODUCED BY KIND PERMISSION OF HERITAGE HOUSE GROUPS AND THE MARQUESS OF SALISBURY/ HATFIELD HOUSE.

rare plants where gardeners could come to learn and yearn for new stock – were characteristic of later commercial enterprises.

Hatfield was then the first show garden to demonstrate John Tradescant's skills for searching out and nurturing prize specimens and using them in the garden designs of the day. Hatfield House established his reputation. He worked there with other notable gardeners and his responsibilities were to plant out the designs rather than to create new patterns (Figure 7.1). He used labouring gardeners to carry out his directions and supervised often from afar during his collecting trips. Although he had home quarters in Hatfield, he seems from the accounts to have been often away and to have had the freedom to collect for himself and accumulate exotics, both plants and the rarities that stocked his own eventual home in Lambeth. He would have specified conditions for fostering rare plants in a nursery area at Hatfield, conditions that would be maintained while he was absent.

The detailed plant lists in the accounts for the Hatfield House gardens – plants initially paid for by Tradescant himself and then refunded, it seems, when his bills were settled – give a picture of Tradescant's impact on the gardens' appearance. The early layout of the gardens had reached the stage in 1610 for Tradescant to be sent to Europe to begin purchasing from his contacts planting material in sufficient quantity to make an impact. Many of his purchases were fruit stock: vines to add to others already given to Hatfield to lay out what was to become a renowned vineyard; many cultivars of fruit trees such as cherries, quinces, medlar, apples, pears and apricots to set beside a brick wall – a wall demanded by Tradescant as the accounts testify – or in the orchard or perhaps they were destined for ornamental walkways underplanted with flowers, offering guests the opportunity to pluck ripe fruit – as noted by Francis Bacon in 1625 in his essay 'Of Gardens'. In Haarlem he bought 800 tulip bulbs as well as Provence roses and anemones, and in Brussels he purchased items such as walnuts, peaches and Hepatica. From Paris came plums, pomegranates and figs, and contact with the famous Robin family of gardeners is noted.[3] Tradescant's finds were laid at Hatfield into the rectilinear and compartmentalised designs fashionable at the time, the planting enhancing the planned spaces.

In the 1620s his own garden in Lambeth, spacious enough in what was then still a market garden area of the city, was laid out in much the same way. In 1634 he made a list of the plants in his collection,

Figure 7.2 *Tradescantia virginiana* (Virginia spiderwort) was given before 1629 to John Tradescant by one of his contacts returning to England after an expedition to Virginia. Linnaeus honoured Tradescant in naming this plant.

which is now preserved in the Magdalen College Library. The plants on the list must include those he collected for himself on all his voyages for his patrons as well as those exchanged or brought to him by others from England and abroad (Figure 7.2). These formed a rare collection available to be seen by those who visited him. In addition to ornamental plants, a great Tradescant interest was fruit varieties and he tried to obtain all that he could as the large number of fruit cultivars in his plant list shows.[4]

Tradescant had, in all, only four years at Hatfield House – from 1610 to 1614 – before moving on, and his work represents only one stage in the long history of the Hatfield gardens. However, he contributed to the realisation of the original design and thus to the estate's continuing fame.

Moses Cook at Cassiobury, head gardener and nursery proprietor
More than sixty years after Tradescant's time at Hatfield House, Moses Cook – another head gardener to an influential owner of great estates,

the Earl of Essex – in 1681 founded with his three partners one of the earliest, most extensive and most renowned of the great London nurseries: Brompton Park. This nursery, established in South Kensington where the museums now stand, was not only a show place for fine and exotic plants, as Tradescant's nursery had been earlier in the century, but was a commercial nursery, selling plants in great numbers. It is thought to have stocked as many as ten million by 1705, and the site may have eventually extended to as much as one hundred acres of ground.[5]

Cook's reputation, owing to his position in the two grand gardens of the Essex family, Hadham Hall near Bishop's Stortford and Cassiobury near Watford, was enhanced by his book, *The Manner of Raising, Ordering and Improving Forest Trees*, published in 1676. His ideas and examples, often taken from the gardens he was working in, were set out as a book of rules gathered at the request of Sir Arthur Capell, employer and patron. Like that of his three partners at Brompton Park, his reputation formed the basis for a profitable business.

Although the estates he gardened were in Hertfordshire, Cook's nursery was established in London, still in the seventeenth century unquestionably the centre for new developments. Not only did the owners of large country estates in nearby counties often have homes in London, enabling the viewing of plants there, where the newest, most exotic and fashionable were available, but the owners' regular travel made transport of materials – whether from the town or the country – unremarkable, simply part of how an estate stocked its gardens. Roads were the means of transport in this age before trains and canals and served that purpose. Rivers, too, were used as transport routes, although slow and, before canalisation, tortuous.

That Cook writes a book is testimony to his own level of education, which extended also, it was said, to mathematics which proved useful for parterres and other exact figures in garden design. John Tradescant the Elder had not this facility for writing but book production after Cook is a common habit of notable gardeners. It is a platform for circulating ideas and publicity for the writer-gardener's pre-eminence, which leads, for nurserymen, to increased renown and profit. At the back of Cook's book are found some designs for forming figures with tree-lined avenues and groups of planting creating vistas (Figure 7.3). His skill at moving and setting out the trees for such vistas is also recorded. 'In November 1672, I had the trees at Hadham Hall nursery taken up as carefully as I

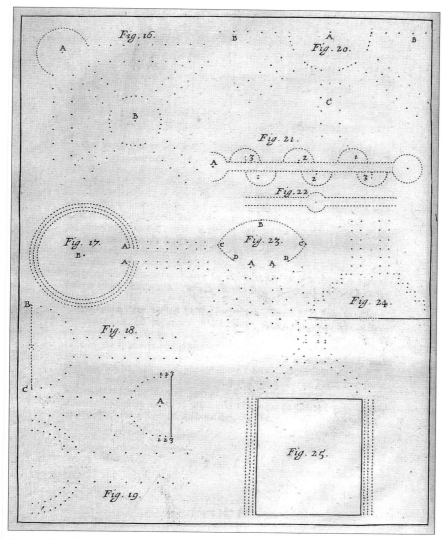

Figure 7.3 Diagrams for planting in Moses Cook, *The Manner of Raising, Ordering and Improving Forest Trees* (2nd edn, 1679). Note Figure 19 to the left and its prefiguring of later avenues.

could, with good help, and carried them to Cassiobury, the place of their new abode, four rows of trees, 296, and of these I lost not one.'[6]

Having come for a visit at the invitation of the Earl of Essex, John Evelyn writing in his diary on 18 April 1680 describes the gardens at Cassiobury (Figure 7.4). He finds them very fine, with the Earl having been 'industrious' in making his home a place of 'Walkes, Ponds, & other

Figure 7.4 Engraving of Cassiobury by J. Kip and L. Knyff in *Britannia illustrata*, 1707. WATF/58. REPRODUCED BY KIND PERMISSION OF HALS.

rural Elegancies' and remarking on the tree-lined walks: 'very handsome avenues: There is a pretty Oval at the end of a fair Walke, set about with treble rows of Spanish firr-trees'. All in all the look of the place is attributed to Moses Cook – 'skillful … Artist', versed in Mathematics and grower of choice fruits.[7] The two men thought well of one another's knowledge, Evelyn in *Silva* of 1664 referring to Cook five or six times and Cook in his book of 1676 referring to Evelyn. Both were concerned to promote the planting of forest trees and to encourage noblemen to set out a variety; both were concerned for the loss of trees over time especially during the Commonwealth period when the felling of timber widely occurred, so that Charles II, too, restored to the throne, wished to remedy the loss.[8] The designs for avenues and vistas placed at the end of Cook's book show perhaps the French influence in the taste for the long views fashionable at the time; in this case Cook lines them, as described, with trees to make an English park-like version. This taste for trees making parks of avenues survives in town-planning schemes, as the wide avenues of Welwyn Garden City, to be discussed later, demonstrate.

In 1681 Moses Cook joined three other famous gardeners – Roger Looker, gardener to Charles II's queen at Somerset House; John Field; and George London, who had been trained by the famous royal gardener John Rose – to found Brompton Park Nursery. This set of gardeners offered knowledge and advice on garden design and practical skills in rearing exotic plants and trees. The nursery could send teams to carry work out and could then stock the gardens, even those grand gardens requiring thousands of specimens, with the plants they raised. The four also set themselves to regularise the naming of varieties – clearly a particular problem for the expanding nursery trade – especially of fruit trees. Fruit continued to be, as it had been for Tradescant, a particular interest and the sourcing of new kinds was high on the list for plant collectors. Cook retired from the nursery in 1689 and went to live in Little Hadham in Hertfordshire as a country gentleman. The nursery continued in business until the site was acquired in 1851 for the building of the South Kensington museums.[9]

Malcolm's Nursery of Kennington – vendor of scientific knowledge and technology

Although Brompton Park continued to flourish, such was the appetite for fine planting that no one nursery, however vast, could satisfy the

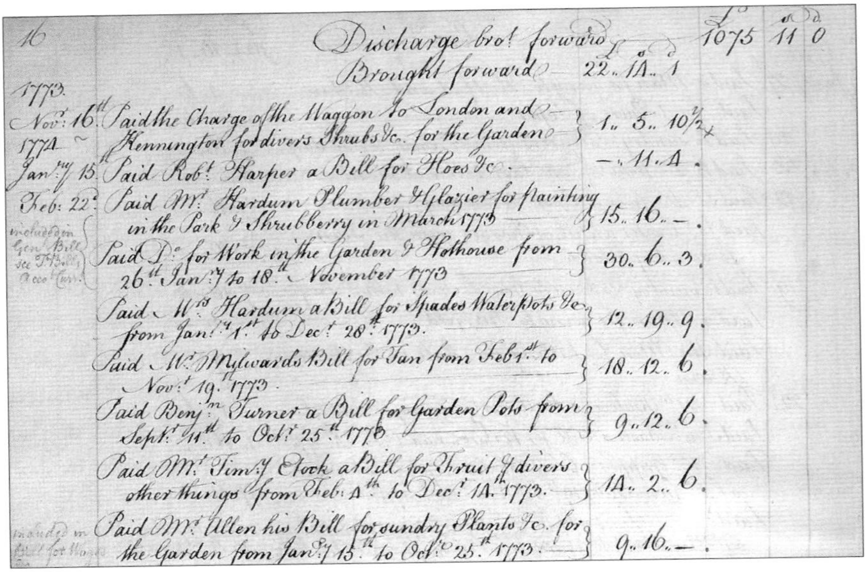
16 Discharge brot forward £ s d 1075 11 0
Brought forward 22.. 14.. 1
1773
Novr: 16th Paid the Charge of the Waggon to London and Kennington for divers Shrubs &c. for the Garden } 1.. 5.. 10½
1774 Jany 15 Paid Robt Harper a Bill for Hoes &c. — .. 11.. 4
Feb: 22 Paid Mr Hardum Plumber & Glazier for painting in the Park & Shrubberry in March 1773 } 15.. 16.. —
Paid Do for Work in the Garden & Hothouse from 26th Jany to 18th November 1773 } 30.. 6.. 3
Paid Mrs Hardum a Bill for Spades Waterpots &c from Jany 1st to Decr 28th 1773 } 12.. 19.. 9
Paid Mr Mylwards Bill for Tan from Feb 1st to Novr 19th 1773 } 18.. 12.. 6
Paid Benjn Turner a Bill for Garden Pots from Septr 11th to Octr 25th 1773 } 9.. 12.. 6
Paid Mr Timy Clark a Bill for Fruit & divers other things from Feb 4th to Decr 14th 1773 } 14.. 2.. 6
Paid Mr Allen his Bill for sundry Plants &c. for the Garden from Jany 15th to Octr 25th 1773 } 9.. 16.. —

Figure 7.5 Brocket Hall account book 1772–3, p.16. The reference to sending a wagon to Kennington for plants indicates a trip to Malcolm's Nursery. REPRODUCED BY KIND PERMISSION OF HALS.

demand. William Malcolm's was another great eighteenth-century London nursery. According to tax records, it was established in Kennington from 1757.[10] There is documentary evidence for its having supplied the great gardens of Hertfordshire, in particular Woodhall Park at Watton-at-Stone and Brocket Hall. At Brocket, some accounts have survived (Figure 7.5), neatly transcribed in great bound volumes for year-by-year expenses, organised clearly under separate headings. There we see that Malcolm's supplied plants and that a 'waggon' was sent to Kennington for them.[11]

This trade between London and Hertfordshire demonstrates that the road connections – existing before the railway age and before the canal system was operational – between areas in Hertfordshire and London were good enough; that wagons were sent as a matter of course; that the expense of travel not considered too great; that the London nurseries were still the suppliers for important gardens; and that there were as yet few provincial nurseries of note for ornamental planting, despite vegetable seeds and produce being acquired locally. Malcolm's had a great reputation and the best gardens would have sought the best plants for their show areas.

Figure 7.6 Frontispiece to William Malcolm's *Catalogue of Hot-House and Green-House Plants, Fruit and Forest Trees, Perenniel and Annual Flower Seeds, Garden Mats and Tools* (London, 1771). REPRODUCED BY KIND PERMISSION OF RHS LINDLEY LIBRARY.

One of the Malcolm's catalogues, itself one of the first plant catalogues to be produced and one of the few to be preserved, is held at the Lindley Library. Issued in 1771, Malcolm's comprehensive list is headed 'A Catalogue of Hot-House and Green-House Plants, Fruit and Forest Trees, Perenniel and Annual Flower Seeds, Garden Mats and Tools'. Its frontispiece (Figure 7.6), crowded with symbolic images, offers pictorially what the nursery can supply to its clients, including those in Hertfordshire.[12] It was drawn by a master of botanical art, J.F. Miller, whose work *An Illustration of the Sexual System of Linnaeus* appeared in parts between 1770 and 1777.[13]

After more than two centuries of collecting and nurturing plants from Europe, the Near East and America, and through propagating native plants, there was available to nurseries a multitude of species and many varieties of each. It was evident that there was no clear naming procedure, particularly as there was no final arbiter for plant names. Moreover, people could and did invent names freely through ignorance or by attempting to claim novelty. The confusion of names was widely recognised and those attempting to make plant lists had to come to terms with the problem. Moses Cook and his partners at the Brompton Park Nursery were known to have tackled the problem of identifying fruit varieties, which suggests the need for nurseries in particular to lead the way for the buyers. Botanical names were already in Latin but in addition to being long and uncertain there were disagreements in how to apply them.

Linnaeus's *Systema naturae* appeared in 1735, describing his new system for classifying plants as well as the rest of the natural world. Linnaeus proposed a binomial system of Latin names for all plants – genus and species – in which the characteristics of the sexual parts of the flower enabled classification by genus and species description was based on examination of other plant structures such as leaves.

Malcolm's preface, 'To the Reader', from the 1771 catalogue, describes the problems and his solution:

> Having presumed in the following catalogue to deviate from the order generally pursued in publications of this nature, I thought it necessary to prefix a few words in explanation of the method which I have chosen ... [to combat] that evil so often complained of, the sending of plants under wrong names and the selling one plant for another ... the collecting of plants and seeds from the

various parts of the globe, and propagating them, has been my favourite study; in the execution of which, I have spared neither expence, labour or attention ... as some system must necessarily be adopted, I know of none, in my opinion, in any degree equal to the Linnaean being by far the most correct and most universally received ... His system then standing so fair with me, no wonder I make choice of his genera and specifick names, to which I have annexed the most intelligent and best known English ones of those that have any...[14]

Miller's frontispiece depicts Britannia being offered plants from America, Africa and Turkey and accepting them with the support of a pile of books, Linnaeus's on top, and with the help of science and technology represented by women diademed with compasses and by glasshouses of various kinds, a thermometer suggesting the warmth required for tender species.[15] Malcolm carefully divides his catalogue into sections advertising plants according to the nurture required: 'they may be justly reduced under three distinct heads; the hot-house; the green-house; and the open air'.

Malcolm's catalogue, powerfully persuasive, offers knowledge and technology to buyers, as well as plants. For gardeners and nurserymen, the problems of plant identification and the search for technologies to nurture exotic species nevertheless continued into the nineteenth century.

Rivers of Sawbridgeworth: The rise of provincial nurseries

By 1842, when the elegantly headed and beautifully inscribed bill from Rivers for special roses was presented to Mrs Delme Radcliffe at Hitchin Priory (Figure 7.7), the nursery trade in England had evolved in various significant ways. Whereas there had been notable nurseries run by Hertfordshire gardeners sited in London, as had been the case with the Tradescant garden and Moses Cook at Brompton Park, or a London nurseryman trading to Hertfordshire gardens, as had been the case for Malcolm's of Kennington, by the nineteenth century there were prominent nurseries established in the county of Hertfordshire, trading widely with Hertfordshire gardeners and others beyond.[16]

This development was both important and widespread. Whereas the showground gardens and later trade establishments had, as the previous discussion indicates, been concentrated in London during the seventeenth and eighteenth centuries, by the end of that period and during the nineteenth century nursery empires were established in the

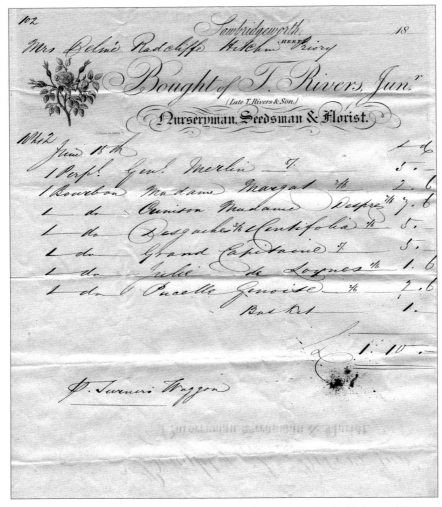

Figure 7.7 Bill from Thomas Rivers Nursery, to Mrs Delme Radcliffe, Hitchin Priory, 20 May 1842. REPRODUCED BY KIND PERMISSION OF HALS.

provinces.[17] There were a number of reasons for this change. London was continuing to grow very quickly and the large areas of rural countryside adjoining the city that had been the centre of the market garden trade where nurseries grew up were being encroached on for building. The long-established famous early nurseries such as Brompton Park were declining partly because the later generations of partners were less gifted, partly because the land could be more profitable if sold for building rather than used for growing stock.

The transport systems were continuing to develop and with them the mobility of those who could work in the city and live at least some of the time in the country, whether the grand gentry or the growing middle class, whose gardens also needed supplies of plants. As can be seen from the letter head of another Hitchin Priory Rivers bill, there is the inscribed notation 'equidistant from the Harlow & Sawbridgeworth stations on the Northern and Eastern Railway' (one of the two main lines which became the Great Eastern Railway).[18] By 1842 the railway age had arrived and instead of having to send a horse-drawn wagon to Kennington by road for shrubs, the Priory could send its wagon to the local railway station for pick-up, just as Rivers could send its delivery wagon down to the Sawbridgeworth railway station to send plants on a line that set down at a station conveniently close to its patrons. This efficient railway system was both a quicker and less expensive form of transport for both nursery and client. Although the canal network was also in place and might have formed part of the journey to and from London for plant materials, it was, as a flexible means of transporting stock in all directions, less useful than railways and slower – a significant factor in transporting fragile plant materials.

The Rivers Nursery had been founded in 1735 probably as a local supplier of common plant requirements. However, it came to prominence in the nineteenth century as it began to specialise first in fine and unusual roses and, later in the century, in fruit of all kinds but notably plums, pears and cherries. With both roses and fruit, the three best-known Thomas Rivers (the name passed from father to son) that succeeded one another in this family firm were able to find new varieties from trips to the Continent or from careful selection and propagation on their own land. The firm became highly successful and grew very large, both in terms of land – up to one hundred acres by the end of the century – and in terms of local people employed. It became second only to the Sawbridgeworth malting industry as employer and a local institution known to provide reliable work. The family moved into the gentry class, as the entry in the *National Trades Directory* of 1839 testifies, and lived as prosperous and well-respected members of the community, supporting the local church and the poor. In these respects Rivers was representative of provincial nurseries, of which there were increasing numbers.[19]

Under the direction of the outstanding Thomas Rivers (1798–1877), the nursery achieved its greatest prominence. Like others of the great gardeners who preceded him, Thomas Rivers had an enquiring mind, a gift for working with others in considering horticultural questions, a ready pen and the success in business that allowed him time to think. Among his achievements was the culture of a number of new varieties of roses and fruit, including the Early Rivers plum, which he developed and which sold as many as up to 18,000 per year at the height of its popularity. He conducted a correspondence with Charles Darwin, which added to the data in relation to Darwin's formulation of theories, as well as with many other important figures in the horticultural establishment. He also wrote several readily readable books that were reprinted in large numbers year after year, including one on glasshouse design. Glasshouses had become more affordable as the glass tax was abolished in 1845 and while large glasshouses continued to be status symbols for the upper classes, smaller configurations were now possible for less wealthy gardeners. The popularity of Rivers' books and their phrasing shows them to have been written for the middle-class gardener as well as for the head gardener of large estates. The yearly Rivers Nursery catalogues, which by the end of the century were fifty pages long, were impressive lists of the multitudes of varieties available for sale. The identification problem had not disappeared and we find Thomas Rivers calling for a Pomological Society in 1854 to deal again with the troublesome issue of fruit names. *The Gardener's Chronicle* – one of the most important gardening journals of the time – had come into being in 1841 founded by Joseph Paxton and John Lindley among others. In its pages were recorded regular visits to the Sawbridgeworth 'grounds' where the *Chronicle* correspondent wandered with the proprietor looking at the new varieties and discussing the horticultural hot issues of the moment.[20]

It was a long-term thriving enterprise linked to the peace and prosperity of the Victorian age and looked set for the next hundred years. Then came the world conflicts of the first half of the twentieth century and with them the great changes to the old way of life. The decline of the great estates and of general prosperity resulting in the loss of markets, mechanisation and employment trends including the demand for higher wages, and social changes that meant the need for more housing saw the gradual loss of profitability for the business and its final collapse when the whole of the remaining Rivers Nursery land was sold in 1987. All that remains now is a five-acre community orchard where Rivers varieties are cultivated on a patch of Rivers land as yet undeveloped for other uses. It is dedicated to the ethos of preservation of the one-time multitudes of English apples and of the Hertfordshire countryside where these were cultivated. The disappearance of this great family nursery firm is similar to the fate of many other nursery empires around the country. These businesses live on in the names of plant varieties and in the memories of the aging local populations who still remember the glory days (Plate 7.1).

Rivers is a notable example of the proliferation of provincial nurseries in Hertfordshire. Bridget Howlett, describing other nurseries the Delme-Radcliffe records of the 1830s and 1840s show as suppliers, points out that Hitchin Priory was 'able to obtain almost all the plants and seeds they required from Hertfordshire nurserymen, including two nurseries in Hitchin'.[21] She cites the bills from Abraham Fells and Daniel Newton in Hitchin, from the Hertford Nursery, from A. Paul & Son in Cheshunt, Lane & Son in Berkhamsted, as well as from Rivers in Sawbridgeworth.[22] Others of the renowned nineteenth-century Hertfordshire nurseries were specialists. One such was the Orchid Nursery of Frederick Sander in St Albans, which achieved its greatest fame in the latter part of the century especially in the period 1887–94. The fashion for orchids, and Sander's part in supplying demand, is described by Harold Smith.[23] Another specialist of a somewhat later period was the Six Hills Nursery in Stevenage which sold alpine plants between 1907 and 1954. Clarence Elliott, the proprietor, worked as an apprentice at Rivers Nursery – a common practice as Rivers was listed by the Ministry of Agriculture as a suitable firm in which to gain grounding in sound horticultural practice.[24] These Hertfordshire businesses were family firms that thrived for a period and then lost competitive ground and were sold by later generations.

Digswell of Welwyn Garden City – A nursery for a new town

Drive into Welwyn Garden City (Figure 7.8) on a sunny afternoon in midsummer – passing down broad avenues with spacious green centres laid out with a variety of well-placed flourishing trees and areas of seasonal well-tended bedding plants – and the many-hued greens, the shade and the calm are striking. Here is successful town design and good landscaping, emphasising the layout of the municipal buildings and town centre amenities. The town centre feels like a park.

The partnership of Welwyn Garden City and Digswell Nursery is a twentieth-century version of the planting work that has taken place in

Figure 7.8 Welwyn Garden City, an aerial view down Parkway, *c.*1950, showing the design of the avenues of trees, reminiscent of designs of Moses Cook. REPRODUCED BY KIND PERMISSION OF HALS FROM THE PICTURE CATALOGUE.

great Hertfordshire gardens over the centuries. In this case the idealistic and imaginative scheme of Ebenezer Howard for a planned new 'garden' community, as realised in the designs of the architect Louis de Soissons, from the start proposed landscaping and planting as an integral part of what might be viewed as one estate with its varied gardens in much the same way as is Hatfield House nearby. The distinct areas of housing, many open in front without hedges to the street, were sections of the whole planting project. The landscaping was essential, as in a great garden, for providing an aesthetic display, healthful avenues and walks, a sense of vista in terms of height – the lombardy poplars and other fastigiate trees reaching up in place of palace heights or chapel spires – and distance, providing delight for the eye, the ready paths to the countryside and the retreats to a planned wildness of woods or 'wilderness'. The nursery, based on Digswell Hill, was brought into being to supply the planting needs of the new town.

The Garden Cities and Town Planning Association in 1919 defined the concept thus: 'A Garden City is a town designed for healthy living and industry; of a size that makes possible a full measure of social life, but not larger; surrounded by a rural belt; the whole of the land being in public ownership, or held in trust for the community.' A later residents' association description is of 'the city in a garden' and 'a city of gardens'.[25] Nowadays, the philosophical and social concept of this Garden City can be perceived more casually as having resulted in a pleasant environment with striking botanical features, particularly trees.

The sense of a whole is striking here. That the town was designed conceptually to be one entity makes it easier to see the landscape design and planting as one, although individual areas have been and continue to be built and planted over time, as took place also in grand estates. In the context of this present study of nurseries and garden planting, what can also be seen is that the mix of trees owes as much to historic botanical adventuring abroad and to plant nurture by generations of nurserymen, as to the preservation of existing grown-up hedgerow trees already in situ and further use of native species. 'Maple, sycamore, red and white flowering horse chestnuts, ash, silver birch and the white-flowered acacia … liquidambar, hazel, various thorns, laburnums, almonds … were planted in groups and rows to give variety of habit of growth, foliage shape and colour, and flowerings at different times of year.'[26]

The history of Digswell Nursery is entwined with its partnership with Welwyn Garden City. In the 1920s, as the planning and early construction of Welwyn Garden City began to take place, Digswell Nursery was established to supply planting material for the new designs and to carry out the work of setting out and maintaining the elements of the landscape.

> Digswell Nursery planted trees and shrubs, hedges and beds, laid out verges and maintained all the public open spaces. A good variety of plants from the nursery was also available for sale to residents busy creating their own gardens out of rubble-strewn ground overlaying old arable land, meadows, coppice woodland and the other earlier uses of their land.[27]

According to a long-term Welwyn Garden City resident the early gardens were exceptionally large, as much as 140 feet, and in the original plan every house was to have an apple tree.[28]

Digswell Nursery was therefore essential to the creation of the town and the town's garden-like aspect. It was established on about fourteen acres of town-owned land off the Great North road, variable in character from clay to gravel and therefore with soil suitable to a variety of growing needs. That site is where it continues to operate today. Digswell Nursery has had a considerable life span of nearly eighty years to this point and during that time has had a variable organisation, although the close relationship with the town and its needs has continued.

No full history of the nursery and its personnel has yet been produced but some of the story is available from different sources. Various planning booklets, for example, describe the landscaping concepts and the important impact planting has always had on the town's design; control of detailed aspects of landscaping and such features as trees and hedgerows was implemented by the Garden City Company at first, then by the Commission for New Towns and later the council from 1978.[29] To this end, the operation of nursery gardens and a tree nursery – that is, Digswell Nursery – has been essential for quality of life not only in the central and residential areas but also in industrial and commercial areas.[30] After the New Town Act of 1946, central government required that the private Garden City Company hand over its responsibilities to the Welwyn Garden City Development Corporation, in 1948. Although Digswell Nursery was initially managed by the Howardsgate Trust, set up after the handover, the necessity for the nursery to operate with the landscaping team of the Corporation meant that it was later transferred to the council.[31]

Digswell Nursery was then the council nursery. However, by the 1990s the nursery site itself had become neglected and photographs show it as disordered and almost derelict. The decline may have been due to outsourcing of the nursery functions by the council in an effort to save money over the years, and other factors, but something had to change and the relationships and identity of the nursery had to be reformed. In 1995 a dramatic reorganisation took place. The worldwide Catholic charity Saint John of God Care Services took over from the council as owner of the nursery. This charity 'provides a wide range of health, social care and pastoral services that support in excess of 1000 people in over 45 projects throughout Great Britain'. The vulnerable and disadvantaged adults who are trained to work in horticulture at the nursery now are the team who grow the summer and winter bedding plants that Welwyn

Garden City continues to contract for.[32] The nursery site, with a different identity, has come back to life; it is adding new features such as a coffee shop and play area and welcomes the community in to buy a limited selection of garden plants. It is intending to add the City and Guilds qualification scheme to its training practices.[33]

In the meanwhile, according to the Digswell Nursery website, the nursery continues to meet the city's bedding plant requirements, supplying annually 150,000 plants to the council to be set in place by Serco, the contractors now responsible for the planting and maintenance of the town's landscape.[34] A further point is made that the nursery has a modern, responsible environmental policy: chemicals are used sparingly, peat-free compost is preferred and pots and trays are recycled. The nursery's modern identity is confirmed by its website.

The historical figures and nurseries that this study has considered span five centuries of planting in Hertfordshire. The ethos of exploration and collection and the joy of discovery that led to the sciences of plant nurture and naming, and to expertise in technology as well as to the experiments, discussion and formation of theories such as those about breeding and inheritance, were always underpinned by more everyday planting purposes. From the arbours and delightful paths of Hatfield House to the vistas of Welwyn Garden City, designers and nurseries had the intention of providing a healthful as well as a pleasing outdoor environment for residents and visitors, whether grand lords or the common man. Plants were to provide medicine, food and beauty for the healthy body and the contented psyche. To meet these requirements, nurseries required capital and had to make a profit. Initially head gardeners used their accumulated stock of plants retained from those raised for their patrons and their own funds to start businesses which in some cases became empires and were highly profit-making, enhancing the social status of the directors in successive family generations. In the twentieth century this model of nursery could no longer exist and more competitive private companies or local governments filled the gap. Nurseries have continued to exist on the bounty collected by historic plant hunters and on the efforts of those who carry on the work of their predecessors, investigating plant characteristics – and nowadays genetic structures – in order to diversify and nurture the countless varieties we can choose from.

Notes

1. J. Potter, *Strange Blooms: The Curious Lives and Adventures of the John Tradescants* (London, 2006) and P. Leith-Ross, *The John Tradescants: Gardeners to the Rose and Lily Queen* (London, 1984) both follow Tradescant the Elder through the accounts at Hatfield House.
2. Potter, *Strange Blooms*, pp. 11–24.
3. Leith-Ross, *The John Tradescants*, pp. 28–43.
4. Potter, *Strange Blooms*, pp. 80, 194–201.
5. J. Harvey, 'The Stocks Held by Early Nurseries', *Agricultural History Review* (1974), p. 19, <http://www.bahs.org.uk/22n1a2.pdf>, accessed 10 August 2011.
6. M. Cook, *The Manner of Raising, Ordering and Improving Forest Trees* (1676), p. 8.
7. E.S. de Beer (ed.), *The Diary of John Evelyn, Volume IV, Kalendarium, 1673–1689* (Oxford, 1955), p. 200 and note 4.
8. *Ibid.*
9. E.J. Willson, *West London Nursery Gardens* (London, 1982), pp. 9–17; J. Harvey, *Early Gardening Catalogues* (London, 1972), p. 10.
10. J. Harvey, *Early Nurserymen* (London, 1974), pp. 88, 197.
11. Brocket Hall Account Book, 1772–1773, HALS Ref 63828.
12. W. Malcolm, *A Catalogue of Hot-House and Green-House Plants, Fruit and Forest Trees, Perenniel and Annual Flower Seeds, Garden Mats and Tools* (London, 1771).
13. G. Saunders, *Picturing Plants: An Analytical History of Botanical Illustration* (London, 2009), p. 92.
14. Malcolm, *A Catalogue*.
15. Discussion with Frances Rankine, Curator Prints and Drawings Department, at the Victoria and Albert Museum, 16 June 2011.
16. Bill from Thomas Rivers Nursery to Mrs Delme Radcliffe, Hitchin Priory, 20 May 1842, HALS D/ER F281.
17. Harvey, *Early Nurserymen*, pp. 5–9.
18. Bill from Thomas Rivers Nursery to Mrs Delme Radcliffe, Hitchin Priory, 9 June 1842, HALS D/ER F281.
19. Pigot and Company, *National Trades Directory* (1839).
20. E. Waugh, *Rivers Nursery of Sawbridgeworth* (Ware, 2009), pp. 82–105.
21. B. Howlett, *Hitchin Priory Park: The History of a Landscape Park and Gardens* (Hitchin, 2004), p. 56.
22. *Ibid.*, pp. 56, 57, 61.
23. H. Smith, 'A Victorian Passion: The Role of Sander's Orchid Nursery in St. Albans', in A. Rowe (ed.), *Hertfordshire Garden History: A Miscellany* (Hatfield, 2007), pp. 155–73.
24. M. Ashby, *Six Hills Nursery, Stevenage 1907–1954* (Stevenage, 1998).
25. M. de Soissons, *Welwyn Garden City: A Town Designed for Healthy Living* (Cambridge, 1988), pp. 37, 214.
26. *Ibid.*, p. 50.
27. *Ibid.*, p. 60.
28. Discussion with Wanda Vanderhornsey, Librarian, Welwyn Garden City Central Library, 28 July 2011.
29. *Welwyn Hatfield Planning Handbook* (1985), p. 29.
30. *Welwyn Hatfield Planning Handbook* (1987/88), p. 27.
31. de Soissons, *Welwyn Garden City*, pp. 122–7.
32. Leaflet, Digswell Nurseries, published by Saint John of God Hospitaller Services.
33. Discussion with David Lingard, Horticulturalist, Digswell Nurseries, 28 July 2011.
34. <http://www.digswell.org.uk>, accessed August 2011.

Bibliography

Primary sources

Cook, M., *The Manner of Raising, Ordering and Improving Forest Trees* (1676 and 2nd edn, 1679).

De Beer, E.S. (ed.), *The Diary of John Evelyn, Volume IV, Kalendarium, 1673–1689* (Oxford, 1955).

Discussion with David Lingard, Horticulturalist, Digswell Nurseries, 28 July 2011.

Discussion with Frances Rankine, Curator Prints and Drawings Department, at the Victoria and Albert Museum, 16 June 2011.

Discussion with Wanda Vanderhornsey, Librarian, Welwyn Garden City Central Library, 28 July 2011.

Leaflet, Digswell Nurseries, published by Saint John of God Hospitaller Services.

Malcolm, W., *A Catalogue of Hot-House and Green-House Plants, Fruit and Forest Trees, Perenniel and Annual Flower Seeds, Garden Mats and Tools* (London, 1771).

Welwyn Hatfield Planning Handbook (1985; 1987/88).

Hertfordshire Archives and Local Studies (HALS):
63828, Brocket Hall Account Book, 1772–1773.
D/ER F281, Thomas Rivers Nursery, Bills to Mrs Delme Radcliffe, Hitchin Priory, 20 May 1842, 18 June 1842.

Secondary sources

Ashby, M., *Six Hills Nursery, Stevenage 1907–1954* (Stevenage, 1998).

Harvey, J., *Early Gardening Catalogues* (London, 1972).

Harvey, J., *Early Nurserymen* (London, 1974).

Howlett, B., *Hitchin Priory Park: The History of a Landscape Park and Gardens* (Hitchin, 2004).

Leith-Ross, P., *The John Tradescants: Gardeners to the Rose and Lily Queen* (London, 1984).

Pigot and Company, *National Trades Directory* (1839).

Potter, J., *Strange Blooms: The Curious Lives and Adventures of the John Tradescants* (London, 2006).

Saunders, G., *Picturing Plants: An Analytical History of Botanical Illustration* (London, 2009).

Smith, H., 'A Victorian Passion: The Role of Sander's Orchid Nursery in St. Albans', in A. Rowe, (ed.), *Hertfordshire Garden History: A Miscellany* (Hertford, 2007), pp. 155–73.

Soissons, M. de, *Welwyn Garden City: A Town Designed for Healthy Living* (Cambridge, 1988).

Waugh, E., *Rivers Nursery of Sawbridgeworth* (Ware, 2009).

Willson, E.J., *West London Nursery Gardens* (London, 1982).

Web sources

Digswell Nurseries, <http://www.digswell.org.uk>, accessed August 2011.

Harvey, J., 'The Stocks Held by Early Nurseries', *Agricultural History Review* (1974), <http://www.bahs.org.uk/22n1a2.pdf>, accessed 10 August 2011.

CHAPTER EIGHT

Salads and ornamentals: A short history of the Lea valley nursery industry[1]

Kate Banister

All the roads round London, therefore, are covered with market carts and waggons during the night, so that they may reach the markets by three, four or five o'clock, when the dealers attend.

Sir Richard Phillips, 1820[2]

Introduction

By the latter part of the eighteenth century Covent Garden had become the greatest market in England for 'herbs, fruit and flowers'.[3] Much of the produce came from the lower Lea valley (Hackney, Tottenham, Leyton, Walthamstow and Edmonton), which, with its combination of fertile soil, plentiful water and good drainage, was noted for its market gardens and plant nurseries (Figures 8.1 and 8.2). Transport to London was easy by river or by horse and cart on the road.

With the coming of the railway to Broxbourne in 1840, which made possible the delivery of coal for heating glasshouses, and the abolition of the tax on glass in 1845, the commercial glasshouse industry developed until, in the 1930s, the Lea valley contained the largest concentration of glasshouses in the world. By 1945 the so-called Sea of Glass exceeded 1,200 acres producing mostly 'salads and ornamentals'. London's insatiable need for land for industry and housing gradually drove the market gardens and nurseries further north up the valley to the areas around Waltham Cross, Cheshunt, Turnford and Broxbourne and, on the Essex side, Waltham Abbey and Nazeing. To support these nurseries

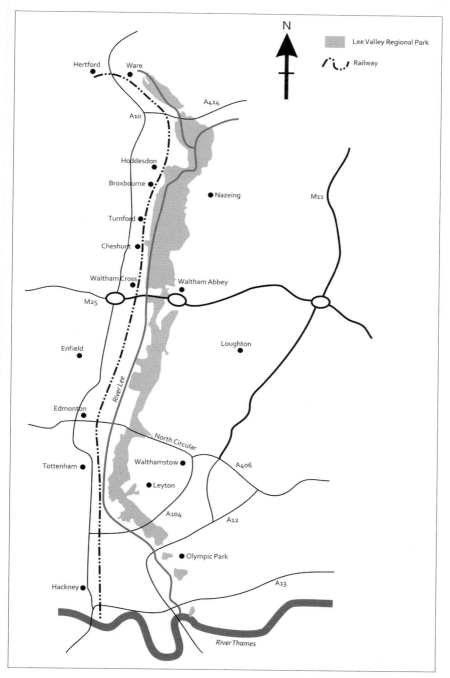

Figure 8.1 Map of Lee Valley. Based on map of Lee Valley Park Authority
<http://www.visitleevalley.org.uk>. REPRODUCED WITH KIND PERMISSION.

Figure 8.2 Light in market hall at Covent Garden, late nineteenth century. PEN AND INK DRAWING BY DIANA JONES, 2012.

various ancillary industries grew up – potteries to make the flower pots (Tuck's at Waltham Abbey and Samuel South's at Tottenham – Figures 8.3 and 8.4); firms which constructed glasshouses; specialists in the steam sterilisation of the soil; suppliers of fertilisers, twine, hosepipes and watering cans. At one time, the haulage branch of Samuel South employed nearly 100 horses for the delivery of clay pots.[4]

The area now under glass is estimated to be approximately 300 acres. But, amazingly, the output vastly exceeds that of fifty years ago thanks to advances in technology and growing skills. Today, the salad section covers cucumbers, which make up three-quarters of the crops, tomatoes, sweet peppers, lettuces and aubergines. The ornamentals include bedding plants, carnivorous plants and aquatics, the latter two reflecting the public demand for the new and unusual.

Figure 8.3 (left) Advertisement for Tuck's flower pots, 1954. REPRODUCED BY KIND PERMISSION OF EPPING FOREST DISTRICT MUSEUM.

Figure 8.4 (right) Advertisement for South's calendar for 1960. REPRODUCED BY KIND PERMISSION OF EPPING FOREST DISTRICT MUSEUM.

Adam Paul (Adam Paul & Son)

The earliest named nursery for which we have evidence (scant though it is) was probably that of Adam Paul. He came from Scotland and rented land from the Whit Hern estate in Cheshunt in 1806. Some thirty years later he bought a house in Cheshunt High Street and with his two sons traded as 'Nurserymen, Florists and Seedsmen' under the name of Adam Paul & Son. Here they grew over 1,500 varieties of rose in an area of more than 40 acres. There is evidence that in 1855 two cases of roses (304 plants) were safely delivered to Philadelphia, U.S.A.[5]

William Paul (William Paul & Son)

In 1848 William Paul (Figure 8.5), the younger son, at the age of twenty-six, published a huge work entitled *The Rose Garden*, lavishly illustrated with colour plates (Plate 8.1). Part I is an exposition of the rose in the arts, with directions for its cultivation. The chapters in Part II are devoted to special groups of roses – Damask, Provence, Moss and Gallicas. The book was very successful and went into ten editions, some of which had fewer illustrations to 'bring the work within reach of the humblest cultivator'.[6] William's reputation as a rosarian grew but his relations with

Figure 8.5 William Paul, 1822–1905. From W. Paul, *Contributions to Horticultural Literature* (Waltham Cross, 1892), frontispiece.

Figure 8.6 Advertisement from gardening journal, 1887.

his brother's family seem to have deteriorated. In 1860 William set up the Royal Nurseries in Waltham Cross, leaving his brother and nephew (both called George) to run The Old Nurseries in Cheshunt. The advertisement in Figure 8.6 carries the advice to any buyer to note carefully the Christian name of the firm. Both William and George are described elsewhere as 'Nurserymen, Seedsmen, Florists and Prize Rose Growers'.[7]

The Royal Nurseries extended eastwards from the High Street to the railway line, a scene described some years later as forming 'a wall of roses, the whole saturated with perfume from the thousand flowers grouped in bold masses' (Figure 8.7).[8] The 1861 census shows Wm. Paul & Son as employing thirty men in an area of fifty acres. William advocated growing roses in pots – a style favoured by the French – and championed standard roses: 'in growing Roses as standards the flowers are brought near to our eyes and noses, and those who … are growing old have not to bend the back or go on all fours to see and smell them'.[9] Although best known for his breeding of roses, William also grew hollyhocks, hyacinths, camellias, hollies, ivies, decorative shrubs and fruit trees. *Country Life* records that there were also extensive nurseries in Broxbourne and Loughton.[10]

In 1871 William bought Waltham House (formerly the home of the writer Anthony Trollope), a large eighteenth-century house with extensive gardens which included terraces, a lake, and a lime and elm avenue estimated to be 200 years old (Figure 8.8). William is described in the *Gardeners' Chronicle* as 'catholic in sympathies' with one exception – he did not grow orchids.[11]

Figure 8.7 Royal Nurseries, Waltham Cross, 1899. *Country Life*, 30 September 1899, p. 406. REPRODUCED WITH PERMISSION.

Figure 8.8 Waltham House, Waltham Cross, 1901. *Country Life*, 2 February 1901, p. 137.
REPRODUCED WITH PERMISSION.

Apart from his book on roses William's writing was not extensive, being mostly articles for journals, magazines and papers delivered to societies ('not a voluminous writer but ever ready to oblige'[12]). His articles covered subjects such as the cultivation of orchards, the values of clarified and unclarified sewage as manure, and trees and shrubs in large towns: 'trees purify the air, render it healthier and more suitable for human consumption'.[13] In one intriguing article he criticises what he calls 'floricultural millinery' as practised in floral shows – the elaborate tricks used to make a plant look 'other or better than it is'. Such practices included the pinning back of pansy petals, the gumming and brushing of petals of pelargoniums, the artificial packing of the petals of carnations, the building-up of dahlias and the pinning of hyacinths.[14] Apparently, one Christopher Nunn of Enfield, a barber and friseur by trade, was in great demand to dress flowers for exhibition.

William also collected books on horticulture: in his extensive library both antiquarian and contemporary books were methodically catalogued. 'From about 1840 I was in a position to see every book on gardening as it issued from the Press.'[15] After his death some of his collection was kept by his son; the rest was sold by Sotheby's.

In company with Dean Hole, William was a promoter of the first National Rose Show in 1858 and a member of the National Rose Society. He was also a Fellow of the Linnaean Society and, together with his nephew George, was one of the first sixty recipients from the Royal Horticultural Society of the Victoria Medal for Horticulture in 1897. Locally he was a supporter of many charitable institutions and was chairman of the Cheshunt Board of Health. He died in 1905, 'an honoured and veteran floriculturalist'.[16]

The business continued at the Royal Nurseries under William's son, Arthur William. After school in Bishop's Stortford he finished his education on the Continent and throughout his career maintained friendly relations with rosarians in Portugal, Spain and Russia. In 1906 he contributed a paper at an International Conference on Genetics and became known for introducing to English gardens varieties of rose raised on the French Riviera.

Following Arthur William's death in 1921, Waltham House was bought by an order of nuns and used as a convent school, and later was owned by the Eastern Enfield Cooperative Society. The nurseries continued under the name of Chaplin; William Chaplin had previously been the foreman of the nursery. But the fears expressed in *Country Life* that 'a devouring builder would seize upon estates likely to prove

Figure 8.9 George Paul, 1841–1921. *Gardeners' Chronicle*, 1921.
REPRODUCED BY KIND PERMISSION OF HAYMARKET PUBLISHING.

a profitable and commercial investment' came true, and house, gardens and nurseries disappeared forever in the 1930s.[17] However, two well-known rambler roses keep the name of Paul alive today – Paul's Scarlet and Paul's Himalayan Musk.

George Paul (Paul & Son)

The Old Nurseries in Cheshunt were run by George Paul and later his son George, who took over the nursery on his father's death in 1867. They traded as Paul & Son, and, like his uncle William, George II was a raiser, cultivator and exhibitor of roses (Figures 8.9 and 8.10). He had spent some time in Hamburg after leaving school and then worked with Charles Fisher at the Royal Nurseries in Handsworth, Sheffield, which specialised in the cultivation of hollies. The *Journal of Horticulture* for 1911 describes the 150,000 seedling briars for budding the following year, the 50,000 standard roses and the half acre of ground filled with roses in pots.[18]

Besides roses, George also supplied hollyhocks, hollies and herbaceous phloxes and won several certificates for his new rhododendron *Rhododendron cantabriense x fortunei*. Apparently £400 worth of these were delivered to Cape Town for the garden of the late Cecil Rhodes.[19] He also won thirteen certificates for *cannas,* although

Figure 8.10 *Rosa,* Goldfinch, bred in 1907 by George Paul. PHOTOGRAPH REPRODUCED BY KIND PERMISSION OF PETER BEALES ROSES.

Figure 8.11 View in Messrs Paul's Garden in Broxbourne, 1880s. WOOD ENGRAVING FROM PHOTOGRAPH © ST ALBANS MUSEUMS.

the improvement of the species was not pursued as the plant seemed not yet to appeal to public taste. The nurseries also bred and supplied fruit trees; the Cheshunt Pippin, a mid-season apple, is listed as a variety raised by George Paul in 1864.[20] Large quantities of *Aucuba japonica* were also grown, mainly to supply London costermongers who sold them on as pot plants for the winter.[21] In 1881 George established a nursery in Broxbourne for alpines (Figure 8.11).

The census for this year records that George's nursery in Cheshunt consisted of 143 acres and that he employed 98 men and 29 boys – quite a sizeable business. He helped to organise the first Temple Flower Show (1888) and for over forty years was an exhibitor and judge. In addition to receiving the Victoria Medal, he was a founder member of the National Rose Society and on the Council of the Royal Horticultural Society. Locally he was a Justice of the Peace and a member of Hertfordshire County Council, with a particular interest in education.

In 1897 his son, George Laing Paul, took over the running of the nursery which continued to specialise in roses and fruit trees but was also involved in the cultivation of ornamental trees. In the 1920s, when his son took over, the firm became Ernest Paul & Son and was still trading in 1948.

Customers of the Pauls

Very few records survive about the customers of the Pauls and the prices of their roses or other plants. There is a reference in *Country Life* to 'a charming rose garden recently formed at Sandringham for the Prince of Wales by Mr Paul'.[22] Archives at Hatfield House mention a rosarium but no records or invoices survive for the late nineteenth century. At Waddesdon Manor the archives show that 12 per cent (in 1904), 14 per cent (in 1905) and 8.7 per cent (in 1906) of the annual expenditure on plants went on plants from Paul & Son.[23] Not surprisingly, E.A. Bowles of Myddelton House in nearby Enfield was a customer and probably on more friendly terms than that would indicate. He was a director with George Paul of the 1912 International Horticultural Exhibition; he gave a hybrid viola to George which the latter bred and named 'Mrs Bowles' (after Bowles' mother)[24] and was the recipient from George of a cutting of *Ligustrum ovalifolium* – 'my most beautiful flowering shrub of mid-July'.[25] George had apparently discovered the plant in a hedge in France and paid the owner ten francs for it, a price which Bowles considered rather high for 'a bit of a hedge'. The shrub is still thriving in the garden of Myddelton House, Enfield.

Other early nurseries

Many of the early nurseries were probably little more than plots where vegetables and plants were grown in the open air. Some had glasshouses for raising plants, as in some places the air was too polluted for outside cultivation. Some had hothouses for exotic fruit such as pineapples and melons. Shirley Hibberd in 1859 warned the amateur gardener that in the suburbs of London there are numbers of small nurseries, where 'a little of everything' is to be had at a moment's notice – fruit trees, evergreens, roses, etc. The way in which most of these are grown is such that they are utterly unfit to be removed when sold.[26]

A large proportion of the well-known nurserymen, however, began their careers as gardeners to large estates. One such was Mr Woolley, a 'pioneer in commercial horticulture' who gained a considerable reputation at the Royal Botanical Shows for his ferns and orchids. He had been gardener to Mr Benjamin Kerr, Clerk to the House of Lords. His employer gave him money to buy a nursery in Cheshunt. Mr Thomas Hamilton, described as the 'universal provider of cucumbers', also came south from Scotland to the Kent garden of Mr Wyn Ellis (MP

for Leicester and High Sheriff of Hertfordshire in 1871) who lived at
Ponsbourne Park and Whitstable. We are told that Hamilton was in the
habit of sending his surplus cucumbers from Kent to London to be sold
and from this he had the idea of making it a business.[27] He bought land
in Cheshunt where he founded Hamilton's Nurseries, which went on to
become very profitable.

Michael Rochford

Another of the gardeners turned nurseryman was Michael Rochford,
founder of the world-famous producers of potted plants. He came
over from Ireland in 1840 and worked firstly for Lord Nugent at
Weedon, near Aylesbury, then for Lord Feversham at Duncombe Park,
Yorkshire, and also at Oak Hill, East Barnet. The gardens of Oak
Hill were famous for two crops – pineapples and grapes. The Black
Hamburg grapes from Oak Hill were sold at Covent Garden for 16s
per pound, when other grapes, grown nearby at Southgate, could be
bought for 1s 6d.[28]

In the 1850s Michael moved to Tottenham, at this time merely a
village, and set up a market garden with glasshouses on two acres of
land. Here he continued to grow grapes (Black Hamburg and Muscats)
and pineapples, employing five men and a boy. Disaster struck, however,
when a violent hailstorm in 1876 damaged the vines, ferns and tender
plants. Undeterred, Michael, with the help of his two sons, John and
Joseph, designed new glasshouses. They went on to design the Rochford
boiler, a modified version of an existing model, which was fuelled by
coal and heated the glasshouse by circulating hot water through pipes.
One other problem with the early glasshouses was ventilation, and this
the Rochfords solved by positioning a lever outside the house to open
and close the lights.

One of the most profitable crops for nurserymen at this time was
ferns – this was the time of fern mania when ferneries (both indoor
and outdoor) were hugely popular and fern designs were added to
everything from garden seats to paper knives. Michael Rochford had
three glasshouses filled with varieties of *Adiantum*, the maidenhair fern.
Popularly known as 'Everybody's Fern', it could be grown in ferneries
or combined with cut flowers. For winter trade he grew *Solanum,* with
roots confined in small pots to encourage fruiting. Three acres of glass
were still kept for vines, for despite foreign competition the Rochford

grapes continued to command high prices. Michael died in 1883 – 'his place as a market nurseryman … second to none in the neighbourhood of London'.[29]

Thomas Rochford (Thomas Rochford & Son)

Of Michael's five sons it was Thomas (Tom) and Joseph who would give their names to the Rochford empire – Tom for potted plants and Joseph for cucumbers and tomatoes. Thomas had set up a market garden first in Tottenham, but with the arrival of what was to become the Great Eastern Railway in the 1840s not only did the population increase (it doubled in ten years) and the land become covered in houses but the smoke and soot from the engines made growing anything much more difficult. So in 1882/4 Tom and Joseph bought 8.25 acres of land on the Turnford Hall estate further north in the Lea valley. Five years later Tom bought Turnford Hall and in a short time what had been merely a cluster of thatched cottages became seventy acres of glasshouses, the beginnings of what was later known as 'Rochfordville' (Figures 8.12 and 8.13). Both brothers grew grapes, but Joseph first of all concentrated on cut flowers and then turned to tomatoes; Thomas specialised in potted plants.

Figure 8.12 Turnford Hall, c.1953. PHOTOGRAPH REPRODUCED BY KIND PERMISSION OF LOWEWOOD MUSEUM.

Figure 8.13 Picking melons at Mr E. Rochford's nursery, 1913. PHOTOGRAPH REPRODUCED BY KIND PERMISSION OF LOWEWOOD MUSEUM.

Among Thomas's specialities were potted lilies of the valley. The means of refrigeration had recently been discovered and Tom installed six freezing chambers in which he laid down lily of the valley crowns (bought from Germany) for retarding. When needed, they were brought out and exposed gradually to the light and warmer temperatures. By this means he could have bowls of scented flowers ready for sale at any time of year. *Lilium longiflorum*, a relatively recent introduction originally from Japan, was also one of his popular lines. Tom's business of potted plants prospered and when, in the 1880s, the London Underground was being built, sub-soil from the tunnelling was brought to Turnford to provide foundations for new glasshouses. By 1895 the workforce numbered sixty men and boys and, besides lilies, the plants included orchids, palms, hundreds of ferns, five houses of hydrangeas and two of double pelargoniums (Figure 8.14). Each year tulips and hyacinths were forced for Christmas. By 1898 four Rochford brothers owned eighty-six acres of glass in the Lea valley and seventy of these in 1905 belonged to Joseph and Thomas.

Figure 8.14 Workforce at Rochford's nursery, *c.*1895. PHOTOGRAPH REPRODUCED BY KIND PERMISSION OF LOWEWOOD MUSEUM.

Tom I was remembered as a hard task master – twelve-hour days with just a one-hour break for lunch and any bad behaviour marked down in the Staff Record Book. But he was also a benevolent one. Terraces of houses were built for the men, a Benefit Society was established as well as a Workmen's Institute with concert hall, library and reading room. He died in 1901; it was observed that 'A Prince of British Horticulture has passed away'.[30]

The firm Thomas Rochford and Son continued under the chairmanship of Tom II, and by 1909 twenty-eight new glasshouses had been built, nine of which were for grapes. Orchids were phased out; palms, ferns, lilies of the valley and others remained the mainstay of the crops grown and there was a steady export trade to America. A shipment of palms (worth £1,000) for an A.H. Dreer of Philadelphia was transported on the *Titanic*. They never reached their destination but a complete replacement was dispatched soon after. During the 1914–18 war the emphasis was on food production, and the growing of tomatoes and cucumbers was stepped up; some grapes continued to be grown but the poor quality of the soil, which had come from the Underground tunnelling, made a total handover to foodstuffs impossible, and the production of potted plants continued. The period between the wars was not easy: plant stocks from Europe were difficult to obtain as all connections with German suppliers had been stopped; most of the best growers had gone to the war; few records had been kept and the standard of maintenance in the glasshouses inevitably dropped. The Second World War again saw a concentration on foodstuffs. Cucumbers were not thought to be nutritious enough to warrant the space given them, so the emphasis was on tomatoes, with a small reserve of decorative plants which would be needed for subsequent re-stocking.

At the end of the war, Tom III now oversaw a major refurbishment of the nurseries. Glasshouses were repaired, new boilers were installed and the Institute renovated. But, most important of all, the stock was reorganised. The Palm House, which had cost £1,000 annually to heat, was pulled down; asparagus was discontinued; and the emphasis was now to be on foliage plants (Figure 8.15). In 1952 *Country Life* reported: 'last year was the first nurserymen remember when the sale of pot plants, both green and flowering, never ceased'.[31] The early varieties of the rubber plant (*Ficus*) and spider plant (*Chlorophytum*) were joined by examples of ivy (*Hedera*), *Peperomia*, Zebra plant (*Aphelandra squarrosa*),

Figure 8.15 Palm House at Rochford's nursery. PHOTOGRAPH REPRODUCED BY KIND PERMISSION OF LOWEWOOD MUSEUM.

Grape ivy and Kangaroo vine (varieties of *Cissus*) until in the mid-1960s there were over twenty-five acres of foliage plants. Needing little care and lasting for much longer than cut flowers, these plants became known in the market as 'Tom's weeds' and the market salesmen, who thought they would lose their profit on cut flowers, dubbed the foliage plants 'Rochford's folly'. The firm moved into flowering plants and the African violet (*Saintpaulia*; named after Baron Walter von Saint Paul-Illaire – the district commissioner of a province of what is now known as Tanzania – who had discovered it in 1892) became one of the best sellers: it was compact, flowered more than once, came in a variety of colours, needed little attention and was happy in centrally heated houses. In 1966 more than half a million of these were sold, the majority of which had been propagated in the nursery. The mainstay of Christmas plants nowadays – the poinsettia – was introduced in 1964, having been bred in America. The years 1958–70 saw many awards for the Rochford plant nurseries – Grand Prix d'honneur at the Floralies in Paris, gold medals at the RHS shows and the Victoria Medal for Horticulture for Tom – and visits to the nurseries by members of the royal family. Along with this prosperity went modernisation: a new propagation block was built, an automatic watering and mono-rail system was introduced, as well as plastic pots, central heating from an oil-fired boiler, and, on the marketing side, new methods of packaging and effective advertising.

Information about how to grow these plants was limited in the 1950s and as a result of the first gardening programme on television the Rochford plant nursery received around 2,500 letters asking for advice. This led to a nursery advice service and the redesigning of plant labels to include information on temperature and watering. Books on the subject by Tom Rochford and others followed – the most successful probably being *Be Your Own House Plant Expert* by Dr D.G. Hessayon, estimated to be the largest selling work of non-fiction after the Bible.[32] In 1965 The Houseplant Centre, a long glass showhouse at the entrance to the nursery, was opened and visitors came in coach loads to see and to buy.

Increasingly, however, the import of foreign plants from Denmark, Holland and Belgium threatened the viability of home production and councils and developers were after land. The acres under Rochford's nursery were sold for building and Rochford's nursery at Turnford Hall closed in the 1980s.

Joseph Rochford (Joseph Rochford & Son)

Joseph Rochford & Son, the salad arm of the family, started with the same crops as Thomas – pineapples, ferns and orchids – and shared some of the same site at Turnford. Soon after moving there 1.5 acres of glass were built especially for tomatoes, producing two crops a year, and by 1900, to keep pace with demand, there were thirty acres for tomatoes, cucumbers and grapes. In 1912 the company bought a new nursery of twenty-five acres in Slough and in 1936 they purchased the old Larsen nursery in Waltham Abbey. At this time 5,000 boxes of tomatoes were going to market from Rochfords each day. Originally sent in wicker baskets (locally called 'strikes'), they now travelled in wooden boxes, each fruit wrapped in different coloured paper to distinguish the grades. With a shortage of wood in 1939 cardboard began to be used for packaging instead. In later years the company bought two more nurseries in the Isle of Wight and Malmesbury.

As with all the nurseries, two World Wars and economics brought about changes: by the 1960s most of the grapes had gone and lettuces and flowers were introduced to keep the workers busy all the year round. During the 1960s and 1970s there was a shift from tomatoes to cucumbers and now peppers have become more popular. Cucumbers are a relatively quick crop and so give a quicker return to the growers.

Paul's and Rochford's are probably the two most well-known nursery names in the history of the Lea valley. There have been many, many more growers, who have battled, some more successfully than others, to make a living out of growing salads and ornamentals. The year 1911 saw the foundation of the Lea Valley and District Nurserymen's and Growers' Association. There were four aims: to study pests and diseases, to learn more about the cultivation of crops, to sort out problems with the railway companies and market salesmen; and generally to act together to help the smaller nurserymen who 'muddled along'.[33] After two years the annual membership fee was increased to one guinea for those with two acres or more, half a guinea for those with less. The year 1913 saw the foundation of an experimental station with two small laboratories, an office and a dark room and with a scientist as director. Later known as Cheshunt Research Station, it was responsible for research into pests and diseases, soil conditions and raising new hybrids. Cheshunt Compound (a treatment to prevent damping-off in tomatoes) and steam sterilisation of soil were started here under Dr Bewley in the 1930s. In 1926 the Association became affiliated to the National Farmers' Union.

Problems faced by nurseries
Atmospheric pollution

In 1961 the Lea Valley Growers' Association, as it became known, produced a summary of its activities over the previous fifty years and this gives us a fascinating insight into the problems faced by growers. In 1929 there was trouble from the power station (the North Metropolitan Electricity Supply Company Ltd) emitting smoke. Action was taken, which led to the lessening of the nuisance. Atmospheric pollution has often been a problem. Earlier, in the 1890s, the soot deposited on the roofs of the nearby glasshouses by the locomotives of the Great Eastern Railway in Northumberland Park led to a claim for damages, and compensation was awarded. Clean air and light is essential for glasshouse cultivation, particularly of tomatoes – hence the gradual increase in the number of nurseries in Sussex and the Isle of Wight.

In 1931 the Association set up a sub-committee to consider the possibility of canning tomatoes and selling them for use in making chutney. Experiments were held but the scheme was dismissed as unprofitable.

Weather damage

Damage from bad weather has been an ever-present problem. In 1876 in Tottenham a storm with hailstones as big as cherries and walnuts that fell to a depth of five inches or more virtually wrecked the vines, ferns and exotic plants of Michael Rochford's nursery and those of other nurserymen, and, as a result, a Hailstorm Relief Fund was launched which raised nearly £800 for those affected. Some twenty years later an independent Hailstorm Insurance Corporation was formed to provide coverage at a premium far lower than that charged by other companies. On the Board of Directors were three Rochfords: Thomas Hamilton, of cucumber fame; George and Henry May, fern growers of Edmonton; and Frederick Sander, the orchid grower of St Albans. Again in 1932 another hailstorm wreaked havoc in west Enfield and on the Rochford nurseries – glasshouses were shattered and the crops inside rendered useless. In 1961 over 1,500 *Ficus* plants were ruined in the Rochford nursery in Turnford by huge shards of ice which had formed on the overhead electricity cables and then fallen on the roofs of the glasshouses. Compensation was forthcoming from the Electricity Board but months had to be spent clearing up. The year 1976 also brought a very damaging storm, as shown in Figure 8.16. Similar damage by enemy action in the Second World War had led to the Association forming a claims commission and helping to procure licences for timber for repairs. Bomb damage had been quite extensive because of the proximity to London, and the relative frailty of the glasshouse buildings meant that they were very vulnerable to the effects of explosions.

Water supply

The supply of water, surprisingly in a river valley, has sometimes been a problem. In 1949 action was taken by the Association to stop water being pumped away to waste when sand and gravel was extracted, thus depriving growers of surface water. Representations were made to Parliament and companies extracting minerals had to undertake not to lower the water table. Ironically the same year excessive rain caused damage to crops from flooding.

Where fortunes have gone with the wind

Figure 8.16 Storm damage at Nazeing, 6 January 1976. PHOTOGRAPH REPRODUCED BY KIND PERMISSION OF THE *EVENING STANDARD*.

Fuel supply

The Association stepped in to ensure fuel supplies during the Second World War – petrol for delivery vans and for agricultural vehicles and coal for heating glasshouses. Later, in 1961, when 2d duty per gallon was levied on fuel oil, it was the Association which represented the disquiet of the growers who had been encouraged to change to oil heating and now felt themselves unjustly burdened. In the next Budget, fuel oils used for horticultural crops were made exempt from this duty.

Shortage of labour

One of the perennial problems for nurseries was a shortage of labour. In small nurseries whole families were involved, but where there were a number of glasshouses outside workers had to be employed. In 1898 the medical officer in Waltham Abbey reported a considerable immigration of young adults as a result of a 'boom in the glasshouse branch of the market garden trade'.[34] The work was hard and unskilled – heaving coal, stoking boilers, cleaning panes of glass as well as digging, planting and watering the crops. The hours were long – fifty-four hours a week in summer, fifty in winter. Records show that in 1914 the local vicar

Figure 8.17 Women workers picking cucumbers, 1916. PHOTOGRAPH REPRODUCED BY KIND PERMISSION OF LOWEWOOD MUSEUM.

addressed the Association on seven-day working. (We are not told what he said or what, if anything, happened.) In 1912 one grower reported to the committee of the Association that one of his employees had asked for a half-holiday on Saturdays. This had not been granted. In 1915 the Association approached the Belgian Refugee Committee to ask for workers. During the First World War, women joined the workforce, as they did in many other industries, and the Association actively supported the local child welfare centres set up to enable the mothers to go out to work (Figure 8.17). After the Second World War better wages could be earned in the light industries in the surrounding area.

Horticulture at all levels has always crossed European boundaries: the rose hybridists included several French nationals, and past officers of the Lea Valley Growers' Association include several Scandinavians who had come to Britain as students and later stayed to set up businesses. Mention has already been made of the Belgian refugees. But the main influx was of Italians from south Italy and Sicily, who came over seeking work after the Second World War. Some were former prisoners-of-war and many of them were joined by their families and, in time, took over the nurseries either as owners or tenants. A sizeable Italian community grew up especially in Waltham Cross and Rye Park, with a vice-consulate in Cheshunt. By 1978 half of the growers in the Lea valley were Italians.[35]

Foreign competition

The two greatest problems that faced growers were competition from abroad and the relentless advance of London. It was, after all, foreign competition which spelled the end of glasshouse grapes grown in the Lea valley between the wars. Outdoor-grown grapes could now be imported from South Africa relatively cheaply. In 1927 the Lea Valley Growers' Association approached the government about the possibility of a tax on imports of tomatoes from the Channel Islands and the Canaries. After lengthy negotiations a duty of 2d per pound in the summer and 1d per pound in the winter was imposed. During the Second World War, when the Channel Islands were under German occupation and the emphasis was on producing foodstuffs, tomatoes were the sole produce of the area and the price was controlled. Not all nurserymen, however, had experience of this crop and not all glasshouses were suitable; but at least there was a guaranteed sale. In the period after the war the foreign markets recovered and imports of tomatoes from Spain and the Canaries began to overlap the British season. Entry to the Common Market brought free trade between members and the Dutch horticultural industry, backed by significant government fuel subsidies, threatened to corner almost the whole European market in the 1970s. This culminated in a huge protest march in Brussels in 1981 and the Dutch government was forced to abandon the subsidies. The production of tomatoes had turned to cucumbers and flowers, but, even here, the growers faced severe competition from countries where no heat was needed for cultivation and labour was cheap. The rising cost of oil at this time added to the anxieties of the growers; the cost of heating oil had increased by 400 per cent in 1973. After the initial costs of changing to oil they had reduced their costs of production but now found themselves trapped.

Land development

Probably the most serious threat to the glasshouse industry has been the ever-increasing need for land for building. Selling up was for many growers more profitable than struggling on. Planning authorities re-zoned large areas for housing development: from 1951 to 1961 the population of Cheshunt Urban District increased by a higher percentage than any other district in England, apart from the New Towns.[36] Developers followed the railway line up the valley with plans for housing. Lengthy public inquiries were held; in some cases the government overruled inspectors. In Cheshunt, Hoddesdon, Waltham Cross, Waltham Abbey, Turnford and Goffs Oak, nurseries gave way to planners and the area under glass dropped to approximately 300 acres in the 1990s.

Present situation

It would be natural to assume that this huge decrease in glasshouse acreage over the last eighty years would have spelled defeat for the growers. But that is emphatically not the case, as technology and automation have transformed the industry. In an attempt to cut down on fuel costs, greenhouses were rebuilt in the 1980s: now the majority are made of galvanised steel and aluminium, the size of each pane of glass has been increased and the number of glazing bars has been reduced to a minimum. The modern glasshouses are around 30 per cent more energy efficient than the old ones.[37] The frames do not rot, like timber, so maintenance costs are reduced. Computers now manage the environment of the plants, controlling light, temperature and humidity, irrigation and feeding. Artificial growing media, such as rock wool (molten rock spun at high speed to form a woven slab), is widely used for cucumbers and other crops, and hydroponic culture (growing in water with mineral nutrient solutions added) is widespread. There is then no need for soil sterilisation. In addition, an integrated system of pest control is used; this includes genetic, biological and chemical means in a balanced combination.

Up until the 1960s all the produce from the nurseries was transported by road or rail to wholesale markets in London and other cities in the Midlands. But a huge change in distribution came about with the advent of supermarkets. Today three-quarters of the supplies of fresh produce are bought by the big food chains, and locally based market organisations have been formed to buy in the produce from the growers, then to pack and deliver it direct to the supermarkets. The time between harvest and point of sale can thus be less than a day, essential for salad crops and cut flowers. However, it must be said that this dominance of the market by the food chains exerts a ruthless pressure on the sale prices for the growers.

Conclusion

After 200 years the industry and the Lea valley have changed. The rose breeders and the display gardens have gone: space is needed for both and the land is needed for housing. The exotics grown in the early glasshouses – pineapples, melons, orchids and palms – have gone. It is now cheaper to import all these from other parts of the world, and, with no Victorian conservatories to fill, the need is for smaller house plants. Ferns are no longer in fashion. There is no need now for clay flower pots or large numbers of timber-framed glasshouses. So much gravel has been extracted from the valley that much of what was once marshes is now dry and the resulting lakes have become part of the Lee Valley Regional Park, twenty-six miles of countryside with facilities for cycling, walking, riding, canoeing, white-water rafting and, of course, the site, at the southern end of the valley, of the 2012 Olympic Games. The names of once well-known nurseries now survive only in street names.

The reformed nursery industry now has no need for large numbers of workers to do heavy work in all weathers: a much reduced acreage supports a highly automated, highly productive industry successfully growing salads and ornamentals in huge quantities to satisfy the demands of large supermarket chains. Both sides of the railway from London to Ware are now developed: the commuters who travel on the trains back and forth to London each day make their journeys in relative comfort, unlike the carters of years ago, who, wrapped in sacks and horse-blankets, are said to have slept while the horses travelled the road by night to take the vegetables and fruit to the market at Covent Garden.[38]

Acknowledgements

My thanks go to Bryan Hewitt, senior gardener at Myddelton House; Diana Jones; Roger Dungey, director of Thomas Rochford & Son; Peter Leach, director of Joseph Rochford & Son; Tony Stevenson, past secretary of the Lea Valley Growers' Association and Lee Stiles, present secretary of the LVGA; Colette Warbrick, registrar at Waddesdon Manor; and Robin Harcourt Williams, archivist at Hatfield House.

I am also most grateful to Ayletts Nurseries Ltd, Peter Beales Roses, the curator and staff of Lowewood Museum at Hoddesdon, the staff of Epping Forest District Museum at Waltham Abbey, RHS Lindley Library, City of Westminster Libraries, *Country Life* picture library, St Albans Museum and the ever-helpful HALS.

Notes

1. In Elizabethan documents the spellings Lea, Ley and Lee are found, with Lee being the most common. Today both Lea and Lee are current. See J. Lewis, *London's Lea Valley: Britain's Best-Kept Secret* (Chichester, 1979), p. 1.
2. Sir Richard Phillips, *A Morning's Walk from Kew* (London, 1817), p. 224.
3. W. Thornton, *The History of London and Westminster* (London, 1784), p. 454.
4. P. Rooke, 'The Lea Valley Nursery Industry: The Growth and Decline of Market Gardening in SW Herts', *Hertfordshire's Past*, 42 (Autumn 1997), p. 6.
5. P.C.A. Archer, *Historic Cheshunt* (Cheshunt, 1923), p. 191.
6. W. Paul, *The Rose Garden*, 1848 (reprint by Earl Coleman, New York, 1978), p. 1.
7. *Kelly's Directory* (1869).
8. 'Flower and Fruit Farms of Great Britain', *Country Life*, 30 September 1899, p. 405.
9. W. Paul, 'Standard Roses', in *Contributions to Horticultural Literature 1843–1892* (Waltham Cross, 1892), p. 181.
10. *Country Life*, 30 September 1899, p. 405.
11. *Gardeners' Chronicle*, i (1905), p. 216.
12. *Gardeners' Magazine* (1905), p. 231.
13. W. Paul, 'On Trees and Shrubs in Large Towns', in *Contributions to Horticultural Literature*, p. 286.
14. *Ibid.*, 'Floricultural Millinery', p. 552.
15. *Ibid.*, 'On the Literature of Ancient and Modern Gardening', p. 551.
16. *Journal of Horticulture and Cottage Gardener*, V, 50 (1905), p. 325.
17. 'Notable Gardens: Waltham House', *Country Life*, 2 February 1901, p. 137.
18. *Journal of Horticulture and Home Farmer*, V, 62 (1911), pp. 194–6.
19. *Ibid.*
20. 'Lost Apples of Hertfordshire', < http://www.applesandorchards.org.uk>, accessed 2011.
21. W. Thomson, *The Gardener VI: Garden Records No. VIII. Messrs Paul & Son* (1869).
22. *Country Life*, 30 September 1899, p. 407.
23. Waddesdon Archives, Accounts and Records for 1904, 1905, 1906.
24. E.A. Bowles, *My Garden in Spring* (n.p., 1914), p. 260.
25. E.A. Bowles, *My Garden in Summer* (n.p., 1914), p. 285.
26. S. Hibberd, *Town Gardens* (2nd edn, 1859), p. 99.
27. *Journal of Horticulture and Home Farmer*, V, 62 (1911), p. 194.
28. *Gardeners' Chronicle*, 24 July 1858.
29. *The Garden*, quoted in M. Allan, *Tom's Weeds: The Story of Rochfords and Their House Plants* (London, 1970), p. 56.
30. *Cheshunt Observer*, 17 October 1900; quoted in Allan, *Tom's Weeds*, p. 76.
31. V. Stevenson, 'The Return of the Potted Plant', *Country Life*, 8 February 1952, p. 350.
32. T. Rochford and R. Gorer, *Rochford Book of House-Plants* (1965); *The Rochford Book of Flowering Pot- Plants* (1967); *Rochford's House-Plants for Everyone* (London, 1969).
33. Jubilee Newsletter of the Lea Valley Growers' Association, *passim*.

34. P. Pennell, *Waltham Abbey through the Twentieth Century* (n.p., 2001), p. 40.
35. Rooke, *The Lea Valley Nursery Industry*, p. 12.
36. *Ibid.*, p. 13.
37. Report by Reading Agricultural Consultants Ltd for Epping Forest District Council, September 2003, p. 7.
38. Memories of Jim South, 1977, <http:// www.samuelsouth.btinternet.co.uk/nurserymen.htm>, accessed 2011.

Bibliography

Primary sources

Golden Jubilee edition of the Newsletter of the Lea Valley Growers' Association (Waltham Cross, 1961).
Kelly's Directory, 1869.
Paul, W., *Contributions to Horticultural Literature 1843–1892* (Waltham Cross, 1892).
Paul, W., *The Rose Garden*, 1848 (reprint by Earl Coleman, New York, 1978).
Rochford, T. and Gorer, R., *Rochford's House Plants for Everyone* (London, 1969).
Waddesdon Archives, Accounts and Records for 1904, 1905, 1906.

Secondary sources

Allan, M., *Tom's Weeds: The Story of Rochfords and Their House Plants* (London, 1970).
Allan, M., *E.A., Bowles and His Garden at Myddelton House* (London, 1975).
Archer, P.C.A., *Historic Cheshunt* (Cheshunt, 1923).
Bowles, E.A., *My Garden in Spring* (1914).
Bowles, E.A., *My Garden in Summer* (1914).
Edwards, J., *Cheshunt in Herts* (n.p., 1974).
Hibberd, S., *The Fern Garden: How to Make, Keep and Enjoy It* (London, 1879).
Hibberd, S., *Town Gardens* (2nd edn, London, 1859).
Horwood, C., *Potted History: The Story of Plants in the Home* (London, 2007).
Lewis, J., *London's Lea Valley: Britain's Best-Kept Secret* (Chichester, 1979).
Lewis, J., *Water and Waste: Four Hundred Years of Health Improvement in the Lea Valley* (London, 2009).
Pennell, P., *Waltham Abbey through the Twentieth Century* (n.p., 2001).
Phillips, Sir R., *A Morning's Walk from Kew* (London, 1817).
Rooke, P., *Cheshunt's Past in Pictures* (Ware, 1994).
Thomson, W., *The Gardener VI: Garden Records No. VIII. Messrs Paul & Son* (1869).
Thornton, W., *The History of London and Westminster* (London, 1784).
Wilkinson, A., *The Victorian Gardener: The Growth of Gardening and the Floral World* (Stroud, 2006).

Journals

'Flower and Fruit Farms of Great Britain', *Country Life*, 30 September 1899, pp. 405–8.
'Notable Gardens: Waltham House', *Country Life*, 2 February 1901, pp. 136–8.
The Garden, vol. 57 (1900), p. 166.
The Garden, vol. 62 (1902), pp. 8–9.
The Garden, vol. 63 (1903), p. 166.
The Garden, vol. 67 (1905), pp. 213–14.
The Garden (2 July 1910), pp. 324–5.
Gardeners' Chronicle, (24 July 1858).
Gardeners' Chronicle (1905), i, pp. 216–17; ii, pp. 405–6.
Gardeners' Chronicle (1921), ii, p. 166.
Gardeners' Magazine (1897), pp. 411–12.
Gardeners' Magazine (1905), p. 231.
Gardeners' Magazine (1909), pp. 739–40.
Gardeners' Magazine (1910), pp. 1–2.
Gardeners' Magazine (1911), pp. 139–40.
Journal of Horticulture and Cottage Gardener, V, 45 (1902), p. 474.
Journal of Horticulture and Cottage Gardener, V, 50 (1905), p. 325.
Journal of Horticulture and Home Farmer, V, 62 (1911), pp. 194–6.
Stephenson, V., 'The Return of the Potted Plant', *Country Life*, 8 February 1952, pp. 350–1.
Report by Reading Agricultural Consultants Ltd for Epping Forest District Council, September 2003.

Rooke, P., 'The Lea Valley Nursery Industry: The Growth and Decline of Market Gardening in SW Herts', *Hertfordshire's Past*, 42 (Autumn 1997), pp. 2–14.

Web sources
'Lost Apples of Hertfordshire', <http://www.applesandorchards.org.uk>, accessed 2011.

Index

Page numbers in *italic* refer to illustrations and/or their captions; plates are referred to as *pl. 1.1*, etc. Main references to subjects have the relevant page numbers in **bold**. n denotes footnote. NB one page may contain multiple references.

Abbots Hill 121, **133–8**, *135*, *136*, 142, 143, 144, 146n35, *pl. 5.2*
Abbots Langley 121, 134, 135
Abbotswood 158
Adam, Robert 106
Albemarle, Earl of 102, 107
Alley 11, 19
Alpine plants 155, 195, 210
American seeds 103
Amersfort, Potten End 157, 160
Amyce, Israel 39
Anderson, James 101
Anson: Admiral Lord 95, **96–7**, 98, 107, 108, 111; Lady Elizabeth 96, 98; Thomas 96
Apsley 124: Mill 124, 129, *130*, 134, 143, *pl. 5.1*, *pl. 5.2*
Aquatics 153, 204
Arbor-Vitae 140
Army 97, 107, 134
Arundel House, London 71
Ash tree 14, 197
Ash valley 61
Ashridge 92, 105, 106, 112: Golden Valley 106
Ashton, Thomas 57
Ashwell Bury 157
Aspenden 5: Hall *22*, **23–5**, 63
Assheton: Ralph 57n65; Rebecca 51, *pl. 2.5*
Aubergine 204
Aubrey: Eli 102; John 14
Aylesbury 122, 212

Bacon: Anthony 11; Francis 5, **9–14**, *10*, 16, 20, 24, 31, 48, 72, 182; Nicholas 5, 7– 9, *8*, *10*, 15
Baillie Scott, M.H. 162
Balcony 70, 71, 72, 156
Balls Park, Hertford 74, 161
Banqueting hall 60, 61, 66, 68, 69, 70, 71, 72, 74, 78, 84, 85

Banqueting house 14, 16, 24, 71, 74, 79, 80
Banqueting House, Whitehall Palace 75
Barclay, David *110*, 111, 116n123
Barn 61, 63, 64, 76, 86n18, 98, 159
Barnes Lodge, Kings Langley 134
Barnet 3, 94
Baskerfield, Thomas 125
Baud family 60, 61, 63, 66, 81, 84, 86n18 and n24: Thomas 61; William 61
Baud's Manor 61
Bedding plants/schemes 139, 148, 151, 153, 165, 195, 198–9, 204
Beech 14, 98, 104, 132, 137, 140, 161
Beechwood Park, Flamstead 92, 98, 105
Belvedere 11, 71, 72, 159
Belvedere Court, Vatican 71
Benington Park 5, 19–21, *20*, 24
Benyon Croft, Richard 150, 165
Berkhamsted 149, 150, 154, 155, 156, 195: Kilfillan 154, 155; The Kraal 154, 156; Staghurst 154, 155; Woodcock Hill 149
Bethell, Christopher 107
Bethel, Wood 154, 165
Betts, John 81; Samuel 81
Bishop's Stortford 61, 63, 68, 123, 184, 208: St Michaels Church 63
Black House or Bleak House Farm 135
Blenheim 100
Blomfield, Reginald 153, 154
Botham, Henry 134
Bowles, E.A. 211
Bowling alley/green 16, 24, 45, 67, 157, 165
Bowood 100
Boxmoor 122, 143, 149
Boyd, Harold Haven de 155
Bramante 71, 74
Brand, Thomas 95, 106–7
Brettingham, Matthew 125

Bridgeman, Charles, garden designer 51, 125, 157
Bridgeman, Charles, nurseryman 101
Bridgewater, Duke 95, 106
Britannia Illustrata 79, 125, *186*
Brocket, Lord and Lady 151, 166
Brocket Hall/Park, Hatfield 50, 50, 166, 188, *188*
Brompton Park 179, 184, 187, 190, 191, 192
Brookmans Park 149, 150, 171n5
Brown, David 107
Brown, Jane 160
Brown, Lancelot (Capability) **92–120**, 133, 157, *pl. 4.1*
Broxbourne 149, 153, 154, 167, 202, 206, *210*, 210
Bryant, A. 53
Bulbourne 122
Burghley, Lord 4, 5, 7, 15, 16–17, 20, 31, 38–9, 40, 41, 55n22, *pl. 1.2*, *pl. 2.1 see also* Cecil, William
Burghley, Stamford 15
Burns, Walter 153, 171n17
Bury St Edmonds, Suffolk 140
Bushey Hall 31, 32, **45–8**, *46*, *47*, 54, *pl. 2.3*, *pl. 2.4a and b*
Bushey 31, 45, 48, 122, 151: Chalk Hill 128; Hollybank 162; Lululaund 155, 171n28; Myholme 162; Roebuck 154, 156; Rose Garden 154–5, 170; Sparrows Herne Hall 167; Tilehurst 162
Byng, Admiral John 107–8
Byng, General George MP 95, 108

Caesar: Charles (1590–1642) 20, 21; Charles 23; Julius 5, 19–20, 21
Camberwell (Lambeth) 60
Canal, industrial 106, 122, 123, 130, 131, 133: Grand Junction 131, 143; Grand Union 131, *131*, 132, 144; Languedoc 106; Midland canal system 122
Canal, ornamental 15, 19, 49
Capel, Capell: Algernon 81; Sir Arthur 67; Arthur, Baron Capel 60, **68–71**, *69*, **77–8**, 84, *pl. 3.3*; Arthur, Viscount Malden and Earl of Essex 79, 84, 179, 184; Sir Edward 63; Elizabeth 68, 70, 74, 77, 79, *pl. 3.3*; Gyles 63; Henry 5, 60, 63, 64, 65, 66, 67, 68, 83, 86n18; John 62; Katherine 63; Margaret 63, 67; Theodosia 77; William 60, 78; Sir William 62–3
Capel Court, London 63
Carey, Henry 5
Carlile, Edward Hildred 16
Carnation 71, 207
Carnivorous plants 204
Caroline Italian garden style 84
Carpender's Park 128
Cashio Bridge 124, 130, 132, 144
Cassiobury 5, 68, 77, 79, 80, 81, 82, 84, **125–8**, *127*, 130, 132, 134, 142, 144, 150, 179, **183–7**, *186*: Beech Lodge 128; Home Park

132; Little Cassiobury 128; Ridgeway Lodge 128; Upper Park 125, 132
Catherine of Braganza 56n41
Caus, Isaac de 72, 74, 75, 76, 85, 88n58
Caus, Salomon de 17
Cecil: Robert 5, 14, 15, 17, 31, 39–41, 45, 54, 67, 72, 178; William 4, 9, 14, 15, 16, 18, 25, 38
Cecil House 16
Cedar 98, 140: of Lebanon 137, 152
Cedars Park, Cheshunt 42
Chambers, William 107
Charles I 42, 68, 70, 77, 78
Charles II 79, 187
Charnock, John 103, *104*
Chatsworth 132, 133, 139
Chauncy, Sir Henry 22, 23, 45, *47*, *93*, *pl. 2.4a* and *b*
Cheshunt 3, 14, 39, 42, 149, 195, 202, 205, 210, 211, 212, 223, 224: Board of Health 208; Cedars Park 42; Compound 219; Old Nurseries 206, 209; Pippin 210; Research Station 219; Wood Green 41
Chess, river/valley 123, 124
Chestnut 14: horse 154, 197; sweet 104
Cheverells 151
Chipping Campden 79
Chorleywood 124, 150, 162: The Orchard 162; Solesbridge 124
Christi, John 101
Church, John 53
Civil War 6, 23, 42, 60, 77, 84
Clarendon, Earl of 125, 127, 128, 129, 144
Clematis 153, 155, 165; wild 139
Clover 104
Cobham, Lord Richard Temple, first Viscount 95, 96, 98
Cocks, John 101
Codicote 151
Cole Green 92, **98–105**, *102*, *104*, *pl. 4.3*: menagerie 92, 102, 112; temple 92, 102–3, 112
Colne, river 33, 45, 46, 124, 128, 129
Conder, Josiah 166
Conifers 83, *130*, 137, 166
Cook, Moses 79, 82, 125, 179, **183–7**, *185*, 190, 191, *196*
Cooke, David *see* Mitchell
Corrie Wood, Letchworth 162
Courtyard 23, 36, 45, 48, 65, 163, 164
Covent Garden 76, 202, *204*, 212, 225
Coventry, Lord 96
Cowper: George, third Earl 104–5; Spencer, Dean of Durham 101–2; William, first Earl, Lord Chancellor 99, *pl. 4.3*; William, second Earl 92, 95, 98, *99*, 100–1, 103, 104, 112
Croome, Worcestershire 96
Croquet lawn 82, 162
Croxley 121, 124, 129: Green 149
Cucumbers 204, 211–12, 213, 216, 218, 219, 220, *222*, 223, 224

Cullings: manor 39, 55n22, *pl. 2.1*; moat 40, 41, *43, pl. 2.1*

Dance, Sir N. *pl. 4.1*
Darcy, Thomas Lord 62
Darwin, Charles 180, 194
Davenport, John nurseryman 98
Deer 40, 55n16, 68, 72, 81, 97: park 24, 33, 38, 57n63, 99, 125
Dickinson archive, Frogmore 140
Dickinson: Harriet 130, *130*; John 121, 123–4, 129, 130, 134, 135, 137, 142, 144
Digswell 92, 112, 117n129
Digswell Nursery 180, **195–9**
Dillistone, George 161, 165
Dovecote 24, 45, 46, 148, 159
Dover 60
Drapentier, Jan, engraver *22*, 23, 25, 45, *46*, *47*, 92, *93*, *pl. 2.4a* and *b*
Drive 49, 63, 83, 157, 162: Abbots Hill 137; Cassiobury 127, 128, 132; The Grove 131, *131*; in a landscape park 103, 107, 108; Shendish 138, 139
Drummonds Bank 97, 107
Duncombe Park 212
Durham Park 92, 107, 108, 112
Dury and Andrews' county map 48, 49, 53, *80*, 81, 98, 102, *102*, 103, 107, 125, 126, 134
Dyrham Park *see* Durham Park

East Barnet 94, 108, 212
Ebury, Lord 130, 157
Edmonton 202, 220
Edward IV 33, 163
Egerton, Francis *see* Bridgewater, Duke of
Egremont, Lord 96, 101
Elizabeth I 1, 5, 7, 19, 31, 60, 63, 83
Elizabethan 5, 15, 42, 60, 72, 135, 138, 153
Ellis, Wyn M.P. 211–2
Elm 14, 152, 206
Enfield 207, 208, 211, 220: Archaeological Society 43
Epping Forest 81
Esher Place, Surrey 33, 36
Essex, Earl(s) of 5, 77, 79–80, 84, 125, 129, 134, 144, 184, 185
Essex, Lady 126
Eusebius 78
Evelyn, John 185, 187
Evergreens 24, 108, 140, 211
Exeter College, Oxford 99

Fagel, Gaspar 76
Fanhams, Ware 150, 165, *pl. 6.1*
Fanshawe, Henry 5, 18–19, 20; Thomas 5, 18
Faudel-Phillips, Sir Benjamin 161
Fells, Abraham 195
Fenwick, H.G. 151, 158, 159
Ferns 128, 211, 212, 215, 216, 218, 220, 225: ferneries 212; maidenhair fern 212

Feversham, Lord 212
Field, John 187
Fir trees 83, 103
Fish 32, 33, 40, 68: fishing 72, 112; fishponds 38, 41, 55n10, 64, 67, 76, 77 *see also* Stew
Florence 104–5, 106
Flower: bed 82, 83, 140, 156; border 160, 162; garden 18, 82, 140, 151; pot 204, *204*, 225
Flowers 1, 11, 18, 19, 70, 71, 77, 140, 159, 177, 182, 190, 202, 206, 207, 218, 223: cut flowers 212, 213, 217, 224
Foliage 153, 197, 216, 217
Forcing-houses 140
Forest garden 5, 79
Foudrinier brothers 123
Fountain 11, 15, 16, 17, 18, 19, 21, 24, 70, 72, 73, 74, 77, 78, 84, 85: in Arts and Crafts gardens 155, 161, 162, 163, 165
France 17, 60, 73, 123, 211
Freman 5, 25: Ralph 23; Ralph (nephew) 23; Ralph (grandson) 23; William 23
Frisketting Room 74, 87n56
Frogmore 140: Mill 123, 124, 129, 144
Fruit 13, 18, 46, 77, 180, 187, 190, 193, 194, 202, 218, 225: houses 140, 179, 183, *189*, 190; trees 11, 17, 42, 71 (espalier), 74, 76, 77, 104, 170, 182, 187, 206, 210, 211; walls 153
Fruits: apples 77, 182, 195, 197: Cheshunt Pippin 210; apricots 76, 182; cherries 42, 76, 182, 193; figs 182; grapes 212, 213, 216, 218, 223: Black Hamburg grapes 212; Muscadine grapes 19; vines 76; medlar 182; melon 19, 103, 211, *214*, 225; nectarines 76; peaches 76, 182; pears 76, 182, 193; pineapples 100, 103, 211, 212, 218, 225; plums 19, 42, 76, 182, 193: Early Rivers plum 194, *pl. 7.1*; pomegranates 182; quinces 182; strawberries 42, 155

Gade, river/valley 121–44, *124*, *127*, *136*
Gainsborough, Thomas 50, *pl. 2.6*
Gallery 9, 11, 15, 16, 36, 66
Garden buildings: arbour 155, 199; banqueting house 14, 16, 24, 71, 74, 79, 80; barn 64, 98; bath house 98; belvedere 71, 72, 159; courtyard 23, 45, 48, 65, 163, 164; ice house 98; menagerie 92, 102, 103, 112; 'Pallisadoe' 42; pavilion 21, 41, 45, 80; rotunda 27n39, 103, 115n71; stand 42; summer house 11, 13, 15, 21, 71, 74, 140, 151, 155, 156, 159, 162; temple 49, 50, 51, 53, 92, 98, 102, 103, 112, 125–6, 128; viewing platform 48
Garden design: formal 11, 16, 24, 41, 45, 49, 50, 51, 88n67, 94, 97, 103, 106, 111, 112, 126, 137, 139, 142, 148, 151, 153, 155, 159, 165; geometric 70, 125, 126, 137, 138; informal 107, 138, 157; natural/istic 95, 97, 139, 151, 152, 153
Garden features: alley 19; avenue 13–4, 49, 53, 79, 82, 103, 105, 107, 125, 206; bowling alley 16; bowling green 24, 45, 67, 157, 165;

bridge 36, 41, 48, 107, 131, *131*, 132, 139, 167; gate 24, 71, 74, 83, *158*, 163, 164, 165; grotto 15, 72–4, 75, 76, 78, 84, 85, 86n23, 87n56, 111; grove 23, 24, 53; ha-ha 98, 101, 103, 139; knot 18, 67; mount 11, 16, 42, 49, 57n68, 67, 166; parterre 21, 70 (*de gazon*), 74, 79, 95, 139, 151, 165, 184; pergola 148, 151, 153, 155, 156, 159, 161, 162, 164, 166; stairs 71, 74, 84, 161, 162; sunk fence 98, 101, 103 *see also* ha–ha; urn 70, 71, 83, 162; view 16, 24, 25, 36, 46, *47*, 53, 60, 70, 72, 98, 102, 108, 129, 132, 133, 137, 138, 139, 143, 154, 159, 161, 187; vista 53, 71, 159, 161, 168, 184, 187, 196, 199; wilderness 49, 57n68, 125, 196 *see also* Canal, ornamental; Fountain; Lawn; Orchard; Pond, ornamental; Terrace; Walk; Walled garden; Water features, ornamental
Gardenesque 139, 140, 142
Gate piers 24, 83
Gatehouse 63–4, *64*, 86n18
George II 99, 209
George III 49
Gerard, John 16
Gibson, Dan 155
Gilbert: Adrian 39–41, 42; Charles J. 155; Sir Humphrey 40
Gingko biloba 104
Glasshouses 157, 179, 191, 194, 211, 212, 213, 215, 216, 225: artificial growing media 224; bomb damage 220; design 194, 212; fuel supply 202, 221, 223; Hailstorm Relief Fund 220; heating 202, 212; pollution 219; weather damage 220
Gorhambury 5, 7–14, *8*, 15, 25, 31, 72, *pl. 1.1*: gardens of Nicholas Bacon 9, 11; Francis Bacon 13–14; Oak Wood 11, *12*; The Pond Yard *13*, 48
Gower, Edward 33
Grand tour 95, 98, 99, 104, 106, 111
Grass 38, 70, 71, 101, 104, 140, 159, 161, 162, 163, 168
Gray, Thomas 57n61
Grey, Margaret 67
Griffith, John 138
Grove, The 125–6, 127, *127*, 128, 130, 131, *131*, 132, 134, 142, 144
Gunning, Elizabeth 106

Hackney 202
Hadham Hall 5, 60–85, *62*, *64*, *65*, *66*, *69*, *80*, *81*, *82*, *83*, 179, 184, *pl. 3.1*, *3.2*, *3.3*: Homestall 76–7, 88n59, *pl. 3.1*
Hadham Old Park Lodge Farm 80
Hadham Parva *see* Little Hadham
Ha-ha *see* Garden features
Haileybury School 153
Halsey, J. *pl. 4.3*
Hamilton, Thomas 211, 220
Hammersmith 96

Hampton Court, Surrey 33, 36, 55n9: The Pond Gardens 55n10
Harcourt, first Viscount 153, 171n17 and n18
Harrington, Lucy (Lady Bedford) 5
Harris, George William 102
Hassell, John 129
Hatfield 3, 17, 18, 31, 50, 53, 123, 163: Goodrich House 163; Morton House 163; Woodside Place 53
Hatfield House 3, 5, 14, 19, 25, 31, 45, 72, 178, 180–3, 196, 199: Archives 40, 48, 211; estate 53; Old Palace 67, 163
Hayes, Middlesex 60
Hazelwood, near Hunton Bridge 134
Head gardener 95, 101, 177, 178, 179, 180, 183, 194, 199
Heather Cottage, Potten End 154, 157
Hedges 102, 110, 157–8, 159, 162, 196, 197, 198, 211: apsidal 156; box 155; yew 148, 151, 152, 153, 159, 160, 161, 165; hedged rooms 163
Hemel Hempstead 121, 122, 123, 126, 129, 134, 143, 144
Henry VIII 9, 23, 31, 33, 36, 55n10, 63
Herkomer, Hubert von 154, 155, 171n28
Hertford 18, 74, 92, 99, 105, 123, 161, 170: Hertford Nursery 195
Hessayon, Dr D.G. 218
Hibberd, James Shirley 211
Hicks, Sir Baptist, Viscount Campden 79
Hill, Thomas 16
Hillside, near Hunton Bridge 134
Hitchin Priory 160, 191, *192*, 193, 195
Holbeach manor *see* Popes
Holland, Mr (Henry) 106
Homewood, Knebworth 151, 159
Hoo, The 92, *93*, 106–7
Hot beds 80
Hot house *189*, 190, 191
Howard: Ebenezer 168, 196; Thomas 71
Howe, Admiral Richard 95, 108
Howes, John 63
Hulls, William 51
Humanist thought 2
Hunsdon House 5
Hunton Bridge 124, 128, 129, 132, 134, 144
Hyacinth 206, 207, 215
Hydraulic system 72

Ireland, William 97
Isle of Wight 218, 219
Italian Renaissance 3, 6, 65
Italianate garden 60, 61, 68–72, 76, 77, 78, 80, 83, 84, 85
Italians 106, 222, 223
Italy 2, 71, 73, 74, 95, 98, 99, 106, 222

James I 1, 15, 17, 67, 74
James II 31
Japanese garden 165–7, *167*, *pl. 6.1*

Jekyll, Gertrude 154, 157–62, 163, 173n67
Jocelin, Ralph 23
Johnson, Cornelius 69, 70, *pl. 3.3*
Jones, Inigo 2, 71, 74, 76, 85

Kemp, Edward 139–42, *141*, 143
Kennington 179, 187–8, *188*, 191, 193
Kent 20, 45, 48, 51, 211–12
Keppel: Admiral Augustus 107; General George, third Earl of Albemarle 107; General William 92, 95, 107
Kerr, Benjamin 211
Kielmansegge, Count Frederick 92
Kings Langley 81, 138: Barnes Lodge 134; Cocks Head Wood 138; Hens Head Wood 138; Home Park 124; Shendish 121, 134
Kip and Knyff 125, *186*
Kirkharle Hall 95
Kitchen garden 49, 67, 77, 82, 98, 108: Arts and Crafts 153, 155, 156, 161; Cole Green 100, 103–4; Shendish 138, 139, 140; walled 49, 108, 140, 153
Kitt's End 108
Knebworth 151, 159, 170

Lake 42, 166, 206; *see also* Landscape park
Lambeth 60, 78, 178, 181, 182
Landscape park 97, 106, 112: belt 108, 135; clumps 98, 105, 108, 137, 138, 139; contouring 97; lake 42, 107, 111, 131, 206; pond(s) 98, 108, 111; seat 98, 110, 126; shrubbery 108, 137; trees 97, 98, 100, 102, 103, 104, 105, 107, 108, 136–7, 138; walk 96, 98, 101, 108, 110, 128; woodland 98, 103 *see also* Drive
Lane, Wilmot Ernest 156
Lane & Son 195
Langley End 159
Langleybury 125, 126, 129, 130, 131, 132, 133, 134, 142
Lantern 65, 166
Lapidge, Samuel 108
Larch 103
Lawn 83, 104, 137, 140, 151, 156, 157, 160, 162: croquet 82, 162; tennis 155, 156, 163
Lawson, William 76
Lea, Lee, river/valley 42, 48, *203*: Regional Park 225; spelling 226n1
Lea Valley and District Nurserymen's and Growers' Association 219
Leewenhorst, Netherlands 76
Leicester, Earl of 7
Letchworth Garden City 150, 162, 168, *169*, 169, 170
Lethaby, William Richard 152
Lettuce 204, 218
Leyton 202
Ligustrum ovalifolium 211
Lilium longiflorum 215
Lily of the valley 215

Lime trees 14, 140, 154; avenue 79, 125, 206
Lindley, John 194
Linnaeus/Linnaean 179, *183*, 190, 191: Linnaean Society 208
Little Court, Buntingford 152
Little Hadham 60, 61, 68, 86n20, 187, *pl. 3.1*: Bury Green 81
Littlegrove, East Barnet 92, *94*, **108**, 111
Lodge 24, 137, 154: Barnes Lodge 134; Cassiobury 127–8; Hadham Hall 80, 81, 87n25; Porters Lodge 108; Sherborne Lodge 40; Theobalds 16–17, 39, 40, 41; White Lodge 156
Loggia/Arcade 9, 11, 15–16, 24, 25, 72, 84, 163, 165
Lombardy Poplar *130*, 196
London 3–5, 6, 9, 15, 16, *17*, 17, 18, 23, 25, 33, 42, 49, 50, 51, 54, 60, 62–3, 71, 79: Tower of 78, 80, 94, *94*, 96, 108, 122, 123, 128, 134, 149, 150, 154, 166, 178, 179, 181, 184, 188, 191, 192, 193, 202, 210, 211, 212, 213, 220, 223, 224, 225; London and Birmingham Railway *see* Railways
London, Bishop of 61
London, George 187
London Plane 133
London Underground 215
Longleat, Wiltshire 100
Longman: Charles 121, 134, 138, 140, 142, 144, 146n51; George 134
Looker, Roger 187
Lord Mayor 23, 63
Lorimer, Robert 161, 173n67
Loudon 139
Loughton 206
Lucas, Geffry 162
Lutyens, Edwin 151, 154, **157–62**, 170

Magdalen College Oxford 183
Magnolia 103, 159, 164
Malcolm, William 179, **187–91**, 189
Malting 123, 150, 193
Markyate 151: Cell 161, 165
Marsham: Sir John 45; Sir Robert 45, 46, 48, 54
Mason, George 108, 111
Mawson, Thomas 151, **154–7**, 166, 172n32
May: George & Henry 220; Hugh 79
McVitie, Robert 149
Melon *see* Fruit
Member of Parliament (MP) 23, 61, 95, 97, 98, 105, 106, 107, 108, 157, 166, 211–12
Mill 45, *46*, 129, 132, 133, 144: corn 123, 132; flour 132, 133; paper 123, 124, 129, 130, 132, 133, 144; pulp 123, 129, 132; water 132, 133
Miller: J.F. 190, 191; Philip 100
Mimmshall Brook 107
Mimram, river 100, 153
Minet: Isaac 60; William 60, 61, *62*, *64*, 64, 65, 66, 70, 72, 76, 80, 81, *83*, 83, 84, 86n4, *pl. 3.1*

Mitchell: Admiral Sir David 51; David né Cooke 51, 53, 57n63
Moat 32: The More 33, *34*, 36, 38; Theobalds 39, 40, 41, 42, *43*, 43, 45, 46, 48; Knebworth House 151; Hadham Hall 61, 64, *77*; Tower of London 78
Moated garden 39, 41, 42, 43
Monson, Colonel 110, 116n118
Moor Park, Rickmansworth 5, *34*, 92, 96–7, 98, 112, 130, 150, 154, 157, *pl. 4.2*
More, The 31, 32, 33–8, *34*, *35*, *37*
Morgan, John Pierpoint 165
Morrison: Sir Charles 68, *75*; Elizabeth 68, 74
Myddelton House, Enfield 211
Mytens, Daniel 71

Nash Mill House 134
Nash Mills 124, 129, 134, 137, 142, 143, 144, *pl. 5.1*, *pl. 5.2*
Navigations 122
Navy 107, 108
Nazeing, Essex 202, *221*
Neville, Archbishop George 33
New River, the 41–2, *43*, 149, 154, 162
Newton, Daniel 195
Niche 71, 163
Node, The, Codicote 151, 166
Norden, John 3, *4*, 16, *17*, 39
North Mymms 153, 171n18
Nugent, Lord 212
Nuneham Courtenay 153
Nunn, Christopher 207
Nurseries, nurserymen and seed merchants 177–99, 202–29: Barr's of Lancaster 173n83; Brompton Park 179, 184, 197, 190; Cook, Moses 82, 183–7; Davenport, John 98; Digswell 180, 195–9; Elliott, Clarence 195; Fells, Abraham 195; Hamilton's Nurseries 212; Hertford Nursery 195; Lane & Son 195; Malcolm, William of Kennington 179, 187–91; Newton, Daniel 195; Old Nurseries, Cheshunt 206, 209; Paul, Adam & Son 195, 205; Paul, George 154, 209; Paul, William & Son 205; Rivers, Thomas and son 179, 191–5; Rochford, Joseph & Son 218–9, Michael 212–3, 220, Thomas & Son 213–18; Royal Nurseries, Waltham Cross, 206–9; Sander, Frederick 195; Six Hills Nursery 195; Tradescant, John 178; Williamson, John 100; Woolley, Mr 211
Nut Walk 61

Oak 11, 103, 104, 137, 140, 150: Holm Oak 140, 151; Red Oak 140
Oak Hill, East Barnet 212
Old North Road 3, 15, 39
Orchard 11, 16, 36, 38, 67, 76–7, 139, 151, 155, 159, 162, 165, 179, 182, 194, 207
Orchids 195, 206, 211, 215, 216, 218, 220, 225
Oxhey 128
Oxnead Hall, Norfolk 74

Paine, James 132, 133
Palladio 74
Palms 215, 216, 225; Palm House 216, *217*
Panshanger 100, 102, 105
Paper-making 123, 144
Papermills: Apsley 124, 129, *130*, 134, 143; Batchworth 124, 130; Croxley 124, 129; Frogmore 123, 124, 129, 144; Hamper 124; Home Park 124, 129; Mill End 124; Nash 124, 129, 134, 137, 142, 143, 144; Scots Bridge 124; Solesbridge 124
Parigi 74
Parliament 42, 77, 98, 122, 220
Paston, Sir William 74
Paul 211, 219: Adam (1780–1847) 205; Arthur William, (1854–1921), son of William 208; Ernest 210; George I (1811–67) 206, 209; George II (1841–1921) 154, 206, 208, 209, *209*, *210*, 210, 211; George Laing 210; William (1822–1905) 205, *205*, 206, 209, *pl. 8.1*
Paul, A. & Son 195
Paxton, Joseph 139, 140, 194
Pembroke, Lord 72
Peppers, sweet 204, 219
Petworth, Sussex 96, 101
Pierrepoint, Lady Caroline 106
Pine (trees) 103, 166: Austrian 140; Scots 140
Pines/pineapples 100, 103, 211, 212, 218, 225
Pishiobury 92, 112, 117n129
Pitt, William the Elder 96, 98
Pleasure ground 110
Poinsettia 217
Pond, ornamental 14, 15, 19, 32, 36, 38, 55n10, 77, 82, 98, 105, 108, 111, 137, 151, 185: Bushey Hall 45, 46, 48; lily pond 155, 167; Popes 49, 51, *52*, 53, 57n68 Theobalds 40, 41, 42, 43, 44, 45 *see also* Fish
Pondyard *13*, 13, 14, 38
Ponsbourne Park 166, 212
Poole: Mrs Jane 108, 110; Josiah 110
Pope, Alexander 51
Popes, Hatfield 31, 48–53, 54, *pl. 2.5*: Popes Farm *52*, 53; Popes Pondholes *52*, 53; Popes Walk 53
Porters Park (also Porter's Lodge), Shenley 92, 108
Presdales, Ware 164, 165
Primrose 42, 128
Privy garden 24, 36
Pymms 67

Quaker 110, 111
Queen Henrietta Maria 70
Queen Katherine 36

Railways: Great Eastern 149, 193, 213, 219; London to Birmingham 122, 128, 133, 135, 142–3, 149; Metropolitan 149, 150 *see also* London Underground
Ralegh, Sir Walter 40

Raymond, Sir Robert 126
Rayne Hall, Braintree 63, 67
Read, Benjamin 101
Red Gables, Harpenden 164
Renaissance 25, 74, 78, 84: English 1–2, 8;
    Italian 3, 6, 65
Repton: Humphry 105, 115n71 and n83; John
    Adey 74
Rew, Charles Henry 155
Rib, river 108
Richard III 33
Richmond, Nathaniel 97
Rickmansworth 31, 33, 96, 124, 129, 149, 150:
    Church 97
Rivers: May *pl. 7.1*; Thomas 179, *192*, 193–4
Rivers of Sawbridgeworth 191–5
Roads 3–4, 107, 122, 134, 146n35, 150, 168,
    179, 184, 202
Roberts, John 40
Robinia pseudoacacia 104
Robinson, William 152–3
Rochford: Joseph 212, 213, 215, 218–19;
    Michael 212–13; Thomas I (1849–1901)
    213–16; Thomas II (1877–1918) 215, 216–18
Rochford boiler 212
Rochfordville 213
Rome 71, 106
Romney, George 50
Rosarium 211
Rose 153, 208, 210, 222: arches 164; bed 156;
    breeder 206, 225; climbing 155; grower
    205–6; rose garden 153, 154, 155, 156, 158,
    159, *160*, 160, 161, 162, 163, 170, 211; *Rosa
    209, pl. 8.1*: Goldfinch *209*; Paul's Himalayan
    Musk 209; Paul's Scarlet 209; Penzance briar
    155; varieties 205, *205*, 208
Rose, John 187
Rosehill, near Hunton Bridge 134
Rothamsted 163–4, *164*
Rousham, Oxfordshire 133
Royal Nurseries, Waltham Cross 206, *206*, 208
Ruislip 150
Russell/Russell Park/Russells/Russells Farm,
    Watford 125, 126, *127*, 130, 134, 142,
    145n15, 154, 157
Rustic seat 82, 126

Sadleir, Sir Ralph 67
St Albans 31, 123, 195, 220: abbey 33; abbot
    of 33
Saint Augustine 78
St Catherine's Estate, Broxbourne 149, 154
Saint John of God Care Services 198
St Loe Strachey, John 158, 169
Salisbury, Frank 164
Salisbury: Lord 31, 53; Earl of 45, 67; Marquess
    of 53
Sandby, Paul 50, *50*, 51
Sander, Frederick 195, 220
Sanders Frewer and Co., Bury St Edmonds 140

Sandringham 211
Savorgnano, Mario 36
Sawbridgeworth 179, 191, 193, 194, 195
Scott: Elizabeth 81; Thomas 81
Scott, John Quaker 111
Sebright, Sir Thomas 95, 98
Sele Mill, Hertford 123
Serlio 74
Service buildings 24, 66, 67
Seymour, Edward, Duke of Somerset 67
Shaw, William Cunliffe 111
Shendish 121, 130, 133–42, *136*, *141*, 143, 144,
    pl. 5.1
Sherborne Castle, Dorset 40: Sherborne Lodge 40
Sheriff of Hertfordshire 49, 67, 212
Shrubbery 108, 137
Shrubs 11, 16, 19, 44, 83, 101, 108, 137, 140,
    165, 169, 177, 193, 197, 206, 207
Shugborough Hall, Staffordshire 96
Six Hills Nursery 195
Social mobility 6, 23
Society of Antiquaries 60
Society of Dilettanti 95, 96, 97, 98, 106, 111
Soissons, Louis de 196
Solanum 212
Somerset House 67, 187
Sopwell 123
South, Samuel 204, *204*
Sparrows Herne: Hall *167*, 167; Trust 122;
    turnpike 122, 126
Spencer: Georgiana Caroline, countess Cowper
    99–100; Hon. John Spencer 100; John, first
    Earl Spencer 100
Spooner, Sarah 51
Spruce 140
Stafford, George 134
Standon Lordship 5, 67
Stane Street 61, 63
Stanstead Bury 5
Statuary 70, 71, 74, 84, 85
Statues 9, 11, 14, 15, 70, 73, 84, 163, 167:
    Ceres 70; Jupiter 70, 74; Cupid 74; Flora 74;
    Venus 74
Stebbing Park 68
Stephenson, George 122
Stew 110 *see also* Fishpond
Stocks, Aldbury 154, 156
Stone, Nicholas 74, *75*, 85
Stowe, Buckinghamshire 95–6
Stroud, Dorothy 92, 107
Styles, Benjamin 97
Summer house *see* Garden Buildings
Supermarkets 224, 225
Sweet chestnut 104
Sycamore 14, 197

Taylor and Chilcott 51, *pl. 2.5*
Temple, Richard first Viscount Cobham 95
Temple Dinsley 151, 158, *158*, 159
Tennis court/lawn 16, 155, 156, 162, 163

Terrace 17, 20, 21, 25, 43, 70–1, 72, 79, 83, 84, 85, 137, 151, 153, 155, 156, 161, 162, 165, 206: of houses 130, 168, 216; roof *47*
Thames, river 33, 71
Theobalds 5, 7, 9, **14–17**, 18, 19, 20, 25, 31, *32*, 67, *pl. 1.2*: Lane 39; The Lodge 16, 17, 39; manor 39, *pl. 2.1*; park 5, 7, 32, **38–45**, *43*, *44*, *pl. 2.1, pl. 2.2*
Thorogood, Jonas 101
Thorpe, John 40, 41, 42, *pl. 2.2*
Thurley, Simon *35*, 36, *37*, 55n5
Timson, Lt Col S.R. 156
Titanic 216
Tomatoes 204, 213, 216, 218–19, 223
Tottenham 202, 204, 212, 213, 220
Tradescant, John 17, 177, 178, **180–3**, *181*, *183*, 184, 187, 191
Tring 122: bricks 150
Truman, Sir Benjamin 49–51, *50*, 53, 54, *pl. 2.6*
Tuck, G. & A., 204, *204*
Tulip 71, 182, 215: Tulipomania 71; Tulip tree 103
Turf 11, 42, 104
Turnford 202, 215, 220, 224: Hall 213, *213*, 218
Turnpike 143: Sparrows Herne Trust 122, 126; Trusts 122
Two Waters 123, 129, 133
Tyttenhanger 33

Van Dyck, Sir Anthony 70
Venice 15, 19, 36
Verulam House 13, 14
Villiers, Thomas, first Earl of Clarendon 125
Vineries 140
Violet 42, 128 : African 217
Voysey, Charles F.A. 151, 162
Vries, Hans Vriedeman de 70

Waddesdon Manor 211
Wages 101, 194, 222
Walk(s) 7, 14, 16, 19, 20, 23, 24, 27n38, 39, 49, 53, 70, 82, 96, 98, 128, 137, 153, 155, 156, 158, 160, 161, 182, 185, 187, 196: gravel 101, 110; nut walk 61; shrubbery walks 108
Walker: Sir George, Baronet 45, 56n41; Sir Walter 56n41
Walkern Park 68, 78
Wall Hall 165, 171n15
Wallace & Co. 161
Walled garden 65, 70, 80, 83, 84, 87n25, 108, 151
Walnut 182
Walpole, Horace 57n61, 97, 104, 107; Robert 126
Waltham Abbey 202, 204, 218, 221, 224
Waltham Cross 31, 38, 42, 202, *205*, 206, *206*, *207*, 223, 224
Waltham House 206, *207*, 208
Walthamstow 202
Ware 3, 42, 111, 123, 150, 165, 225

Ware, Isaac architect 108
Ware Park 5, 18–19
Water features, ornamental 38, 40, 42, *52*, 53, 56n29: artificial river 32, 40, 41, 45; basin 70; Chinese boat 50–1, *50*; island 14, 39, 41, 42, 46, 48, 49, 153; octagonal basin 49; pond *see* Pond, ornamental; canal *see* Canal, ornamental
Water garden 5, 9, 11, 13, 14, 19, 31–54, *32*, *46*, 165, 166, 167: definition 55n1
Watford 33, 68, 122, 123, 124, 125, 126, 128, 132, 143, 144, 149, 150, 154, 157, 170, 184: church *75*; Hamper Mill 124; Watford Junction 129; Watford Tunnel 129, 133
Webb: Daniel Carless 125; Philip 151, 152
Welwyn 151, *152*, 153, 154, 157: Lockleys 153; New Place *152*, 152; Thatched Rest 154, 157
Welwyn Garden City 170, 180, 187, 195, *196*, 197, 198–9: Development Corporation 198
West, Richard 57n61
Westminster 33, 78
Whately, Thomas 97
Whippendell Wood 125, 126
Wickham Hall 80
Willes, Edward Judge 108, 111
William III 81: and Mary 31
Williams, Henry 128, 132, 133
Williams-Ellis, Clough 158
Williamson: John 100, 101; Tom 149
Wilson, Richard 97, *pl. 4.2*
Wilton House 56n29, 72, 74, 75, 76: Holbein Porch *73*
Woburn Abbey 74, 75, 86n23
Wolsey, Cardinal Thomas 33–8, *35*, 54, 55n5 and n10
Wood, Robert 106
Woodhall Park 188
Woolley, Mr 211
Worshipful Company of Drapers 62
Wrest Park 96
Wright, Thomas 125
Wrotham 92, 108

Yew 83, 137, 148, 151, 152, 153, 159, 160, 161, 165: Irish Yew 140
Yewlands, Hoddesdon 162
York Place, London 33, 36
Yorke, Jemima 95
Young, Arthur 98, 127
Youngsbury 92, 108–11, *109*

Zig-zag walls/crinkle-crankle/*slingenmuren* 76